Advance Praise for *A Rift in the Earth*

"The divisions that ripped the country apart during the Vietnam War were rekindled in the struggle to bring the Vietnam Memorial to life. But unlike the war itself, that second struggle resulted in a shared reconciliation this extraordinary book charts."

—Ken Burns, filmmaker

"Searing and sweeping, Reston's narrative captures the political, cultural, and social ferment of those heady days of Vietnam and its aftermath with great skill and erudition. *A Rift in the Earth* is an indispensable guide through the cultural wars at the heart of the memorial itself, and a powerful reminder why it was so important that we find a way to move forward from the division of war to begin a healing within our country and between the United States and Vietnam."

—John F. Kerry, 68th US Secretary of State

"This is a story that needs to be told, and James Reston, Jr., tells it very well. I believe that readers will soon find themselves taking and even changing sides as the Art War in his account heats up and then reaches its conclusion. For me, the Wall and the entranceway that resulted from the Art War controversy provide a place to find closure for those who fought the war, those whose loved ones did not return, and even those who violently opposed it."

—Lieutenant General Ron Christmas, USMC (Retired),
Former President & CEO, Marine Corps Heritage Foundation

"*A Rift in the Earth* is an absolutely fascinating account of the artistic, political, personal, and cultural tensions that arose from America's most divisive war, and that led to one the country's greatest works of public art. I followed the controversy over the Vietnam Veterans memorial when it was underway, but I learned from almost every page of this book. This is a great narrative and reportorial success."

—James Fallows, *The Atlantic*

A RIFT IN THE EARTH

Also by James Reston, Jr.

To Defend, To Destroy: A Novel, 1971

The Amnesty of John David Herndon, 1973

The Knock at Midnight: A Novel, 1975

The Innocence of Joan Little: A Southern Mystery, 1977

Our Father Who Art in Hell: The Life and Death of Jim Jones, 1981

Sherman's March and Vietnam, 1987

The Lone Star: The Life of John Connally, 1989

Collision at Home Plate: The Lives of Pete Rose and Bart Giamatti, 1991

Galileo: A Life, 1994

The Last Apocalypse: Europe at the Year 1000 A.D., 1998

Warriors of God:
Richard the Lionheart and Saladin in the Third Crusade, 2001

Dogs of God:
Columbus, the Inquisition, and the Defeat of the Moors, 2005

Fragile Innocence:
A Father's Memoir of His Daughter's Courageous Journey, 2006

The Conviction of Richard Nixon:
The Untold Story of the Frost/Nixon Interviews, 2007

Defenders of the Faith:
Christianity and Islam Battle for the Soul of Europe, 2009

The Accidental Victim:
JFK, Lee Harvey Oswald, and the Real Target in Dallas, 2013

Luther's Fortress: Martin Luther and His Reformation Under Siege, 2015

A RIFT IN THE EARTH

Art, Memory, and the Fight for a Vietnam War Memorial

JAMES RESTON, JR.

ARCADE PUBLISHING • New York

First Edition

Arcade Publishing books may be purchased in bulk at special discounts for sales promotion, corporate gifts, fund-raising, or educational purposes. Special editions can also be created to specifications. For details, contact the Special Sales Department, Arcade Publishing, 307 West 36th Street, 11th Floor, New York, NY 10018 or arcade@skyhorsepublishing.com.

Arcade Publishing® is a registered trademark of Skyhorse Publishing, Inc.®, a Delaware corporation.

Visit our website at www.arcadepub.com.
Visit the author's site at www.restonbooks.com.

10 9 8 7 6 5 4 3 2 1

Library of Congress Cataloging-in-Publication Data

Names: Reston, James, Jr., 1941– author.
Title: A rift in the Earth: art, memory, and the fight for a Vietnam War memorial / James Reston, Jr.
Description: First edition. | New York: Arcade Publishing, 2017. | Includes bibliographical references and index.
Identifiers: LCCN 2017012314 (print) | LCCN 2017029092 (ebook) | ISBN 9781628728583 (ebook) | ISBN 9781628728569 (hardcover: alk. paper)
Subjects: LCSH: Vietnam Veterans Memorial (Washington, D.C.)—History. | Vietnam War, 1961-1975—Monuments—Washington (D.C.) | Lin, Maya Ying. | Hart, Frederick, 1943- | Washington (D.C.)—Buildings, structures, etc.
Classification: LCC F203.4.V54 (ebook) | LCC F203.4.V54 R47 2017 (print) | DDC 959.704/36—dc23
LC record available at https://lccn.loc.gov/2017012314

Cover design by Brian Peterson
Cover photo: iStock photo

Printed in the United States of America

In Memoriam

· RONALD E RAY ·

CONTENTS

INTRODUCTION

This is a book about the memory of the Vietnam War and the five-year battle, from 1979 to 1984, to define that memory in the building of a memorial in Washington, DC. Initially, the effort was intended to honor those men and women who fought in the war, and by doing so, to aid in healing the wounds of a fractured nation. But the healing balm did not emerge from the ferocious fight over what manner of public art would serve the purpose. Indeed, the reverse was true. It was as if the Vietnam War was being fought all over again.

The competition for an appropriate design to commemorate America's first national experience with a lost war was, at the time, the largest contest of its kind in the history of American or European art. The 1,421 entries represented a remarkable explosion of creativity. The surprising winner was a twenty-one-year-old Yale undergraduate named Maya Lin. But her concept of a simple, chevron-shaped black granite wall was instantly controversial. A cabal of well-connected, forceful veterans led the charge against it, denigrating the design as shameful and nihilistic, an insult to veterans and a paean to anti-war protesters. They did everything they could to scuttle the winning design and replace it with something more heroic . . . and they almost succeeded. When that effort failed, they did ultimately manage to impose an entirely different work of art on the winning design: a classical sculpture representing three soldiers in combat gear, fashioned by another remarkable artist, Frederick Hart.

Thus, the eventual memorial was really two memorials in one, and the "art war" featured a clash of two entirely different concepts of art—one modernist, the other traditional—while raising questions about the inviolability of an artist's work. The process of compromise came to involve politicians at the highest level of the American government, both in the US Congress and at the White House. Art organizations and veterans' groups also entered the fray, and the opposing positions were argued with force and passion. At several moments in the struggle, it seemed as if the contentiousness was simply too great for any memorial to be built at all. And yet, once the art war ended and the dream of a memorial was realized, it was embraced with near universal acceptance and has become a place of reflection about not only the Vietnam War but all wars.

The roots of this book reach back to my own service in the US Army (1965–1968), through the shock of losing a comrade during the Tet Offensive in January 1968. His story is told here as well. His fate could easily have been my own. Those three years as a soldier gave me a deep and abiding empathy for any soldier in harm's way, regardless of the rightness or wrongness of the conflict. Like many soldiers of that generation, I turned against the war while I was still in the service. Afterward, perhaps by way of penance, I became deeply involved with the amnesty movement that sought relief and return for the tens of thousands who fled the United States to avoid the military draft. I probably wrote more about that issue than any other American writer, and I ended up advocating for universal amnesty in debates held all over the country.

Just as the Vietnam War memorial in Washington has transcended the specifics of the war it memorializes and ascended to the level of the universal, so the issue of reconciliation and reconstruction after a divisive war has also become timeless. Through the conflicts in Iraq and Afghanistan and beyond, the period of peace in a war's aftermath will be, and should be, a time for reflection, and hopefully, for renewal. To have a permanent physical space to ponder those issues, a space that is almost sacred in feel, defines the brilliance of the Maya Lin and Frederick Hart creations. But there is also great value in revisiting the fierce struggle over divergent concepts of art and patriotism that brought their creations into existence.

In the essay accompanying her submission to the original memorial design competition, Maya Lin described her vision as a "rift in the earth." Whether wittingly or unwittingly, that vision became a metaphor for the rift in the entire Vietnam generation. Those who came of age from 1959 to 1975 faced difficult choices. Many like my friend, Ron Ray, answered the call of their president without question as an obligation of citizenship. Others supported the war overtly, thought it was the right thing to do, and served willingly. But those who opposed the war faced an impossible moral choice: whether to serve in an ill-conceived and immoral war effort or to resist and avoid service . . . with all the consequences that entailed. The rift pitted soldiers against protesters, sons against fathers, citizens against politicians, friends against friends, veterans against veterans, all in the context of a war that should never have been fought and that involved terrible loss, not only of the soldiers who were killed, maimed, or driven crazy but to the moral standing of the nation before the world.

PART I

ART AND MEMORY

Chapter One

IT SHALL NOT COME NEAR YOU

On January 20, 1977, when Jimmy Carter assumed office as the thirty-ninth president of the United States, he faced the monumental task of national reconciliation after the most unpopular war in American history and the most divisive since the Civil War. At that time, the Vietnam War had been the country's longest war, lasting from 1959 to 1975. As the first elected peacetime president afterward, his challenge to heal the nation's wounds was paramount and daunting. Over 58,000 American soldiers had been killed in the conflict; more than 300,000 had been wounded, and some 245,000 would file for compensation for injuries they had suffered from exposure to the toxin-laced herbicide Agent Orange. These figures do not include the hundreds of thousands more who suffered from debilitating psychological wounds. More than two million Vietnamese, Cambodians, and Laotians died during the war.

Moreover, an entire generation of young Americans that came to be known as the Vietnam Generation was said to have "dropped out." That was especially true of the best educated. The vast majority of them had found loopholes to avoid the universal military draft. The "trick knee" became the symbol of escape, but bone spurs, marriage, graduate school, and a psychiatric diagnosis of dire mental illness were just as effective. Of the 26.8 million men of the Vietnam generation, the majority—15.4 million men—received deferments or exemptions. Only a year into the first escalation in 1966, the unease and disenchantment of the American people toward the war was already being felt. By the summer of 1968, 65 percent of those Americans polled by the Gallup organization considered the war to be a mistake. The country had definitively turned against the conflict, partly because of the high casualty rate, partly because of the graphic images of death and destruction that were conveyed nightly on television, partly through the presidential candidacies of Eugene McCarthy and Robert Kennedy, partly because of the incessant street demonstrations by the young and vulnerable, and partly because of the shock of the Tet Offensive in January and February 1968 and the fall of Khe Sanh several months later, after the country had been reassured by its president and his generals that the war was being won. By early 1971, only 28 percent of those polled supported the war, and 72 percent favored withdrawal.

In his agenda for healing, President Carter reached out first to the young men in exile abroad in Sweden, Canada, and elsewhere. On his second day in office, he pardoned 12,800 draft evaders (deserters were not covered by the offer). Immediately, both vocal war hawks and passionate dissenters ridiculed the presidential action. By this time leaders of a well-established "amnesty movement" were arguing that to accept a pardon implied a confession of wrongdoing. What they wanted was a universal amnesty, wiping the slate clean of any criminal infraction in an act of collective amnesia. Only such a sweeping gesture would satisfy the anger of a generation faced with the impossible choice between service or flight in a bloody national endeavor that they viewed as sorely misguided. Those opposing Carter's measure argued that to absolve draft evaders would dishonor the heroic service of those who did serve the nation when they were called. The debate would continue throughout the Carter presidency and beyond, as those in exile struggled with what they viewed as a moral dilemma. Was one to accept Carter's pardon, accept guilt, and return home? Or stay abroad? Many stayed, smug in their moral rectitude. And those who had served, unpleasant and dangerous as their choice was, struggled to resume a semblance of normal life. That life was often conducted in a smoky netherworld of disgust and alienation and resentment.

Almost forgotten in this early period of the Carter presidency was the torment of the Vietnam veteran. More than 2.1 million men and women deployed to Vietnam over the course of the war, and returning soldiers were often scorned and humiliated as purveyors of death and torture and dupes of a discredited policy. As a veteran, having enlisted in the Army and served three years, from 1965 to 1968, I experienced this derision myself, even though I had not been to Vietnam. My college friends looked upon my service with mystification and disapproval, while they moved forward with their graduate careers or cared for their trick knees.

This identification of the American soldier with atrocity worsened after the revelation of the My Lai massacre in November 1969, twenty months after it took place. The image of blood-soaked women and children littering a ditch in that tiny village became an unforgettable snapshot of the war. My own disenchantment with the war had grown during my tour in the Army, and it grew more intense after a comrade of mine was killed, pointlessly, in Hue during the Tet Offensive.

How then should a country begin a healing process after a failed, divisive war? How was the rage and recrimination to end? How should President Carter act? How long would the process of reconstruction and reconciliation last, if indeed that healing would ever be accomplished? And what scars would endure, and how deep were they?

From 1978 to 1984, these profound questions were encapsulated in a brawl over how to commemorate that war, the first that the United States had lost. It was an extraordinary fight between groups with different attitudes toward what some called the lost cause of the twentieth century. It was also a fight between different notions about public art.

It came to involve powerful forces in American politics and business, and it provoked debate over what constitutes honor and courage in times of national crisis. It prompted the question of how to thank the soldier who prosecuted the war at the same time as the protester who ultimately stopped it.

Long after the Vietnam conflict, these questions remain intensely relevant for all wars America may fight and try to end in the future.

The brawl over these issues would break out in an unusual forum: the largest competition for a public works project in the history of American or European art until that time. From this torturous battle, a work of genius emerged, and even more remarkably, that work has changed in its significance. The memorial on the National Mall is no longer just about veterans and their loss and sacrifice, no longer just about Vietnam, but about all wars and all service to country and all moral opposition to governmental authority. Its significance has profoundly changed. No one could have predicted this. It is no wonder that this simple space of contemplation remains one of the most visited of places in the nation's capital. Even in its inscrutability, this simple V of black granite has risen to the universal.

—

The process of reconciliation after a divisive and protracted war can take years, and even longer for the losers, for the bitterness on all sides of the issue is always severe. A process of coming to terms with what actually happened and why must precede a healing, a forgiving, and a forgetting. Dealing with the American defeat in Vietnam and digesting it into the national consciousness did not really begin until about five years after the last American soldier was lifted off the roof of the American Embassy in Saigon.

The Vietnam generation—those who came of age from 1965 to 1975—could roughly be split into four groupings. There were the soldiers who were drafted or volunteered, many of whom fought in

Vietnam and were then scorned by the nation when they came home. Then there were the active, passionate dissenters who fueled the protests against the war and who gathered by the hundreds of thousands beneath the Washington monument in 1969. They deserve the lion's share of credit for eventually stopping the war. Third, there were the malingerers, who had done everything they could to avoid service and sat silently on the sidelines, smirking with contempt at both the soldiers and the protesters. As the television toggled between horrific images of bloody combat and angry demonstrations in the streets of America, politicians pitted these three groups against one another with the cynical purpose of tamping down the turmoil that roiled the nation. And finally, after a lottery began in late 1969 and the volunteer military was established in July 1973, two years before the official end of the war,

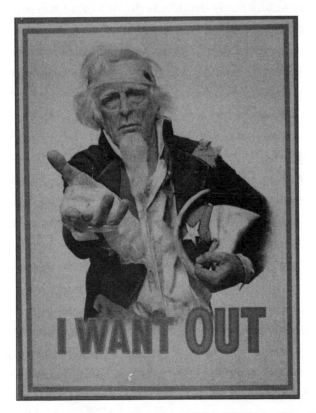

I Want Out *protest poster, Committee to Help Unsell the War, 1971*

there were the lucky ones who were excused with high lottery numbers or who came of age after the draft was eliminated altogether.

The debate over the Vietnam War featured a new concept in American discourse: the immoral war. By that was meant a war that was undeclared by Congress, that was initiated under the false pretense of a nonexistent attack (such as the alleged incident that led to the Gulf of Tonkin Resolution), that was based on a bogus geopolitical premise (the domino theory), and that was waged, colonialist-style, against an Asian people who possessed legitimate aspirations to be free of foreign domination. Policy makers concluded that the path to victory was the pacification of those peoples.

Well after the war was over, popular media spearheaded efforts to acknowledge what happened and why. Only with the passage of time was the wider public ready to address the profound issues of the war as presented in books, articles, and films.

There was one exception: a documentary film called *Hearts and Minds* (1974) that came out shortly before the last Americans fled Vietnam. Garnering an Academy Award for best documentary feature from liberal, anti-war Hollywood, it took its title from a phrase President Lyndon B. Johnson invoked multiple times as a definition of what had to happen—to "win" the hearts and minds of the Vietnamese people themselves—if America was to win the war. The film had several indelible interchanges. In one, General George Patton, Jr., son of the World War II hero, was shown at a funeral of several war victims, when he turned to the camera and said soberly, "They're reverent, determined, a bloody good bunch of killers." The second was even more revealing. The supreme commander of American forces, General William Westmoreland, remarked, "The Oriental doesn't put the same price on life, as does the Westerner. Life is plentiful there. Life is cheap in the Orient." But the timing was too early for the film to have a lasting effect on the reconciliation process.

Toward the end of the 1970s the psychological toll on soldiers who had been in Vietnam rose to the surface as a major issue, taking its place alongside the enormous casualty rate. It gradually became clear that hundreds of thousands of surviving veterans were suffering from severe psychological distress, including depression, anxiety, alcoholism, and insomnia, not to mention thoughts of suicide. This was, of course, not a new issue. After World War I, Virginia Woolf defined the problem best through the main character of her novel, *Mrs. Dalloway*. Septimus had been a brave warrior, but after the war he descended into an abyss of desolation. "Now that it was all over, truce signed, and the dead buried, he had, especially in the evening, these sudden thunderclaps of fear. He could not feel." He had expended all his bravery on the battlefield, Woolf imagined, and could not relate either to his fellow man or to postwar England. Dating back well beyond World War I to ancient Greece and Rome, the issue transcends Vietnam. The veterans of Iraq and Afghanistan know this all too well. Only in the late 1970s was this mental disorder given a new, medical diagnosis: post-traumatic stress disorder, or PTSD.

On the official side, President Carter's administrator of Veterans Affairs, Max Cleland, led a campaign for "readjustment" therapy with a modest proposal to Congress to fund treatment counselors around the country to deal with servicemen's psychological problems. Cleland himself is an amazing case. A captain in the First Cavalry Division who joined the army for the most noble of reasons, he had experienced the Tet Offensive and then volunteered for the perilous mission to relieve the siege of Khe Sanh. But on the day the siege was finally lifted, April 8, 1968, after three months of "total war," Cleland was horribly wounded by friendly fire. A grenade exploded immediately behind him as a fellow trooper carelessly handled his weapons. Cleland lost two legs and an arm.

As a triple amputee, he spoke with great authority and feeling in support of a modest allotment to counsel returning soldiers for drug and alcohol addiction. He likened coming back to civilian life to the explosions that often followed an airstrike in combat. "Coming home [was like] a series of secondary explosions, where the Vietnam veteran

is left alone with his pain and his agony, to try to explain it by himself. That was one reason why we needed the support of psychological
counseling in the Veterans Administration which had never been done
before unless you're psycho."

Max Cleland in Vietnam, circa 1966 (left) *and with President Jimmy Carter
at the White House, July 28, 1978*

After 1971, Congress repeatedly rejected proposals for veterans'
counseling services. As VA administrator, Cleland pleaded for a mere
$10 million to start a nationwide network of three hundred counselors.
At the time, there were only nineteen Vietnam-era veterans in Congress, whereas in 1946, sixty-nine World War II veterans were elected
to Congress. But with dogged persistence Cleland finally carried the
day, and on June 13, 1979, Public Law 96–22 finally passed.

Coupled with the awareness of widespread mental disease among
returning veterans was the discovery of the physical damage that the
toxic defoliant known as Agent Orange had done to the thousands
who had come into contact with it. In *GI Guinea Pigs* (1980), authors
Todd Ensign and Vietnam veteran Mike Uhl chronicled the wanton
disregard for soldiers' well-being that the broadcasting of this poison
throughout Vietnam had caused for the soldier on the ground.

Each side in the debate over the war had their heroes and their
villains. For the hawks, the icon was John Wayne in the 1968 film

The Green Berets. For the war protesters, there were the songs of Joan Baez and the brazen actions of Father Daniel Berrigan and others. The symbols of this dissent were the unforgettable images of the massacre at My Lai, the murder of four students at Kent State University during an anti-war protest, the naked Vietnamese girl fleeing the fire of American napalm, the last helicopter to lift off from the roof of a Saigon apartment house, flower-wielding protesters confronting soldiers with fixed bayonets at the Pentagon, and a Vietnamese police chief assassinating a Viet Cong soldier.

The most incendiary figure of the anti-war movement was actress Jane Fonda. She would later say that her anger over Vietnam began after seeing US carpet bombing on French television when she lived in Paris with her first husband, Roger Vadim. Between 1970 and 1972, while the war was still raging, she barnstormed the country on an anti-war road show and lecture tour. She then famously traveled to North Vietnam and visited with American POWs. John McCain, the navy flyer and later US senator, who was held in the infamous Hanoi Hilton, refused to see her, saying later that he did not think she would be a very good emissary of the truth back home. During this provocative two-week visit to the enemy's lair, she made broadcasts on Hanoi radio, denounced the bombing of Hanoi's dikes, and blasted American war policy in general, earning her the label "Hanoi Jane." She also allowed herself to be photographed next to a North Vietnamese anti-aircraft gun. In later years that photograph was the only aspect of her anti-war campaigning that she came to regret. For many, her behavior qualified as bald-faced treason for giving aid and comfort to the enemy.

Meanwhile, in early 1972, as she was divorcing Vadim, she collected her first Oscar as best actress for her performance in *Klute*. She wore a black Maoist pantsuit—itself a provocative statement—to the ceremony, and Academy Award officials cringed at the possibility that she might use the platform to rant about Vietnam.

"I wanted to make a speech about Vietnam," she said later, but her father, Henry Fonda, counseled against it. "He said to me: 'Just say: There is a lot to be said. But tonight is not the time.'"

Counterintuitively, Fonda developed and starred in *Coming Home* (1978), a moving film about returning veterans. Contrary to her harsh reputation in real life, Fonda's character, Sally, is shy, torn by divided loyalties, and married to a hard-bitten Marine (Bruce Dern). But after her husband goes off to Vietnam, she falls in love with a war-scarred paraplegic (Jon Voigt) in a veterans' hospital. The movie did a great deal to refocus public attention on the war wounded, both physical and psychological. Despite Fonda having conceived the film and gotten it made, the movie did not change her reputation as an inflammatory symbol that hawks and many veterans would resent for decades to come.

Another powerful and tragic movie, released in late 1978, reflected the shifting mood of the American public toward the war. *The Deer Hunter* is the story of three Russian-American steel workers from Pennsylvania who live in grimy houses, labor near the cauldrons of molten steel in the smoky factories, and who play and dance with tremendous gusto, especially with Linda (Meryl Streep) before they go off to experience horrific combat and imprisonment in Vietnam. "Do you think we'll ever come back?" one of them asks another. Only the lead character, Michael (Robert de Niro), outlives the horrors, while one buddy, Nick (Christopher Walken), survives the war only to kill himself during a game of Russian roulette. The third (John Savage) ends up a paraplegic after being badly wounded in an escape from a barbarous Viet Cong prison. Michael is the only one strong enough to bear the numbing dislocation of returning home.

The movie was received as a relentless indictment of a war that had destroyed lives in a purposeless endeavor. Yet the characters themselves try to hold on to their love of country even as they are disconnected and aimless in their return. The film ends with a gathering after Nick's funeral, as the victims sing "God Bless America" quietly and sadly. An editorial in the *Washington Post* observed that *The Deer Hunter* "depoliticizes the war almost entirely, exchanging considerations of historical rightness for strictly human concerns. Depoliticization is what you do to a war you haven't won. It makes its memory easier to take."

"The evidence of these two movies," wrote commentator Stephen S. Rosenfeld, "is that we are halfway, but only halfway, home from the war."

In the literary world three strong voices emerged to challenge conventional wisdom. The first belonged to Tim O'Brien, whose novel, *Going After Cacciato*, caused a stir when it was published in 1978. (In Italian *cacciato* means "hunted.") The story is about a soldier who goes absent without leave to walk from Vietnam to Paris and the men who went after him. To endure the endless slog of war, the protagonist deludes himself. "Waiting, trying to imagine a rightful but still happy ending, Paul Berlin found himself pretending, in a wishful soft way, that before long the war would reach a climax beyond which everything else would seem bland and commonplace. A point at which he could stop being afraid. Where all the bad things, the painful and grotesque and ugly things, would give way to something better. He pretended he had crossed the threshold." The novel received the National Book Award for Fiction in 1978.

Philip Caputo's book, *A Rumor of War* (1977), had a different take. It is a classic war memoir that chronicles Caputo's searing experience as a Marine lieutenant in Vietnam in 1965–66. He had arrived in-country as a twenty-four-year-old romantic, a literature major in college, entranced by the novels of Rudyard Kipling and Saul Bellow and the poetry of Wilfred Owen and Dylan Thomas. He was an adventurer for whom war had seemed like the ultimate "chance to live heroically." He arrived in Vietnam with swagger and idealism. But after his first blistering summer in the combat zone, he aged, technically, three months, "but emotionally about three decades." In the fierce fights for one forgettable numbered hill after another, in watching his unit depleted from 175 to 95 men in one four-month period, and in rebelling against his superiors' obsession with body counts, he chronicles his descent into disillusionment. Caputo is appalled when his fellow soldiers go berserk. Of all the ugly sights in Vietnam, he wrote, the ugliest was seeing that "the change in us, from disciplined soldiers to unrestrained savages and back to soldiers, had been so swift and profound as to lend a dreamlike quality to the last part of the battle." The book ends with his humiliating court-martial for allegedly encouraging the assassination of a Vietnamese informant in a case of mistaken identity. After seventeen months in Vietnam, having witnessed unspeakable carnage, Caputo survived without a scratch, but he emerged as a "moral casualty." The book was later made into a television mini-series.

Finally, there was Michael Herr's *Dispatches* (1977). It is a compilation of a few long pieces he had written as a journalist for several leading magazines. Adopting a stream-of-consciousness style and writing primarily from the viewpoint of the grunts in the field, Herr delivered a tour-de-force portrayal of the combat soldier and the landscape of battle. Herr's writing is beautiful and intimate, empathetic and terrifying, especially in its treatment of the siege of Khe Sanh, America's version of the French debacle at Dien Bien Phu, in the winter of 1968. "All that anyone could see of the hills had been what little the transient mists allowed," he wrote of Khe Sanh's surroundings, "a desolated terrain, cold, hostile, all colors deadened by the rainless monsoon or secreted in the fog. . . . Mostly, I think, the Marines hated those hills; not from time to time, but constantly, like a curse. . . . I heard a grunt call them 'angry,' . . . So when we decimated them, broke them, burned parts of them so that nothing would ever live on them again, it must have given a lot of Marines a good feeling, an intimation of power." And Herr is brilliant in locating what Virginia Woolf called the "creative fact or the fertile fact," the fact that elucidates character. Once he finds himself seated next to a Marine in a helicopter ride from Cam Lo to Dong Ha. The soldier is overweight, but "you could see from his boots and his fatigues that he'd humped it a lot over there." The Marine pulls out a Bible, leafs to Psalm 91:5, and shows it to Herr:

Thou shalt not be afraid for the terror by night; nor for the arrow
that flieth by day.
Nor for the pestilence that walketh in darkness; nor for the destruction that wasteth at noonday.
A thousand shall fall at thy side, and ten thousand at thy right hand;
but it shall not come nigh thee.

Amid the noise of the chopper Herr scribbled "beautiful" on a piece
of paper and handed it to the Marine. But later he would write that he
was thinking to himself of a counter verse, Psalm 106:39:

Thus were they defiled with their own works
And went a-whoring with their own inventions.

It was these works—and even soldiers' poems—that did so much to
drive a cultural shift in the late 1970s. A time of gestation was needed
for the country to absorb the defeat and come to terms with it. Such
powerful, intimate, and emotional works that made the experience of
the soldier real and immediate did far more to move the nation than
the words of politicians and activists.

One noteworthy poem was written by Lewis Bruchey, who had
performed perhaps the most dangerous mission any soldier could
endure in Vietnam. As the leader of a five-man Long Range Recon-
naissance Patrol for the Army Rangers, his job was to roam far from his
unit in lonely scouting missions searching for the elusive enemy. He
was later awarded the Silver and Bronze Stars for bravery. The awards,
he said wryly, were for "staying alive for a year, I guess." His poem,
"Cold, Stone Man," includes these lines:

They pin
A star
Upon my chest,
A subtle nod,

No more, no less.
Alone
I stand.
I AM THE BEST.

But wait.
Remember
The rockets,
The jungle,
The rain?

Remember
Evil, masked
In pain?

Remember
Night sounds
Eyes strain'd
To see?

Remember
Death stalking
The darkness,
A reaper
To reap me?

I do! I do!

So speak softly
To me,
And do not
Stare.

Save your judgment,
Your sorrow,
Your pity,
Your prayer.

For I am
A cold, stone man
Of Vietnam.
Beware! Beware!

Chapter Two

REMEMBER US

Jimmy Carter finally turned to the anguish of the Vietnam veteran late in his presidency. On Wednesday, May 30, 1979, at a White House reception for veterans after the Memorial Day holiday, the president proclaimed that the nation was, at last, ready to change its heart and mind toward the Vietnam soldier and recognize his valor, sacrifice, and commitment. For the melody of the moment, he drew on Philip Caputo's book and the author's moving tribute to a fallen comrade:

"You were part of us, and a part of us died with you, the small part that was still young . . . . Your courage was an example to us, and whatever the rights or wrongs of the war, nothing can diminish the rightness of what you tried to do. Yours was the greater love."

The president's focus had been nearly a year in coming, and Jan Scruggs, a shy, somewhat awkward twenty-nine-year-old veteran, deserved much of the credit. As a teenage member of the 199th Light Infantry Brigade, Scruggs had been badly wounded by a rocket-propelled grenade in a bloody battle northeast of Saigon in May 1969. In the time he spent in a hospital in Cam Ranh Bay recovering, he came to accept his injury without bitterness but as a predictable event of war. He had earned his "red badge of courage," he would say. Two months later he returned to duty. Then in January 1970 he saw twelve of his comrades pulverized when an ammunition truck exploded. "That's what gave me PTSD," he would say later. Over the course of his tour, he had seen half of his company killed or wounded.

Meeting at the US Capitol, December 1979. From left to right:
Senator Mack Mathias, Senator Robert Dole, Jan Scruggs,
Tom Carhart, Senator Dale Bumpers, and Robert Doubek

Back home he graduated from American University in 1975 and went on to earn a master's degree in psychology a year later, focusing on Vietnam veterans' painful readjustment to civilian life and Post-Traumatic Stress Disorder (PTSD), from which he himself suffered. In May 1977, he penned an article for the *Washington Post* entitled "Forgotten Veterans of that 'Peculiar War.'" "Perhaps a national monument is in order to remind an ungrateful nation of what it has done to its sons," he wrote. Fifteen months later he published his second bitter editorial about the "continued indifference" toward the Vietnam veteran. He had come to believe that something more than hypocritical political rhetoric was needed to honor soldiers like himself who had answered the country's call.

Scruggs's notion of a national memorial for Vietnam veterans was percolating. And he was channeling Carl Jung's concept of "collective unconscious," which he had encountered in his psychology classes. Jung argues that all humans share certain fundamental values, one of which is the deep appreciation for those who give their lives for others. And Jung's definition of the archetypical hero—one who overcomes immense obstacles, achieves extraordinary goals, and transcends inner darkness—also captivated him. From these Jungian notions, Scruggs imagined a memorial of names. The names of the fallen on a memorial, he felt, would guarantee overwhelming public and political support. Ultimately, however, it was seeing *The Deer Hunter* in early 1979 that galvanized him, solidifying his idea of building a memorial to his fellow soldiers and realizing that, if it was to happen, he would have to lead the effort himself. As he remembered later, "I was thinking things over and I got very depressed. I started getting flashbacks, it was just like I was in the Army again and I saw my buddies dead there, twelve guys, their brains and intestines all over the place, twelve guys in a pile where mortar rounds had come in."

A month later the movies again had an impact on public awareness when 64 million viewers watched a television program entitled *Friendly Fire* about a mother in rural Iowa, fighting against government obfuscation to find the truth about her son's death from soldiers on his own side. Starring Carol Burnett, Ned Beatty, and Sam Waterston, the movie is based on a 1976 book of the same title by C. D. B. Bryan.

That spring, with $2,800 of his own money and being somewhat clueless about the immense hurdles he would be facing, Scruggs began to mobilize a campaign for a memorial that would honor the poignant sacrifices of US servicemen in Vietnam. He imagined such a memorial in a prominent place on the National Mall in Washington, DC, with a garden-like setting where visitors would come for rest and reflection. He hoped as well that there might be some sort of a realistic sculpture of the Vietnam soldier. In late April, Scruggs and friends formed a corporation called the Vietnam Veterans Memorial Fund (VVMF). They held a press conference over Memorial Day weekend and boldly announced their intent to raise one million dollars to build their memorial.

But the effort got off to a rocky start. In June, Roger Mudd of CBS News reported that the group had raised exactly $144.50. Shortly afterwards, their efforts were spoofed on late night television.

Then there was the matter of the creation and its execution: who could design and build such a memorial? Scruggs thought he knew the very people who could provide just the right combination of setting and art: Joseph E. Brown, a prominent landscape architect who was already engaged in designing a park and pond on the Mall to honor the fifty-six signers of the Declaration of Independence and Frederick Hart, a brilliant young artist who was then working on a sculpture for the main entrance of the Washington National Cathedral. That early relationship with Scruggs and company gave Brown and Hart an inside track to be chosen for creating and building the memorial, should the project go forward.

But Hart would have the misfortune of attending an elegant dinner party on July 29 at the home of Wolf Von Eckardt, the art and architecture critic for the *Washington Post*. Von Eckardt was already a big fan of Hart's: he had written glowingly about the sculptor's classical works at the cathedral. Also present at the soiree was the critic's friend and colleague, Judith Martin, the future etiquette advice columnist known as Miss Manners, who was then a drama and film critic at the *Post*. To the surprise of all, Hart announced, with a certain pride and humility, that he had been chosen to provide the sculpture for the Vietnam Memorial. Von Eckardt rose up in a passionate outburst, voicing strong objection. Martin thought her friend might leap across the table with a knife. This memorial was far too huge and important,

Von Eckardt fumed. How could Scruggs and company blithely award such an important prize to their favorite sculptor, no matter how nice and talented that artist might be? There had to be a national competition, Von Eckardt insisted, and he, by golly, would see to it that it happened.

The idea of design competitions for public art has a long and storied tradition in America. After George Washington's death, a number of proposals surfaced for honoring the first president. The first attempt was Horatio Greenough's sculpture of Washington as a seated and half-naked Roman hero draped with a toga. His statue was received with universal scorn. Meanwhile, a memorial commission of prominent Washingtonians was formed with Chief Justice John Marshall as the honorary chairman. Subsequently, artists presented designs from Greek, Roman, Renaissance, and Mayan traditions. The winning design by Robert Mills called for a five-hundred-foot Egyptian obelisk whose base was a pantheon of thirty columns and whose top featured Washington in a horse-drawn chariot. Construction began in 1848, but the Civil War interrupted the work, leaving the obelisk at 150 feet, well short of its planned height. After the war, Mark Twain described the unfinished stump as "a factory chimney with top broken off [and] cow sheds around its base, and the contented sheep nibbling pebbles in the desert solitudes that surround it, and the tired pigs dozing in the holy calm of its protecting shadow." Not until 1884, through the intercession of many architects and politicians, was the Mills design modified to its current, simple pyramid finish with all the embellishments scrapped. Upon its completion critics again lambasted it, but the public quickly embraced its spare, simple elegance.

A century later the protracted and troubled campaign to craft a memorial in Washington for Franklin Roosevelt met with disappointing results. For that design competition Congress established an advisory committee in 1955 that was to include such luminaries as historian Lewis Mumford, Pietro Belluschi, the dean of architecture at MIT, and Hideo Sasaki, head of the Harvard School of Design. Even with such a distinguished panel, the initial efforts for an FDR monument woefully failed, when the winning design was contemptuously dubbed "instant Stonehenge" and then discarded. Lewis Mumford provided the dirge: "The notion of a modern monument is veritably a contradiction in terms. If it is a monument, it is not modern, and if it is modern, it cannot be a monument."

It was not until 1978 that a design was finally approved; another nineteen years would pass before FDR's memorial opened to the public on the Tidal Basin near the Jefferson Memorial.

Nevertheless, the failure of the FDR effort notwithstanding, Von Eckardt argued forcefully that something similar should be organized for this memorial. Eventually, he calmed down and became again the good host that he was. All congratulated Hart on his good fortune.

In a subsequent column in the *Washington Post*, Von Eckardt stated his case. He cited a few memorials around the world that moved him: the Fosse Ardeatine in Rome that holds the graves of Italian villagers murdered by the Nazis, the Ossip Zadkine sculpture in Rotterdam called simply *May 1940*, the month that the Luftwaffe destroyed that city, and the Hall of Remembrance in Jerusalem that inscribes in stone twenty-one of the largest Nazi death camps.

"None of these . . . is 'good art' or popular art, abstract or representational, 'modern' or 'traditional,'" Von Eckardt wrote. "They are simply powerful ideas translated into a powerful emotional experience. And that is what I think the Vietnam Veterans Memorial group needs. To elicit powerful ideas, there must be a competition. It would be corrupt for some more or less self-appointed committee to pick some favorite." He did not mention Hart by name. The critic would have his way. And Frederick Hart would feel as if the prize had been snatched away from him.

In August, the group got its first political breakthrough when Senator Mack Mathias of Maryland contacted the organizers and offered help. In the year that followed, a bill to erect some sort of a Vietnam memorial began to make its way through Congress. Senator John Warner of

Virginia joined Mathias, and together they spearheaded the congressional effort. But central to the plan was the Congressional requirement
that funds for the memorial be privately raised. Early in 1980 VVMF
sent out two hundred thousand fundraising letters for the cause, and
later, on Memorial Day, they sent out a million more. A disparate group
of celebrities lent themselves to the effort, including Jimmy Stewart and
Bob Hope. The money began to pour in. Scruggs became the face of the
endeavor, and he proved himself to be an adept promoter.

In November 1979, he wrote a powerful op-ed piece in the *Washington Post*, railing against the media's portrayal of Vietnam veterans
as "violence-prone, psychological basket cases." Such a characterization was, he wrote, "collective character assassination." The title of his
piece was "We were young. We have died. Remember us," a line bor-
rowed from Archibald MacLeish's poem "The Young Dead Soldiers
Do Not Speak," which the poet had written when he was Librarian
of Congress during World War II. The poem, often etched on war
memorials, reads in part:

> They say, We have done what we could but until it is
> finished, it is not done.
>
> They say, We have given our lives but until it is
> finished no one can know what our lives gave.
>
> They say, Our deaths are not ours: they are yours:
> they will mean what you make of them . . .
>
> They say, We leave you our deaths: give them their
> meaning: give them an end to the war and a true peace: give
> them a victory that ends the war and a peace afterwards: give
> them their meaning.
>
> We were young, they say. We have died. Remember us.

Tom Chorlton, a dissident who had spent six years protesting against the war, responded to Scruggs's piece.

"If this memorial is to serve any positive purpose, however, it must include those who also suffered by recognizing the tragedy of this war and therefore resisted the draft. . . . I must resist any attempt to apologize to those who served in the military by white-washing the realities of that brave struggle. . . . We must make absolutely clear to ourselves and to history that we are not honoring the Vietnam War itself. At the very least, this memorial must include all war resisters who were imprisoned for resisting the draft. This is the minimum, the very least that must be demanded by the tens of thousands of us who also suffered by trying to bring our country to its senses."

No one was listening.

—

As the push behind the idea of a memorial grew stronger, Scruggs was shown a number of possible sites for his tribute. The guardians of Washington's public spaces were stingy in ceding ground in central Washington. The US Commission on Fine Arts suggested space near the Arlington Cemetery. But the organizers were not disposed to accept some small, out-of-the way niche. To hide the memorial was to sideline the war, as if it was something to be ashamed of. Scruggs had his eye on something far more prominent: a corner of the National Mall itself, a two-and-one-half acre plot of rolling ground just northeast of the shrine to Abraham Lincoln. On its face, this was an outrageous proposition. There was still no World War II memorial in Washington to honor the sixteen million Americans who served and the four hundred thousand who were killed. And there was no national monument in the nation's capital to commemorate the 116,000 Americans who died in World War I. But Scruggs was very persistent.

For decades "temporary" military structures set up during World War I had occupied the area. With the American bicentennial celebration in 1976, the cleared area was set aside as a pastoral place of reflection and eight years later became a tribute, known as Constitution Gardens, to the founding fathers. The resistance to any further "improvement" was great among the city's planners, who believed that this portion of the Mall should remain a quiet byway of planted trees, serene waters, and twisting pathways somewhat like the Bois de Boulogne in Paris. During his presidency, Richard Nixon had noticed the area's pristine emptiness on one of his helicopter rides off the White House lawn and seized on the idea that this would be a perfect spot for an amusement park along the lines of Tivoli Gardens in Copenhagen, replete with a carousel, bandstand, puppet shows, jugglers, and café. Fortunately, as the Watergate scandal came to dominate Nixon's attention, this proposal, like Nixon, languished.

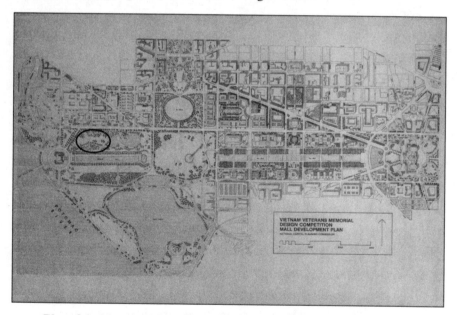

Plan of the National Mall, Washington, DC, circa 1980, with the projected site for the Vietnam Veterans Memorial indicated on the left.

Ultimately, Senator Mathias and twenty-five cosponsors introduced a bill specifying Constitution Gardens as the site for a Vietnam War memorial. As Memorial Day of 1980 approached, it passed unanimously in the US Senate and sailed easily through the House of Representatives.

The critical government agency to approve or reject the project was the National Commission on Fine Arts. Immediately, the commission chairman, J. Carter Brown, voiced strong objection to the designated site. "It is the commission's belief that if Constitution Gardens should become the setting for major memorials . . . the intended character of the park will be seriously diminished, if not lost altogether." This objection created a momentary hiccup in the process. But patriotic fervor always trumps artistic quibbles. This would be the first of many instances in this saga in which political forces would override artistic considerations. The objections were ignored.

On July 1, 1980, President Carter signed the bill into law. In celebrating its passage, the president returned to the words of Philip Caputo. This time, however, he quoted a Caputo passage he had omitted a year earlier. In the continuation of Caputo's letter to his fallen comrade, the author mourned that the country had not matched the faithfulness of his friend. There were no monuments or memorials, no statues, or plaques, the author insisted, because such symbols would make Vietnam harder to forget.

Now, at last, that would change. There would be a remembrance, *if* the right artistic concept could be found that would pass the muster of the Washington salons, and *if* the money for its construction could be raised. When the ground in Constitutional Gardens was finally consecrated, after the strains of the Battle Hymn of the Republic echoed to the Lincoln Memorial, a clergyman delivered the hopeful invocation.

"For those who yet suffer wounds, for those not yet home, let this be a mecca for healing." Some saw this as equivalent to tears as well as joy at a wedding, appreciating what trials lay ahead.

For more than a year the VVMF had toiled on in the thankless task of soliciting donations for an abstract idea. Things had started slowly, but there were a few early successes. Most significant was a call Jan Scruggs made to the Texas billionaire Ross Perot. A proud navy veteran, Perot was one of the greatest fast-talking salesmen in America. His data collection company, Electronic Data Systems (EDS), had had a stratospheric rise into the top ranks of American business, fueled by fat government contracts and deals with corporate giants such as General Motors. He was also passionately involved in POW/MIA issues, partly because his roommate at the US Naval Academy had been killed in Vietnam. In 1979, he achieved considerable publicity after several of his EDS employees were taken hostage in Iran, then in the throes of the Ayatollah Khomeini revolution.

To rescue his employees, Perot had recruited a band of seasoned warriors, led by a notorious ex-Green Beret colonel, Arthur "Bull" Simons. In 1970, Simons led a perilous mission into North Vietnam to free Americans, including a navy fighter pilot named John McCain, from a prison at Son Tay. The mission failed, but it forced the North Vietnamese to consolidate American captives in a prison at Hòa Lo in central Hanoi. That prison would be dubbed the "Hanoi Hilton." In the Iran operation, the Simons team melted into a huge pro-Khomeini rally and freed the EDS employees as well as a large number of political prisoners. Simons then successfully spirited them out of the country to safety.

So, Perot, now among the richest men in America and an acknowledged super-patriot, was a good target for a donation. Scruggs's first call to him netted a cool $10,000.

Another success came at the hands of Scruggs's most important political connection, Senator John Warner. In December 1979 Warner hosted a breakfast with thirteen corporate executives at his tony Georgetown mansion across from Dumbarton Oaks. He would later claim that when his wife, Elizabeth Taylor—he was her sixth husband—made a grand entrance in a pink bath robe with dangling fluffy white balls and pink slippers, the businessmen tripled their donations.

Warner and Taylor had a much more public encore ten months later when they hosted a black-tie extravaganza at the old Pension Building in downtown Washington. Warner looked grand in his tuxedo with the medals he earned as an ensign in World War II and as a marine in the Korean War prominently on display over his left lapel. Besides Senators Warner and Mathias and a number of crusty veterans, the headliners for this event included Perot, General William Westmoreland, Veterans Affairs administrator, Max Cleland, twenty-five generals and admirals, and a handful of corporate chairmen from such firms as General Electric and General Dynamics. Perot, gabby as ever, gave a breezy rendition of his now-famous Iran rescue operation and told of how he had insisted that his commandos be Vietnam veterans. "You take these young guys out and give 'em a mission and cut out all the chatter and they do just fine," he told a reporter.

Elizabeth Taylor looked pretty good too that night in a blousy red dress with Greek designs that the *Washington Post* described as "flimsy." In the estimation of some, the actress did not really look like she wanted to be at the gala, as if she had been trotted out for show against her will. Perhaps as a result, she displayed a flash of her famous temper. When she passed a table and a brash veteran shouted out, "Hey, Miss Taylor, can I take your picture?" Taylor turned on him with a fiery look and said, "It's Mrs. Warner, chump," whereupon the veteran's wife, a tough-looking, no-nonsense woman, jumped up to defend her man, and the two started jawing at one another. The muscle was called in to break up the fight.

There would be other awkward moments. General Westmoreland looked very much the marble man as he assumed the podium. When he began to spout the usual stuff about honor, duty, and country, a veteran in a wheelchair whispered to his dinner partner that he thought Westmoreland was "out of his fucking mind. If they'd given him what he wanted over there, he would have blown the hell out of everything." And even Scruggs, whom the audience might have assumed to be an uncritical flag-waver, gave voice to inner conflict. The author of the memorial to honor soldiers perfectly represented the overwhelmingly anti-war sentiments of most Vietnam veterans and indeed the inner conflict of the entire Vietnam generation.

"I basically think that the war was a serious mistake," he told a reporter. "I'm not pro-war, and not a right-wing warrior. . . . I later protested against the war. I gotta admit I'm still quite confused about the damn thing."

So, it was left to a stocky ex-Marine with curly red hair to express an unqualified love of country. "The key thing that's been missing is simply according to the people who served, the dignity of their experience," he said. "The hardest reentry point for Vietnam guys was their own peer group." His name was James Webb. By this time, he was best known for his gritty Vietnam novel, *Fields of Fire* (1978), which had sold more than seven hundred thousand copies. Webb had convinced his publisher to provide several hundred copies of his book as party favors at the gala, and he was on the VVMF's advisory committee.

All the same, for all the fun and folderol the event at the Pension Building grossed $85,000 for the Memorial Fund. By mid-March 1981, the patrons had $820,000. Then at the end of April, only days before the winner of the grand design contest was announced, Perot stepped forward with an additional $160,000 to underpin the entire cost of the competition.

Chapter Three

NOTHING TO ADD, NOTHING TO TAKE AWAY

I n 1980, the campus of Yale University had settled into a malaise of relative quiet after an era of turbulence over civil rights and the Vietnam War. Students had turned their gaze inward to their courses and their grades. Indifferent toward national and international concerns, their minds and hopes were fixed on their future careers. The Vietnam War was now a distant memory. The draft had been scrapped seven years earlier as the volunteer army had relieved every young male of concern over conscription. Apart from the revolutionary regime of the Ayatollah Khomeini that had taken American hostages in Iran and the Soviet invasion of Afghanistan, the world was experiencing a comparative lull from large-scale bloody conflict. Ronald Reagan had been elected that fall in a landslide and Mount St. Helens had blown its top in Oregon. But among the top news stories that year, students on campus were inclined to be most upset over the assassination of John Lennon.

A decidedly cynical view of the world had replaced outrage. It was easy to hear complaints about America's militaristic tendencies, though none were then in force. The Watergate scandal held more sway over

the minds of Yale students than Vietnam, and it encouraged the view
that all politicians were essentially corrupt. Public service was not
respectable. If the subject of America's most unpopular war arose—a
war that had ended when these students were young adolescents—the
protesters against it were generally seen as long-haired, drug-happy
hippies. The fall semester began with a well-attended lecture by Barry
Commoner, the famous biologist and founder of the modern environmental movement who was then running for president as a candidate
for something called the Citizens Party. The students applauded when
Commoner suggested resuming diplomatic relations with Iran.

If the students at Yale were mostly indifferent to national and
international issues, the same could not be said of the faculty. A large
proportion of them had been very active in the anti-war movement in
the 1960s and early 1970s. That was especially true from 1967 to 1969,
when more than forty thousand American soldiers were killed. Protest
in the country at large against the war rose in concert with this hor-
rendous casualty rate, climaxing with the march of a hundred thousand
protesters at the Pentagon in 1967 and an even larger demonstration at
the Washington Monument in 1969.

Most prominent among the activists on the Yale campus was Reverend William Sloan Coffin, Jr., the mesmerizing university chaplain
and one of the most visible and charismatic leaders of the anti-war
protest. A great teddy-bear of a man, full of good humor and fun and
much beloved by students for his bombast and principles as well as
for his booming singing voice and raucous piano playing, he had proposed in 1967 to make Battell Chapel a sanctuary for fugitive draft
evaders. In 1970, activist students sought to bar a US Marine Corps
recruiter from Yale, and in May Day protests of that year they went on
strike, shutting down the campus with a complete cessation of classes
(although no buildings were occupied, unlike at Harvard and Columbia). National Guard troops deployed to New Haven and downtown
shops closed and were boarded up as fifteen thousand people gathered
on the town green. The following Monday, May 4, Ohio National

Guard soldiers opened fire on war protesters at Kent State University, killing four, only two of whom were demonstrating.

In that same year, a federal grand jury indicted Coffin for abetting draft resistance. Though he was convicted, an appeals court eventually overturned the verdict. Coffin left Yale in 1977 to become the senior pastor at the Riverside Church in New York, and thus the university lost a mobilizing force.

In 1970 Vietnam and civil rights were joined in an incendiary mix as New Haven became the rallying point for black militancy. The town was the setting for the trial of Bobby Seale, a co-founder of the Black Panther party. Seale was already famous as one of the original "Chicago Seven," the group charged with violently disrupting the 1968 Democratic Convention in a protest over the Vietnam War. At their trial, Seale engaged in constant outbursts against the proceedings, and, as a result, was gagged and bound to his chair. This incident inspired a popular protest song by Crosby, Stills, and Nash called "Chicago," which included the lyrics, "So your brother's bound and gagged, and they've chained him to a chair." For his interruptions, Seale was sentenced to four years in prison for contempt of court.

Before he was incarcerated, however, the Panther leader spoke at a raucous gathering on the Yale campus. Later that night, Alex Rackley, an alleged informer within the Panther ranks, was murdered, and Seale was said to have ordered the killing. The Panther among the "Chicago Seven" now became the principal in a trial of the "New Haven Eight." The evidence against him was slim, and protesters denounced the trial as a travesty. The case against Seale was ultimately dismissed, but not before Reverend Coffin stepped forward to castigate the process and underscore the moral imperative of personal witness: "All of us conspired to bring on this tragedy—law enforcement agencies by their illegal acts against the Panthers," he said, "and the rest of us by our immoral silence in the face of these acts." Yale's president, Kingman Brewster, Jr., joined in Coffin's denunciation, doubting that black revolutionaries could receive a fair trial anywhere in the United States.

In 1977, there was a brief flurry of activism at Yale, when food service workers on campus went on strike. Activists took sides, but most students, including a quiet, scholarly Asian-American sophomore from Ohio, were merely annoyed by the disturbance and inconvenience of the strike.

Given the changed circumstances of the time, the protest and pacifism that had once been in the life-blood of Yale did not run through the veins of the Class of 1981.

—

In the summer of 1980, Andrus Burr, a junior architecture professor at Yale, had spent his vacation in Europe looking at famous cemeteries. For a slight man with an unfailingly sunny disposition, this might seem like a depressing way to spend a holiday. But Burr was fascinated by the way human beings over the centuries memorialized their dead and how certain tombs and burial grounds can uplift the spirit. In Paris, he meandered through the famous Père Lachaise cemetery, not only for the elaborate tombs of its famous residents, including Chopin, Balzac, Molière, and Proust, but because the burial ground seemed to him collectively like a "city of the dead." He made a note to himself that there was nothing quite as grand as this in America, except perhaps the Greenwood Cemetery in Brooklyn. Burr tarried at the bizarre tomb of Jim Morrison, the charismatic singer-songwriter of The Doors, whose bust, just above ground, made it look as if he had been buried from the neck down. He missed the tomb of Oscar Wilde with its inscription from the Irishman's famous poem, "The Ballad of Reading Gaol."

> And alien tears will fill for him
> Pity's long-broken urn
> For his mourners will be outcast men
> And outcasts always mourn.

But there was no missing the amazing sculptural and architectural piece by Bartholomé at the end of the entrance boulevard with its inscription, *Upon those who dwelt in the land of the shadow of the dead, a light has dawned.*

After Paris, Professor Burr concentrated on war memorials. Among the many cemeteries he would visit that summer was the overpowering Thiepval Memorial in Sommes, France, which commemorates some 72,000 soldiers killed in the unimaginable battlefield slaughters there from 1916 to 1918. Amid the ocean of simple white gravestones a gargantuan, monumental cenotaph with intersecting triumphal arches, designed by the great British architect Sir Edwin Lutyens, presides over the assemblage. Burr would note that there was no image of the human figure. And at Étaples, also appointed with a Lutyens structure, Burr marveled at the commemoration of the military hospitals that were located there and where more than ten thousand war dead are buried.

This tour paid dividends when Burr returned to Yale. His dean, César Pelli (later the architect of some of the world's tallest skyscrapers), determined that the department of architecture needed another course. Burr suggested "funerary architecture," a study of memorials to the dead.

This was a new idea for Yale, but the topic was very much in the air after the assassinations of John F. Kennedy, Robert F. Kennedy, and Martin Luther King, Jr., and Burr was given the go-ahead. The course title was Funerary Architecture from the Stone Age to the Present. Nine students signed up. Among them was a bright, happy senior from Ohio named Maya Lin. The professor took his students through a number of exercises. He asked them to define the word "sublime" and to visualize it with a sketch. They were to imagine a design for a crematorium and a sarcophagus, and they were shown the famous design of French Beaux Arts architectural theorist Étienne-Louis Boullée for a memorial to Isaac Newton: a huge geometric sphere that was supposed to be the height of the Washington monument, but was never built.

The main requirements for Burr's course were several design projects. Channeling Bartholomé at Père Lachaise, the students were to design a cemetery gateway at Durham, a charming little town north of New Haven. Next, with the memory of the 72,000 dead at Thiepval in the Sommes valley fresh in his mind, Burr asked his class to design a war memorial for the next future American war of their imagination, World War III.

As the semester proceeded, Maya Lin turned out to be an indifferent, prickly, and difficult student, one who did not take criticism well and developed a testy relationship with her professor. She neglected to finish assignments, notably the required notebook called "visual diaries" that were to preserve the student's sketches. For the assignment to design a memorial for World War III, she turned in a dismayingly depressing drawing of a concrete tunnel strewn with trash and urine. It was a tomb, a study in frustration, where visitors would be trapped and unable to get out.

When Burr challenged her that this was not exactly an uplifting concept for a war memorial, Lin responded that she intended her concept to be ugly, since war itself was ugly and revolting. Would she want to visit such a place if her brother or friend were memorialized there? he asked. Lin characterized his question as "angry." Her professor had not understood her concept, she wrote later. Nobody would still be alive after World War III, and she meant it to be empty and depressing. Burr took this simply as an excuse for a poor design.

—

The open competition for a Vietnam War memorial was officially announced in November 1980, and a brochure and a rules packet for it were sent to every art and architecture school in the United States, as well as to architecture and landscape firms. The planning commenced for what was anticipated to be an enormous response. But how was the contest to be administered? The VVMF board chose Paul Spreiregen to be its professional adviser. Spreiregen was a noted architect in Washington who hosted a weekly design program on National Public Radio and had written a book on design competitions.

Spreiregen's first challenge was to oversee the selection of jurors who would determine the winning design. Eight distinguished architects and artists were tapped. Pietro Belluschi was an architect of elegant and sleek modernist towers, including the Pan Am Building and the Juilliard School of Music in New York, and a winner of the American Institute of Architects' gold medal. The former dean of the architecture school at MIT, he was, at eighty-one, the oldest juror. Significantly, he was also a veteran of the Italian army in World War I. Harry Weese had designed the highly regarded Washington, DC subway system's grand, commodious stations with coffered ceilings in the Brutalist style. He had a reputation as a sharp-tongued and witty contrarian. Jurors three and four were two notable landscape architects with national reputations: Garrett Eckbo, who had written a seminal book, *Landscape for Living* (1950), and Hideo Sasaki, former chair of Harvard's Graduate School of Design, whose masterworks were the plan for Copley Square in Boston and the grounds around Foothill College in Los Altos, California. There were also three renowned sculptors: Constantino Nivola, Richard H. Hunt, and James Rosati, whose various works were on display in the major art museums of Washington and New York.

And finally, Grady Clay, a gentle Kentuckian and the editor of *Landscape Architecture* magazine, was chosen as the jury chairman. He was a veteran of the Italian peninsular campaign in World War II, and his combat service would become important later.

With the eight jurors in place, the next consideration was the rules. Submissions would be accepted beginning in January 1981 and ending on March 31. The jury would examine the entries and choose the winner in late April. The purpose of the memorial was "to recognize and honor those who served and died." The submissions should be "reflective and contemplative" in character, as a catalyst for a process of healing and reconciliation. Through the memorial, it was hoped that "both supporters and opponents of the war may find a common ground for recognizing the sacrifice, heroism, and loyalty which were a part of the Vietnam experience." Artists and architects were to submit two rigid 30-x-40-inch panels with their concepts, including a visual representation of their idea, a description, and a statement of purpose. The description had to be handwritten, not typed or printed. Every concept had to include all of the names of those who had died in the war. All competitors had to be US citizens. No competitor was to indicate their identity on the illustrations. To do so would result in immediate disqualification, and the design would not be presented to the jury.

The most important rule was that entries be non-political. They were to express no opinion whatsoever about the rightness or wrongness of the Vietnam War itself.

The final footnote in the rules surely made many eyes roll. "Amateurs" were to have as much of a chance of winning as "professionals." If an amateur should happen to win the contest but not have the skill or experience to execute their concept, the VVMF had the right to "supplement the skills of the winner with other necessary experts and consultants." This too would become important later.

After the competition was announced, Professor Burr changed his course plan and assigned his students to design a memorial for the contest. On her Thanksgiving break, Maya Lin and three classmates traveled to Washington and walked the landscape of Constitution Gardens. There, her vision of a memorial was born. "Some people were playing Frisbee," she would recall later. "It was a beautiful park. I didn't want to destroy a living park. You use the landscape, you don't fight with it. You absorb the landscape, fit the building into it and both are stronger."

Of the eventual submissions for Professor Burr's class, Lin's was the most arresting. It consisted of a horizontal V, with tapered ends, and its vertex below ground. A series of slabs curved from the higher knoll above and ran downhill to the vertex, and it was upon these slabs that Lin proposed to carve the names of the Vietnam dead.

In the world of architecture this is called a pun, for Lin saw these slabs as dominos falling, suggesting that the dead were victims of the "domino theory," the discredited rationale for the war which posited that, if Vietnam fell to the Communists, the countries around it—Laos, Cambodia, and Thailand—would then fall in quick succession. And so, the origin of the most successful, all-inclusive war memorial in American history was, in its inception, certainly not non-political. Quite the opposite: its foundation was a brilliantly devastating political commentary on the Vietnam War: that the "kids" of Vietnam took a dizzying ride on a series of falling dominos to their collective death.

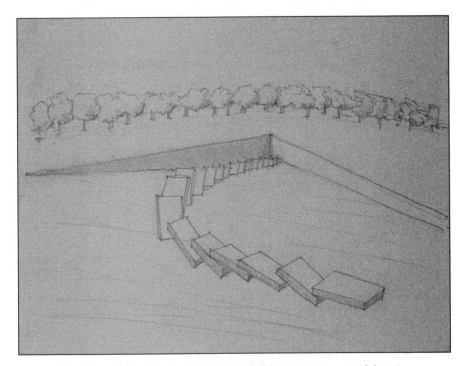

Professor Andrus Burr's sketch recalling Maya Lin's memorial drawing
for a class assignment

To mirror the professional process of an architectural firm, Professor Burr recruited several faculty members to "jury" the class submissions. When it came to Lin's design, the consensus was that a structure below ground was entirely appropriate for a failed war. It was remarked that Lin's V actually suggested the edge of a coffin peeking above ground. But what were these slabs? What was their purpose? Did they not make a pointedly political statement that was forbidden by the competition organizers? It was suggested that she scrap the slabs altogether and leave the simple V as the final draft for this class exercise.

Lin had also proposed initially to arrange the names in the chronological order of their deaths. But that would diminish the importance of the V's vertex, objected a juror. Lin acknowledged this as a weak point of the design. And so, in her revision, she changed the order for the final critique, making the chronological sequence begin and end at the apex, "so that the timeline would circle back on itself and close the sequence." Besides closing the sequence, the configuration might also, metaphorically, be seen as closing a wound.

Lin received an A for her Vietnam assignment. Professor Burr would say later of the dominoes, "I, and my colleague Carl Pucci, criticized it as too literal and dumb. But we suggested that the V-shaped cut in the earth was a very strong gesture, and it alone conjured images of death, a coffin, entombment. We liked it."

But at the end of the course, because of her other unfinished work, Burr first gave her a grade of incomplete. Upon seeing the grade, Lin stormed into his office and amid tears demanded that the grade be changed. She would never get into graduate school now, she wailed. Burr relented and changed the course grade. "I thought she understood that she was lucky to get a B+," he wrote, later noting that "In the end, she certainly got back at me." Maya Lin never forgave him. And Burr himself would resent her ingratitude for all he and his class had done for her.

—

The competition officially opened in early January 1981, and the entries began to pour in. Certain critical questions arose at the outset. Would the winner have a direct role in supervising the actual construction? Answer: "Our intention is that the author(s) of the winning design will participate in all appropriate aspects of the realization of the memorial, commensurate with skill and experience." Who owned the winning design? The answer from the directorate was clear: the Memorial Fund would own it and have the exclusive right to build it. It would also own the rights to publish, display, reproduce, and publicize the winning design. For Maya Lin, this would become a sore point later.

But the most important question dealt with the requirement that the entries make no political statement about the war. How was a "political statement" to be defined?

Answer: "For purposes of the competition a political statement regarding the war is any comment on the rightness, wrongness, or motivation of US policy in entering, conducting or withdrawing from the war."

There were also important, far-reaching questions that hovered over the contest. What segment of the population would ultimately control the memory of Vietnam? Would it be the veterans who were looking for vindication of their service? Would it be the artists who simply wanted to make a stylistic statement? Would it be the war resisters who sought a validation for the American defeat in Vietnam? Or would it be the politicians who simply wanted to allay the political pressures on them and put Vietnam to rest?

Professor Burr himself was among the early entrants to the contest. At his farm outside Williamstown, Massachusetts, where he kept his prized vintage tractors, he had gathered three other architects for a weekend of work and booze and jolly inspiration. Burr described his effort as a kind of "lark," in which the professionals tried to channel what they saw as the "jingoism" of the contest. They came up with a wheel-and-spoke design with a raised central star and a series of upright slabs that were to contain the names of the dead. Ultimately, he and his colleagues went away unsatisfied with their "whiskey-fueled" work and acknowledged that it was scarcely competitive. They submitted it anyway, and then it was back to teaching.

Andrus Burr's design entry for the Vietnam Veterans Memorial competition

Though the entrants had, by rule, to remain anonymous, the competition would include a number of architecture professors and well-known regional practitioners, as well as scores of art and architecture graduate students. Though most of the prominent architectural firms in the country passed up the contest, a handful of luminaries did participate. Charles H. Atherton, who was the chief executive of the US Commission of Fine Arts, the very body that would ultimately authorize the winning design, submitted an entry,

as did Kent Cooper, the architect who was eventually chosen to execute the winning concept. More competitive was Samuel "Sambo"
Mockbee, who already was exerting a huge influence on American
architecture with his "rural studio" program in Alabama and who
would be awarded the American Institute of Architects (AIA) gold
medal after his death in 2001. Mockbee's design featured a grove of
pink dogwood trees and a raised circle, held up, in lieu of columns, by
draped sculpted female figures, suggestive of the ancient Greek *kary-
atids*. Another entrant was a well-known California architect, Thom
Mayne, a principal in the internationally notable firm Morphosis.
Mayne was not only an AIA gold medal winner but in 2005 would

Samuel Mockbee's design entry for the Vietnam Veterans Memorial competition

also be awarded the Pritzker Prize, the equivalent of the Nobel Prize for architecture. His design presented a linear corridor of raised panels beneath an enclosed slit roof.

None of these luminaries made it into the semifinals.

At the time, the eventual 1,421 submissions represented the largest number of entrants of any design competition in the history of American and European art. Collectively, the contest produced a tremendous effusion of creativity, some of which was remarkably original and some which was outrageous kitsch. In reaching for monumental grandeur, many of the entries overlooked the enjoinder to be "reflective and contemplative." The most common offering was a circle or spiral such as that of Andrus Burr, where the names of the dead would appear on low-slung walls or slabs, so as not to compete with the temple of Lincoln to the southwest or the Washington Monument to the southeast. Stars and columns, pyramids and serpentine pathways were recurring features, as were dominos and pools of water. In one submission, soldiers waded through a pool toward a wounded, drowning comrade. A few submissions had the feel of a spaceship, while many others featured groves of decorative trees and scrubs. The central feature of one entrant was a giant teardrop, while another was entitled *Tower of Lost Souls*. A third displayed the gnarled detritus of a battlefield. Perhaps the most memorable absurdities were a pair of sixty-foot-tall combat boots and a rocking chair atop a forty-foot-high column, although a design featuring a massive combat helmet with two big bullet holes was also striking. From inside the helmet the visitor would gaze at the names of the fallen on dog tags that lit up.

Several notable submissions were overtly patriotic. One proposed an American flag that would cover the entire two acres of Constitution Gardens, while the central feature of another was a huge map of Vietnam itself. Several submissions had inscriptions. One read:

Let us to the end dare to do our duty as we see it

while another was:

Please join me in a prayer for a better tomorrow
When the horrors of war and the infamy of men
Will belong to a forgotten people in a forgotten past.

Most of the designs were abstract, and there were relatively few real-istic sculptures. A few had birds both lovely and grotesque. Gigantic bald eagles with wings spread wide were common. One displayed an epic man with wings; another, the Hand of God; while still another featured the figure of a combat soldier reaching out to a seated Viet-namese woman in a conical hat. And inevitably, in a bow to the movie *Apocalypse Now* (1979), a submission portrayed the three Valkyries rid-ing heroically to heaven in Wagnerian glory.

The architecture critic Von Eckardt would write that the entries ranged from "architectural stunts to sculptural theatrics, from the pompous to the ludicrous, from the innovative to the reactionary."

On April 27, 1981, the eight jurors gathered at Andrews Air Force Base outside Washington. In the vastness of Hangar Three, the 1,421 entries were arranged in long rows and mounted on pan-els at eye level. The display panels stretched some 1.3 miles along the corridors. There was a glitch during their installation, however, when in a far corner of the hangar an Air Force pilot revved up the engine of his jet and blew down all the panels. Once reinstalled, the display boards were identified only by number. Before viewing the entries, the jurors reviewed the rules. The enjoinder against any political message was again emphasized. They were reminded that the goal was to find a concept that was reflective and contemplative in character. One juror remarked that the memorial had to have "an expression of human tragedy." While it should look at both death and at life, it should also look "forward to life." As if in a psychiatric counseling session, they were all asked to express any preconcep-tions they had.

Then off the jurors went in their separate ways, pondering this hugely diverse display of imagination and inspiration, hoping for genius, and taking their personal notes. To facilitate the judging, Spreiregen had classified the entries as grotesque or weak, superior merit, and somewhere in between, although he was intent to tell the jurors that they were free to ignore his categorization. Occasionally in their meandering, jurors checked back with Spreiregen. Midway through the first day, Grady Clay, the chairman, said to Spreiregen in a gleeful stage-whisper, "I think there are several that might just work!"

On Day 2 each juror selected his favorites, less than 40 for each, and these were moved to a separate room. That reduced the number of designs under consideration to 232. The jurors then gathered as a group for the first time and paused in front of each entry for discussion. By Day 3, they had narrowed the number down to 39. At one point James Rosati thrust his finger in horror at a squiggle on one panel as if he had uncovered the black spot of Treasure Island. "What's that?" he demanded of the pirate mark. Initials! The entry was immediately disqualified and removed.

Of course, some entries may not have been quite as anonymous as the organizers professed. For example, there were only a handful of entries featuring sophisticated sculptures with distinctive styles. One of those was Frederick Hart's. The landscaper he had worked with to develop his design, Joseph E. Brown, was a principal in EDAW, a prominent landscape architecture firm; among the firm's founders was Garrett Eckbo, one of the jurors. And Brown had worked on other monuments in Washington. He was confident of winning.

On the fourth day, the jurors had their eighteen semifinalists, as prescribed by the competition rules. As they tarried before each entry, the text describing the concept was read aloud to them.

At last they proceeded to the difficult choice of third place, runner-up, and winner.

For the third prize, they chose Frederick Hart and Joseph E. Brown's design. It imagined a cove, a low, white granite wall of human scale, comprising two-thirds of a geometric circle that would have the feel of a sanctuary. Brown had cut windows to frame the Washington Monument and the Lincoln Memorial. At ground level in the horse-shoe, the names of the dead were carved into a scooped wall, at close proximity to the pathway, so that the visitor could sweep his fingers down the names. At various points in the wall, water seeped through small slits from the top down to a small channel along the base, sugges-tive of weeping. At the terminus of each of the wall's prongs, there were two sculptures, facing one another across a meadow and an invisible line of tension. One portrayed a soldier carrying a wounded comrade, reaching out and calling for help. The other was a figure with an out-stretched arm, rushing to help. Later, this concept would be described as heroic, but Hart had specifically tamped down the notion of hero-ism in favor of distress, poignancy and tragedy. The description of the design, however, *was* heroic: "The sculptures are meant to honor and evoke the sacrifice and valor" of the Vietnam soldier and be a "met-aphor for reconciliation." In denying this entry first place, one juror remarked that, while the design might be perfect for World War II, it was not so for Vietnam.

The second prize went to entrant #343. It was a fascinating com-position of two facing U-shaped walls of different heights bearing the names of the dead. Joining the walls was a massive overhang-ing abstract sculpture that formed a bridge between the two walls. Where the sculpture joined the higher wall, the wall was fractured, as if to suggest the war that had fractured the United States. The crumpled bronze artwork reminded some of the cubist sculptures of Lithuanian artist, Jacques Lipchitz, or the lumpy expressionist sculptures of Reuben Nakian, though others found it more in the vein of socialist-realist, Soviet-style art. As it happened, the team responsible for the design was a Long Island group of Russian emi-grés led by Marvin Krosinsky. It bore an inscription that Vietnam veterans would have found uplifting but that protesters might find debatable:

The Nation Divided, its People in Turmoil
A Conflict Unending and Controversial . . .
But their Spirit made This Nation One Again . . .
Its people United and its Principles Resolved and Firm.

The concept was perfect for World War I, a juror remarked, as if they were channeling Professor Andrus Burr's assignment at Yale. But it was not right for Vietnam.

Competition design entry by Marvin Krosinsky, awarded second place

Throughout the competition, the jurors came back time and again to the haunting submission identified as #1026. "He must really know what he's doing," a juror remarked, "to dare to do something so naïve."

Submission #1026 was startling in its differences from all the other entries. Against an abundance of precise drawings by more sophisticated competitors, this entry was a triumph of simplicity. At first glance, its two panels looked almost like the work of a high schooler by comparison, with the elemental black chevron like a floating mustache against a light blue pastel wash. In contrast to the fine geometric renderings of the other top contenders, this entry was ethereal and distinctly Asian in feel. Instead of the heroic labors of the others to fold softly into the existing landscape, #1026 proposed to cut deeply into the earth. Instead of comfortable words about heroism and service, valor and sacrifice, this submission had only a simple inscription: a large, gray rectangular panel with the words *In Memoriam.*

The handwritten words that described the vision of the artist imagined a "rift in the earth" in which a long polished black granite wall would emerge from and recede into the landscape. "Walking into this grassy site contained by the walls of the memorial we can barely make out the carved names upon the memorial's walls." The multitude of war dead would convey "a sense of overwhelming numbers." And these names would be carved into the wall in the order in which they died in Vietnam, so that a stroll along the wall would become a chronicle of the Vietnam War from its first to its last American casualty. It would be up to each visitor "to come to terms with this loss."

For death, in the end, the words proclaimed, is "a personal and private matter."

The entry did not impress every juror. Chairman Clay found the display "sketchy" and "vague." On the first pass, only three of the eight jurors thought well of it. But its strength and "deceptive simplicity," in Clay's words, grew on the jurors, and they kept returning to ponder its beautifully descriptive words. Hideo Sasaki, the influential landscape architect (who had been interned in the Poston, Arizona, camp for Japanese-Americans during World War II), was especially enthusiastic. In time, a consensus developed around it. They considered it to be far superior to all the rest.

On the morning of the fifth day, Clay gathered his notes along with the comments of the others as he prepared to write the jury's verdict. The commemoration must have a sense of serenity, he wrote, and the wall of #1026 below ground would cut out traffic noise and thus achieve that desired effect. "Washington," noted one juror, "is a city of white memorials, rising . . . this is a dark memorial, receding."

"Many people will not comprehend this design," one juror said of #1026.

"It will be a better memorial if it's not entirely understood at first," responded another.

But perhaps the most compelling juror observation was this: "Great art is like an unfilled vessel into which you can pour your own meaning. . . . Each generation continues to do that. . . . A great work of art is never complete and forever fresh."

Clay later wrote, "The winning design is a great one. We believe it should be built as designed. It reflects the precise nature of the site designated by Congress. It is aligned beautifully with the Lincoln Memorial and Washington Monument . . . a unique horizontal design in a city full of vertical 'statements.' It uses natural forms of earth and minerals, without attempting to dominate the site. It invites contemplation and a feeling of reconciliation. The design, by creating a place of utter simplicity and serenity, is a work of art that will survive the test of time."

When the label of #1026 was ripped off and the name revealed, the surprise winner was unknown to any of the jurors, an amateur and a young Asian-American woman by the name of Maya Lin. Of the winner, the juror Pietro Belluschi would say that a family's background "has a way to penetrate and show in her work: [there is] a natural sophistication and sensitivity traditional in Chinese work." And he would see her youth and naiveté as central to her achievement. "Her design rises above [politics]," he said. "It is very naïve . . . more what a child will do than what a sophisticated artist would present. It was above the banal. It has the sort of purity of an idea that shines."

In the joint statement of all the jurors, there was this final praise: "This is very much a memorial of our own times, one that could not have been achieved in another time or place."

Paul Spreiregen, the impresario of this extravaganza, was bursting with pride. He believed that his competition had been a model of fairness and professionalism. The result was a stroke of genius. The very simplicity and transcendence of entry #1026 reminded him of what that French writer Antoine de Saint-Exupéry had once said: *"Il semble que la perfection soit atteinte non quand il n'y a plus rien à ajouter, mais quand il n'y a plus rien à retrancher."*

"Perfection is finally attained not when there is no longer anything to add, but when there is no longer anything to take away."

Chapter Four

AND THE WINNER IS . . .

"We believe it should be built as designed." Those words of the final jury decision were fraught with latent significance.

In the few days after the jury's decision, Paul Spreiregen began planning for the formal public announcement of the winning design. The chances of the memorial actually ever being built, he surmised, were extremely slim, much less built as designed. For that to happen, millions of dollars would have to be raised, not just one million as Jan Scruggs initially imagined, but seven million. Multiple Washington bureaucracies would all have to confer their blessing—the National Park Service, the National Capital Planning Board, the Commission of Fine Arts, and perhaps, most daunting of all, the acerbic, ultra-conservative secretary of the Interior, James Watt. Pencils were sure to be sharpened.

There were more immediate concerns. Maya Lin had won only with an idea, just a figment of her fertile imagination. She had no expertise in building or in landscape architecture or in engineering. There would certainly be technical issues with a structure that was built below ground level. If the wall at its vertex was ten feet high, there was real danger of people falling off. What was the impact of that danger on the design? A need for an unsightly fence or an additional wall? For the impending press conference, what would the critics say, especially the prickly architecture critic of the *Washington Post*, Wolf Von Eckardt? Would there be sore losers, especially the luminaries of art and architecture who might set out to denigrate the winner? And finally, what would the VVMF veterans think and say, not only in public but also in private? Their initial reaction seemed positive. When the patrons were taken to see the winning design, there was a pause before Jan Scruggs said "I like it." And another veteran and colleague, John C. Wheeler, said, "I think it is a work of genius."

They got it, Spreiregen told himself. What about the others?

In fact, Scruggs instantly had private doubts. His first thought was that the design looked like a bat. Then he saw it as a boomerang that people would latch onto as an analogy to the lost war: that the thing was flung out, and then it would come screaming back to coldcock you. Then he saw a black hole in the ground. The choice was sure to occasion an immense public relations headache, he thought prophetically.

The announcement had to have maximum dramatic effect.

Additionally, there was the question of the winner herself. When they pulled off the number of the entry to reveal the name and then her details, they had to wonder: Who was this undergraduate? What did she look like? How mature was she? How would she act and react? Were there implications from the very fact that she was of Asian extraction? Building her up as a credible choice was central to a successful launch. But would she satisfy?

It was the last day of spring semester classes when her roommate rushed to tell Maya Lin that a call had come to her from the Washington competition committee. They wanted to come and see her; they had a few questions to ask about her design.

"Don't get your hopes up," a voice on the line said. Lin did not confer much importance to the impending visit. She might have made it into the top one hundred, she thought. They were probably coming with disqualifying technical concerns like drainage. Besides, she was preoccupied with packing up and getting out of town.

At her dorm door the next day, along with two other colleagues, stood a retired US Marine colonel, Donald E. Schaet, an artillery offi-cer with the infantry in Vietnam and a recipient of a Bronze Star medal with combat V, denoting combat valor. He was an unusual visitor in the corridors of Saybrook College at Yale. For all his record of mili-tary bravado, Colonel Schaet turned out to be rather soft-spoken and unpretentious, in a very un-Marine kind of way. But he was also skilled in recruiting and press relations. He would make a good defender later.

His discourse began with words on the unparalleled magnitude of the competition itself, the largest of any art contest in all of Europe and America, and how many truly worthy contenders there were. The preamble sounded like a rejection. Maya Lin braced herself for the inevitable.

Oh, and by the way, Colonel Schaet said at last, she had won the competition.

—

With the formidable Marine dispatched to New Haven to invite the winner to Washington, Paul Spreiregen began his frantic preparations for the public announcement. At the competition offices, the phone was ringing constantly, with competitors in high anticipation of the results. Joseph Brown, the landscape architect whose horseshoe and weeping water design with its Frederick Hart sculptures made a strong contender, was especially persistent and aggressive. Should he be pre-paring his remarks for his acceptance speech? he asked. Spreiregen was appropriately mum.

Meanwhile, the architect-juror Harry Weese quietly offered the services of his Washington office to build several scale models of Maya Lin's design. They had only an idea, and now the idea had to be devel-oped and given a sense of reality, far beyond the mysterious, floating chevron in a sea of azure blue. A professional, experienced firm was needed to execute the design. Not only did a memorial below ground level present serious engineering problems, but the dimensions of scale had to be made larger to accommodate all the names. That required that the wall be about ten feet tall at its vertex, and that in itself made safety an even greater issue. The challenges were formidable.

Once the models were hastily finished, they were photographed from different angles for a parallax view, and these were rendered into a slide show. A slick press release was crafted to create an aura around the surprising winner. Maya Lin's story was as important as the memorial itself.

"It has to be love at first sight," Spreiregen thought. "Or it is dead."

On the day of her graduation from Yale, Maya drove to Washington. Once there, she was taken immediately to see the models . . . and she was horrified.

"You have changed my design!" she exclaimed and turned on her heel to walk out. "I never want to see you for the rest of my life!"

The managers looked at one another in amazement and befuddlement. Was she crazy? Was she out to scuttle the whole thing? She was going to be a problem.

Good reporter that he was, Wolf von Eckhart was immediately onto this remarkable outcome. Soon enough he found out where the winner was staying and sought her out, taking with him his friend and colleague, Judith Martin. When Lin appeared, they were amazed. She looked much younger than her twenty-one years, especially in her oversized Yale sweatshirt and horizontally striped knee socks. Von Eckhart was lavish in his congratulation, gushing his enthusiasm for the design, extolling its simplicity, its naturalness, its lack of jingoism.

"It's so Taoist," he exclaimed.

"I don't know anything about that," Lin replied flatly.

They had expected her to be over the moon with triumph and a bit in shock. Instead, she was visibly in distress. Their hearts went out to her.

"They look at me, and they don't see an architect," she cried. "They" were Spreiregen and his imposing, self-important colleagues.

They were taking her design away from her, she burst out, and they were beastly and patronizing besides.

Von Eckhart and Martin exchanged meaningful glances. This was a young lady who needed to be taken in tow. Maya Lin's debut was only a day away. And so, the future Miss Manners, feeling very maternal, hustled her off to the toniest store in town, Garfinckel's, for a do-over. There, on the spacious third floor for exclusively designer clothes, Lin tried on a number of outfits, feeling quite out of sorts. Wasn't Frank Lloyd Wright an eccentric dresser? she asked.

"Honey, when you become Frank Lloyd Wright, you can dress any way you like," Martin replied tartly. They settled on a gray suit and stylish shoes. Lin balked at a hat. And then it was downstairs for makeup to make her look just a little bit older.

On May 6, 1981, the circular jury room at the headquarters of the American Institute of Architects had been made ready for the announcement. Fifteen honorable mention entries would be identified first. For suspense, the first, second, and third place finishers were under cover. Amid the crush of press and cameras, the landscape architect, Joseph Brown, stood with his sculptor, Frederick Hart, reasonably certain now that they had not won. He was confident that their entry had all the right aesthetic and political elements for victory. And he had all the right connections in the Washington architectural community and in the even smaller community of public art mavens. But he was getting the sinking feeling that all those factors might not be enough.

Spreiregen made a few remarks on the breadth and fairness of the competition, and then uncovered the second and third place finishers. Brown and Hart took a disappointing third place. And then it was Scruggs's turn to announce the winner. Off came the cover, and there was an audible gasp as petite Maya Lin stepped forward to greet the assemblage, her luxuriant hair cascading to her shoulders over a simple, demure white shift. When she addressed the assemblage, only her head peeked over the podium. She giggled as she told of Colonel Schaet's visit to her dorm room and his remark not to get her hopes up. Joseph Brown could scarcely mask his surprise. Their effort as a leading architectural firm with a sculptor of national reputation and an associate who had won the distinguished Rome Prize for architecture had been bested by a college student with a class exercise. And yet, he saw instantly that his entry had lost for being too complicated. As the chairman of the jury told him later, their entry was "too literal." Maya Lin had captured something Brown and his associates had missed. Her design was simple and strong, if "negative." Brown felt no resentment, only resignation. Hers was better.

She took a few questions. Eventually, the inevitable question came. Since she was an "Oriental person," and since many Asians had died in the war, how did she feel about that?

With the inscrutability of the Dalai Lama, she answered, "It doesn't matter."

Jan Scruggs and Maya Lin at the announcement
of the winning design, May 6, 1981

Afterward, she was escorted to a number of individual interviews. Openly and without hesitation, she admitted that she didn't know much about the Vietnam War. When asked about her artistic intention, she quotably answered, "I wanted to describe a journey—a journey which would make you experience death."

The next day, the headline in the *Los Angeles Times* was:

STUDENT WINS VIETNAM MEMORIAL CONTEST
CHINESE WOMAN, 21, GETS $20,000 FOR WAR MONUMENT DESIGN

In the *Washington Post*, reporter Henry Allen, a Marine combat veteran himself and more skeptical than his colleague Wolf von Eckhart, led his story with this sentence: "For the dead whom few wanted to remember after a war few could forget, a woman who was four years old when the first bodies came home has designed a national memorial to be built on the Mall." And deeper in the story, Allen wrote, "Her design does not mention the war itself, or the Republic of South Vietnam, only the names of the dead."

The naysaying had begun.

—

Maya Ying Lin was born in 1959 in the southeastern Ohio town of Athens. She was the daughter of Chinese immigrants; her father was raised in Fujian province in southeastern China and later in Beijing in a family of well-to-do scholars and statesmen. Her grandfather had been the Chinese delegate to the League of Nations in 1921, and the family could trace its ancestry back to the eleventh century. Her father's upbringing had been strict, at a time when children of the upper classes were drilled in calligraphy and music along with other core subjects. As the Sino-Japanese War began in 1937 and then merged into World War II, Huan Lin nevertheless enjoyed a comfortable, carefree existence as a university administrator. Maya Lin's mother, Ming-hui, hailed from a family of doctors that included women physicians. But as the Communists took over the country in 1949 and set out to quash the upper class, the specter of re-education camps loomed, and it was time to flee. With fifty dollars sewn into her coat, Ming-hui was smuggled out of Shanghai in a junk as Nationalist planes bombed the harbor.

In fleeing China, the refugees had lost everything and, once in America, had to begin anew. Huan Lin gravitated back into academic administration, but he also schooled himself in the art of pottery, an avocation that was probably inspired by *his* father, who had possessed a magnificent collection of Chinese ceramics and porcelain. The style of Huan's pottery was decidedly more Japanese than Chinese, accentuating the rustic simplicity of the Zen aesthetic. No doubt, the Japanese wartime occupation of Fujian province influenced him. (That simple, minimalist, Japanese-influenced aesthetic would come to characterize Maya Lin's later work.)

Her parents met in Seattle and were married in an Episcopal Church in 1951. The family moved to Athens after Huan, now calling himself Henry Lin, was invited to join the faculty of Fine Arts at the University of Ohio. In time he rose to become the Dean of Fine Arts. He would also achieve considerable renown as an award-winning potter, displaying his work in exhibitions far beyond Athens. When their daughter was born, they gave her an Indian name, Maya, the name of Buddha's mother, that means *illusion* and evokes emptiness. In Hinduism, Maya is a sobriquet for goddess.

"I've been an artist from probably the first time I stepped into my dad's ceramics studio," Lin would say. Her mother, meanwhile, earned a graduate degree in English and Chinese literature, with a thesis that fused the poems of William Butler Yeats with Indian philosophy. In 1965, now known as Julia Lin, she got her doctorate with a dissertation on modern Chinese poetry and taught in the university's English department.

As a child and a "faculty brat," Maya Lin found the hilly landscape of southeastern Ohio beautiful and fascinating. The Lin house was deep in the woods, and she came to imagine the trees on the ridges above the house as spines growing out of the earth. A great lover of birds and animals, she mourned the devastating damage that DDT, the chemical scourge about which Rachel Carson wrote in her seminal book, *Silent Spring* (1962), was visiting on Lake Erie and on bird populations.

"This is so unfair that one species can do this to another species," the young Maya said to her mother once. "We have more of a responsibility."

Inwardly directed in her close-knit family, with its concentration on art and learning, she excelled at school, especially in math and science. With her love of animals, she supposed that she would become a veterinarian or a field zoologist. Even as a superior student, she was constantly making things with her hands in deference to her father. The Department of Fine Arts was her playground. A "clean aesthetic" epitomized the art of the family household, and there was great respect for the creative process.

Her adolescence, however, had been a struggle for identity. Her parents wanted her and her brother, Tan, to fit in, to assimilate, and told them both that they only wanted their children to be happy. Henry Lin was intent not to repeat the strictness of his own upbringing in China. The children were left alone to grow as typical Americans and follow their own passions without heavy-handed direction. But in that small Midwestern town, their differentness was evident. Though Lin did not regard herself as anything other than an ordinary American kid, she was something of a misfit. By her own admission, she had only a few friends. Somehow, she did not "belong."

When it came time to apply for college, she was in a good position to reach high. She had the highest grade point average in her high school class and was its valedictorian. Yale admitted her swiftly. Once there she was seen as reserved and apolitical. She was disinterested in extracurricular activities. In her third year, she gravitated toward a major in architecture.

"I chose architecture," she would say later, because "it was this perfect combination of science, math, and art." Architecture was her harmony of opposites, art and science, her yin and yang. She would say that she had to suppress the analytic side of her brain to do her art. She began to lay her groundwork with courses in form and function, place and dimension, and the basic theories of architecture.

Importantly, she would take what was then the best-known undergraduate course in Yale's Architecture School, "History of Modern Architecture and Urbanism," taught by its most famous professor, Vincent Scully. As it happened, it was in Scully's class that a seed was planted for the future. Like Professor Burr, Scully too had covered the World War I monument at Thiepval in Sommes, France, in his course. The "yawning archway" of the great cenotaph, incised with names of the dead, was like a "gaping scream," Scully told his students, as the tombs of seventy thousand soldiers were spread before you. It was a realization of immeasurable loss.

It wasn't until her junior year that Lin's consciousness about her ethnicity rose to the surface. During a semester abroad in Denmark, tanned under the brilliant northern sun, she was often mistaken for an Eskimo, and it was not a pleasant experience since the Danes tended to discriminate against the aboriginal "Greenlanders." It was as if her eastern sensibility was bubbling up from within. When she would disabuse the Danes of their Eskimo fantasies by saying she was Chinese, a common response was: "Oh, so do your parents own a restaurant or a laundry?" Or if, back in the States, she would get in a taxi, a common question was, "Where are you from?" Answer: "Ohio." Counterresponse: "No, no, I mean where are you really from?" And then there was the stereotype in the movies that especially infuriated her, of the docile, servile Asian woman.

"No matter how long you've been here," she would say about her roots, "you're not going to be quite allowed to be American."

While in Denmark, Lin, now fully committed to her architecture major, took an interest in the Nørrebro cemetery in Copenhagen. The psychological and emotional power of cemeteries fascinated her. In a small European country where land is scarce, cemeteries double as parks, and people spend pleasant hours in leisure with no reference to the dead. This tie to the land became central to her aesthetic development.

"All my artworks," she would say later, "deal with nature and the landscape. . . . It's how you experience the land. . . . The Vietnam Memorial is an earth work."

She would eventually bring that Danish insight to her work in Professor Burr's class. For his Vietnam memorial assignment, she began to channel her deepest instincts, returning to the aesthetic of her upbringing. After visiting Constitution Gardens over Thanksgiving and back at her Yale cafeteria, she sketched her idea of a simple V in a helping of mashed potatoes.

Her impulse was simply to cut into the earth. "I imagined taking a knife and cutting into the earth, opening it up, and [with the passage of time] that initial violence and pain would heal," she told Bill Moyers in a 2003 PBS interview. "The grass would grow back, but the initial cut would remain a pure, flat surface in the earth with a polished, mirrored surface, much like the surface of a geode when you cut it and polish the edge." Her design was not a wall, she would insist, but an edge to the earth, an opened side. She chose black granite to make the surface reflect like a mirror. The effect, she surmised, would double the size of the park.

A name can bring back every memory one has of a person. A name alone is more "comprehensive" than a still photograph or a sculpture. "Literally as you read a name, and touch a name, the pain will come out," she would say. "I really did mean for people to cry . . . of your own power, [you have to] turn around and walk back up into the light, into the present. But if you can't accept death, you'll never get over it." Her memorial, she insisted, was about honesty.

Moreover, her decision to place the names in the order in which soldiers died would provide a timeline for the longest war in American history. The names then would become the memorial, but also a narrative of the war. In the sparseness of the simple V, there was no need to embellish the design further. "The cost of war is these individuals," she would say. "It's [about] the people, not the politics." It would be, she said, the interface "between our world and the quieter, darker, more peaceful world beyond." Its apolitical nature was its essence.

"I did not want to civilize war by glorifying it or by forgetting the sacrifices involved," she wrote later. "The price of human life in war should always be clearly remembered."

As the issue would later be drawn, this was the dialectic between abstract and realistic art. When she began to think about Vietnam, there was no single image that came to her mind, like the photograph of the Iwo Jima flag-raising from World War II. Moreover, a realistic sculpture was only one interpretation and specific to only one time. She thought of a memorial as music in the way music can make a person laugh or cry, totally in the abstract.

"That abstraction can be human and relate to you. And that's where the name . . . everything about that person will come back in the name."

In the winter of 1981, when she was completing her entry to the grand competition, she seemed to realize that her elemental chevron floating in a sea of pastel blue would not be enough to make her entry competitive. The design was too simple to be noteworthy, and the overall concept was focused only on the dead. She doubted that it would be chosen.

"It wasn't a politically glorified statement about war."

Her entry's accompanying description was everything. It had to be right. And on that, she had writer's block. So, she sought out Vincent Scully, whose course had had such an impact on her. Sensing her struggle, Scully again pulled out slides of the Thiepval Memorial in France that had so moved Professor Andrus Burr the preceding summer. As she viewed the simple graves and the gargantuan cenotaph, the dam broke, and she picked up her pen and began to write. Her poetic brother, Tan, who was then studying at Columbia University, became her literary adviser.

"Writing is one of the purest arts," she would say years later. "I value writing. I respect it. I find it the most difficult thing for me to do, but when I'm done, I am unbelievably just at peace. If you think about art as being able to share your thoughts with another, writing is totally pure."

Walking through this park-like area, the memorial appears as a rift in the earth- a long, polished black stone wall, emerging from and receding into the earth. Approaching the memorial, the ground slopes gently downward, and the low walls emerging on either side, growing out of the earth, extend and converge at a point below and ahead. Walking into the grassy site contained by the walls of this memorial we can barely make out the carved names upon the memorial's walls. These names, seemingly infinite in number, convey the sense of overwhelming numbers, while unifying those individuals into a whole. For this memorial is meant not as a monument to the individual, but rather as a memorial to the men and women who died during this war, as a whole.

Portion of Maya Lin's handwritten paragraph, from her
competition entry, describing her design

Though she could not know it then, it was ultimately her writing that won the competition for her.

From the fortunate timing to Professor Burr's guidance, to the minimalizing and depoliticizing of her concept of falling dominos, to her realization about the value of simplicity, to her gritty persistence and her essential talent, developing her design had been an evolutionary process. She had succeeded in making history apolitical.

"I have just dealt with facts," she would say. "It's what facts you choose to portray that focus you. It's always about giving to people information and letting them read into it what they will."

PART II

ART, MEMORY, AND POLITICS

Chapter Five

FIGHT AS HARD AS YOU CAN

A week before the official announcement of the grand competition for a Vietnam War memorial, Ronald Reagan trounced Jimmy Carter in the 1980 presidential election. During the campaign, Reagan had addressed memory of the war only once. On August 18, at the convention of Veterans of Foreign Wars, which was endorsing his presidential bid, he rattled the rafters with a stemwinder. "America has been sleepwalking far too long. We need to snap out of it," he proclaimed. The United States could have defeated the Viet Cong and the North Vietnamese Army, if only Americans had not been bamboozled by North Vietnamese propaganda. Presidents Johnson and Nixon had let American soldiers down when US officials had suffered from a lack of will. That war was a "noble cause," he thundered, in which the United States came to the aid of a small, beleaguered country, fresh from colonial rule, a nation that called out for help against a "totalitarian neighbor bent on conquest."

And now, Reagan said, America was suffering from a malady called "Vietnam syndrome." Moral anguish over war's devastation and despair over the loss of life were gripping the country and paralyzing American leaders, making them timid in employing American power. "We dishonor the memory of fifty thousand young Americans who died in that cause when we give way to feelings of guilt, as if we were doing something shameful," the Republican nominee said. In all this Reagan found a lesson. "We will never again ask young men to fight and possibly die in a war our government is afraid to let them win."

Afraid to win? This revisionist fantasy—that the United States could have "won" in Vietnam, if only more bombs were dropped, more lives were lost, more years of struggle were endured—would persist for decades, infecting the way the Pentagon itself dealt with this dark chapter of its past. Meanwhile, a Harris poll earlier in the year reflected a contradiction in the public mind. Sixty-four percent agreed with the statement that Vietnam veterans "were made suckers" by their government, while at the same time more than 90 percent felt those same veterans deserved more respect for having served their country during a difficult time.

In January 1981, as the design submissions for the memorial began to pour in, the new president chose his cabinet. Little noticed at first amid his higher-profile choices was his pick for secretary of the Interior. James Watt, a Wyoming lawyer, would become a central player in the Vietnam Memorial saga. Before Watt resigned under pressure nearly three years later, he gained a reputation as the most hostile steward of the environment in history, pushing for aggressive drilling and mining on public lands and significantly reducing the number of endangered species under federal law.

Watt also had authority over what happened on the National Mall and what could be built there. In the spring of 1983, he banned rock concerts on the Mall, which was regarded as rebuke toward the Beach Boys, who had performed the previous year. Watt justified his decision by saying that rock acts attracted "the wrong element" and encouraged drug abuse and alcoholism. Suddenly, Watt became arguably the most reviled man in America, and even President Reagan's wife, Nancy, announced that she was a fan of the Beach Boys. Later, Watt confessed that he'd never heard of the Beach Boys, one of America's most popular and successful bands.

"If it wasn't 'Amazing Grace' or 'Star Spangled Banner,'" Watt later said, "I didn't recognize the song."

—

After Maya Lin's design was chosen and announced, the public reaction was intense. Letters from outraged veterans poured into the Memorial Fund office. One claimed that Lin's design had "the warmth and charm of an Abyssinian dagger." "Nihilistic aesthetes" had chosen it. The design evoked the digging and hiding that a soldier had to do to survive in Vietnam. The proposal reflected the true situation of the Vietnam veteran: "bury the dead and ignore the needs of the living." An Army major called it "just a black wall that expresses nothing." Predictably, the names of incendiary anti-war icons, Jane Fonda and Abbie Hoffman, were invoked as cheering for a design that made a mockery of the Vietnam dead. There was positive reaction too, but the negative feedback captured the attention of the organizers.

This was only the beginning. Things were to get much worse.

The divide between a potent veterans cadre and critics with authentic artistic sensibilities was beginning to take shape. In a laudatory editorial, the *Washington Star* found Lin's design contemplative with healthy doses both of pride for the veteran and reconciliation for the nation. The *New York Times* architecture critic, Paul Goldberger, pronounced the concept as "one of the most subtle and sophisticated pieces of public architecture" ever proposed for a city known for its haughty and grandiose installations.

And Wolf Von Eckardt, the dean of the architecture critics and arguably the godfather of the competition, gushed with enthusiasm. In a *Washington Post* piece entitled "The Serene Grace of the Vietnam

Memorial," he conceded that the design was unconventional, as unconventional as the Eiffel Tower. "It is," he wrote, "a direct evocation of an emotional experience, which, one way or another, is what art is all about." It might take time for its grace and power to be appreciated. "Its emotional impact . . . will take effect slowly, taking hold of the mind before the understanding quickens the heart."

Not all the critics were so smitten. Paul Gapp, the architecture critic at the *Chicago Tribune*, called the design "inane" and bemoaned the sheer poverty of modern architecture to have produced something so dreadful. The judges were simply disconnected from public taste, he fumed, and he did not think the public would stand for it. The design, he wrote, was akin to "an erosion control project." A colleague of his on the *Tribune*, Raymond Coffey, a Vietnam veteran, wrote in an opinion piece, "It is as if the very memorial itself is intended to bury and banish the whole Vietnam experience." Charles Krauthammer, at his acerbic best, wrote in the *New Republic* that the only purpose of the design was to emphasize the "sheer human waste, the utter meaninglessness of it all." It treated the Vietnam dead like "victims of some monstrous traffic accident."

This mixed reaction among the critics and vets paled next to the critical arena of fundraising. What would the donors, especially Ross Perot, think of the design?

With his large financial investment in the competition and swelling with patriotic fervor, Perot had waited anxiously to hear about the winning design. When he was told about the black wall, the Texan was decidedly negative, and when he saw the design model, he was apoplectic. Dismissing Scruggs's plaudits for the design as a magnificent work of art, Perot remarked that it might be great for those who died, but it said nothing about the two million who served and survived. Scruggs pleaded with him, at least, not to broadcast his disapproval. If the press asked him, Perot replied, he would say he didn't like it. But he promised, for the time being, that he would not overtly publicize his attitude.

As for the winner with Chinese ancestry, Perot began referring to her as "egg roll."

—

Maya Lin moved into an apartment on Capitol Hill in Washington in June 1981 and stayed for a year. After her momentary shock at her triumph, the weeks and months that followed were excruciating for her. She came to think of that horrible year as a war between herself and the entire Washington establishment. At every turn, she felt, politicians, architects, landscapers, veterans, and bureaucrats were trying to alter, water down, and defile her design, forcing her to cede control to lesser, prosaic individuals. In her dogged defense of her vision, she alienated almost everyone with whom she came into contact. She was abrasive and undiplomatic; compromise was not in her blood.

The first challenge was to find a collaborator who could execute her brilliant design, for at least she acknowledged that she was inexperienced in architectural practicalities. This problem led to the first real skirmish in the coming war. The veterans were indebted to Paul Spreiregen for his deft and professional handling of the complex competition, and so he seemed like the natural choice to become the "architect of record." Stiffly and high-handedly, the VVMF patrons presented their choice to her as a *fait accompli*.

She reacted badly. She had already taken a considerable dislike to Spreiregen (and he to her), largely because he had told her bluntly of the flaws and difficulties of her design. Perhaps more annoyingly, according to Kent Cooper, who eventually became the architect of record, Spreiregen pushed for equal billing for implementing the design. On that point, she put her foot down: no one would share equal credit with her. Weeks of tense, angry discussions followed. At one point, according to Lin, the VVMF veterans warned her that she would come to regret her uncooperative, hostile behavior. Soon enough, her tormenters said, she would come "crawling back on [her] hands and knees." It was not a good way to win her cooperation.

She fled to Yale. There, the entire university, especially among the luminaries in the architecture school, stood in awe, disbelief, and soaring admiration at her accomplishment. Her renowned mentor, Vincent Scully, shook his head in astonishment. "There's nothing really like it at all. It doesn't make any specific gesture which can date it in time or in place. It's all wars, all death, all living and all dead . . . at once! It's a remarkable thing and done by a girl of twenty or whatever, it's really unbelievable. It's really hard to grasp."

The dean of the Architecture School, César Pelli, was also among her fervent admirers. To him, her design was amazing in capturing the enormity of the Vietnam conflict. It had touched his heart profoundly, as a triumph of the abstract. That an undergraduate student had conceived this stroke of genius was all the more impressive. In New Haven, she threw herself on Pelli's good graces for advice and protection. The tall, smiling, easygoing Argentinian, who was already a towering figure in American architecture, listened sympathetically as she spilled out her anguish at being eaten alive by the Washington insiders. When she was finished, he began by instructing her in a fundamental truth: in the world of construction a marked difference exists between the designer and the builder. She was the artist, and once a design of an artist is accepted and paid for—she had collected her $20,000 prize—that person has virtually no rights.

Pelli knew what he was talking about. At that very time, he was engaged in a renovation of MOMA (the Museum of Modern Art) in New York. Once his concept was accepted and he was paid for it, the entire project was summarily changed in the subsequent iterations, and his plans ended up in the waste basket. He mentioned how many times the same thing had happened to the brightest lights of their firmament, known as "starchitects," including Philip Johnson himself. Pelli spoke of how in the Renaissance great paintings were painted over, cut up, and the canvas reused. "If I design a building and get paid for it, the buyer can paint it purple, and I have no say in the matter," he told her. Her design had won, and she had been paid. She had to deal with that fundamental fact.

"You may not be able to do anything," he counseled. "But fight as hard as you can!"

The dean did, however, have a specific suggestion. He recommended an old friend, a Washington architect named Kent Cooper, as her collaborator.

"He will protect you," Pelli assured her. And moreover, he could be a mentor.

Kent Cooper was a well-known figure in Washington architectural circles. He had been a brilliant, prize-winning student, and Eero Saarinen had recruited him in 1958 straight out of graduate school to work on the completion of Washington's Dulles International Airport. In that association, he had learned patience. The airport was supposed to be finished in eighteen months; it took seven years. And in his later years, Cooper hung a large portrait of the modernist hero, Le Corbusier, in his office with his dictum, "Creation is a patient search."

Cooper had gone on to develop a reputation as the avatar of modernism in Washington architecture, designing churches, schools, community centers, and libraries—even an installation at the Washington Zoo that earned the word "humane." On his arrival in the capital, he found Washington architecture a boring wasteland of neoclassical buildings. But Dulles Airport, and later the Washington subway system (1976) and East Wing of the National Gallery of Art (1978) became prime examples of a new, modernist trend. In due course, Cooper would add Maya Lin's memorial to that distinguished company. He would refer to it as the landmark and iconic memorial of the postwar era.

"There hasn't been a commemorative piece before or after that has had the same impact," he would say. But that flattering remark came long after his difficult collaboration with Maya Lin.

Though Lin did not know it, Cooper had submitted his own design to the Vietnam Veterans Memorial competition. It featured a long row of aluminum pylons upon which the names would be photographically etched. By design, those names were meant to fade in twenty years, and this fading was central to his notion of fleeting memory. The centerpiece of the design was a crumpled piece of bronze that symbolized death. Cooper's design had made it into the top forty-eight, but no further.

Kent Cooper's design entry for the Vietnam Veterans Memorial competition.
The hands on the lower left are part of the design and show how visitors
might touch the names inscribed on the columns.

Lin returned from Yale and her talk with César Pelli and presented Cooper's name to the skeptical veterans, who were set on Spreiregen. The resistance in the VVMF to an unfamiliar outsider was considerable. Brusque and uncompromising as always, Lin saw her relationship with her patrons deteriorate further. Once again, her newfound booster, Wolf von Eckhart, stepped into the fray to calm the waters, pushing the veterans to listen to her. She was the winner of their contest after all, and besides, she had retained legal counsel to protect her interests. Eventually they had no choice but to capitulate, for she still possessed a semblance of veto power. Spreiregen was out, and Cooper was in. It was a victory that Cooper could only half celebrate. And in his ousting, Spreiregen could only half mourn, saying, "Working with Lin had no great appeal for me." In her first meeting with Cooper, Lin delivered a stiff warning.

"You have no responsibility for the memorial. You will get no credit for it. Just make my design work!"

It was a good thing that patience was Cooper's watchword, for in the coming months his patience would be sorely tried. Through the entire saga in which she was the central figure, Maya Lin would keep a steely focus on her artistic vision and cared little about hurting the feelings of her collaborators. It would be jarring later to hear a participant say, "Maya did not walk away from Washington with a single friend." Friendship was never her concern.

Diligently, Cooper set about making detailed drawings for the construction. An early challenge was to determine the size of the wall's surface, so that it could accommodate all 58,000 names. This required that the size of the wall as originally conceived had to be doubled and its height extended. Cooper wanted a railing, so people wouldn't fall off the top. The military wanted a raised bandstand above the wall for their events. Lin vetoed both ideas.

A more difficult issue was her insistence that the names be inscribed in the chronological order of their deaths, thus providing a timeline for the war itself from 1959 to 1975. This was a startlingly original idea. Her collaborators, however, groused that such ordering would be an inconvenience or worse, an annoyance for visitors. The requirement to search a telephone book-sized index for the name of a loved one would be a turnoff, and if that system was adopted, the tattered book would probably have to be replaced every month. Lin fought back. A timeline of names was central to her vision.

"I knew the time line was key to the experience," she would say. "A returning veteran would be able to find his or her time of service when finding a friend's name." Only when she pointed out the obvious—if you listed all the slain Smiths in alphabetical order, the effect would be prosaic and mind-numbing—did the patrons come around on the issue.

Another area of contention was the thickness of the wall itself. The granite had to be razor-thin, Lin insisted, consistent with her vision of a cut or a rift in the earth. Cooper wanted it thicker and thus more durable, since thin granite would be fragile and difficult to work. The notion of reflective granite was new to him. But, as she would later say, "a massive, thick, stone wall . . . was not my intention at all." To thicken the wall was to undermine her metaphor. She would not have it.

"I always saw the wall as a pure surface, an interface between light and dark, where I cut the earth and polished its open edge," she would say later. A thin surface reflected the vulnerability and pathos of the soldier's experience. Reflection was the point. It allowed the visitor to see himself mingled within the names of his fallen comrades and thus ponder the bracing thought of "there but for the grace of God go I." While Cooper argued against her thin, granite panels as too fragile, others argued against a polished surface as too feminine.

Then there was the matter of color. What was the significance of black anyway? "I do not think I thought of the color black as a color," she wrote later, sharing the widespread artists' view that black is the absence of color. "[It was more] the idea of a dark mirror into a shadowed mirrored image of the space, a space we cannot enter and from which the names separate us, an interface between the world of the living and the world of the dead." White granite does not reflect the image of the viewer.

"If it were white," Lin would say, "it would blind you because of the southern exposure. Black subdues that and creates a very comforting area. . . . [Black] makes two worlds. . . . It's a mirror." In listening to such an esoteric argument, the veterans were in over their heads. Black was black, dark, intimidating, soul-withering.

The last contention was the matter of the inscription. The veterans were pushing for a pithy phrasing to glorify their service, heroism, and courage. Lin resisted. She wanted only the "In Memoriam," as stated in her proposal. She argued forcefully that a politically charged statement would destroy the apolitical nature of her design . . . and narrow and limit the appeal of the place over time. At this early stage, she was operating only on instinct. Her vision of her monument as all-encompassing, embracing the entire Vietnam generation, both for and against the war, was still inchoate. Only later would she state openly that this was not merely a *veterans'* memorial but a memorial to the nation's tormented experience with the entire war.

"Throughout this time," she said, "I was very careful not to discuss my [political] beliefs. . . . I played it extremely naïve about politics, instead turning the discussion into a strictly aesthetic one."

On July 7, 1981, the US Commission of Fine Arts, the agency charged with approving public artworks in the nation's capital, held its first public hearing on the Vietnam Memorial. Its presiding chairman was J. Carter Brown, a formidable figure in Washington and a Rhode Island patrician whose family traced its American roots back to the Revolutionary War and was responsible for the initial endowment of Brown University in Providence. His father had been an assistant secretary of the Navy. After a stellar career at Harvard and study in Florence, Italy, with the legendary art historian Bernard Berenson, Brown became the director of the National Gallery of Art in Washington when he was just thirty-four years old. In that post, he would supervise the building of the gallery's groundbreaking East Wing, designed by I. M. Pei, and preside over spectacular King Tut and Thomas Jefferson exhibitions. He was also the longest serving leader of the US Commission of Fine Arts, from 1971 to 2002.

The director's judgment and appreciation of artistic merit was refined. Around Washington Brown was a leading public intellectual, a familiar figure on the social scene, always elegant and thin in his English suits, and noted for his charm, courtesy, and savoir faire. Sometimes called America's art czar and the country's "arbiter of excellence," it was said that if the United States had a minister of culture, J. Carter Brown was the ideal choice. Unlike other Washington dignitaries, Brown always looked good in white tie and tails.

J. Carter Brown and Diana, Princess of Wales, National Gallery of Art, 1985

At the hearing, Paul Spreiregen addressed the commission first, speaking of the competition and then of the winning design. It had no precedent in public art. He praised its absence of a representational symbol. "A symbol," he said, "would tend to arrest thought rather than to arouse and expand it." And then the microphone was turned over to Maya Lin.

Instead of some new defense, she chose simply to read her soaring, compelling description from her submission. Somehow, spoken in her soft voice rather than absorbed on a printed page, her words were even more magical. The rift in the earth . . . the long, polished stone wall . . . emerging and receding. . . . The metaphor was riveting, and the panel was mesmerized and amazed at this astounding result.

Lin was thrilled by the hearing. "Fine Arts went superbly," she wrote in her journal. "It was reassuring, elating, i like my work to be liked, what would happen if it were criticized by intelligent people? people i respect? would i feel wrong or wronged, am i arrogant in my personality and in my work . . . [people should] lift their eyes up to the magic right within their reach, the joy felt in making something that flows from reason to reality." Then she added the word "burp."

Predictably, the hearing contained one sour note, the first adverse public testimony against the design, a spark that would soon burst into a raging flame. A translator and radio operator named Scott Brewer, whose Vietnam duty had been in Saigon and Bien Hoa, stepped forward as the first public detractor. Lin, wearing a porkpie hat and long skirt, stood to the side, listening intently. Countering the lavish praise of the design, Brewer found it to be "abstract, anonymous, inconspicuous, and meaningless, and it is so unfulfilling as a lasting memorial that *no memorial* would be a better alternative."

Robert Doubek and Maya Lin listen as veteran Scott Brewer, left, pillories Lin's design before the US Commission of Fine Arts, July 7, 1981.

But Brewer's criticism was a mere hiccup in the air of congratulation and did little to mar the day. After praise was heaped on Lin for the design, Brown had the last word. "Nobility . . . is the great hallmark of this design," he said in his sonorous voice. Pointing to the design's deference to the nearby the Washington Monument and the Lincoln Memorial, he continued, "It is an understatement of sensitivity . . . and is highly commendable . . . we give the Commission's blessing to the jury and to the designer."

The public battle was just beginning.

Chapter Six

BLOWBACK

I n the fall of 1981 the battle over the memorial turned starkly political and decidedly ugly. Amid the tumult, Maya Lin, designer,
worked quietly and productively with Kent Cooper, the architect
of record, on practical and aesthetic problems: the stone, the drainage,
the safety barrier, the lighting, the problems of etching. There was a
natural, healthy tension between them, Lin the artist with her strong
vision, Cooper the architect, dogged by the considerable challenges
of making her below-grade emplacement both safe and workable. But
Cooper respected the artist-architect divide for what it was, and while
he argued his positions forcefully, he deferred to her on all design
questions.

In October, the issue of the memorial's inscription was joined. If
Lin had won the veterans' competition, then the veterans had paid for
it, and so some gesture of gratitude to them was appropriate, even if an
epigraph about duty and honor, country and sacrifice was counter to
her vision for the memorial. The veterans threw themselves into the
process with gusto, asking for suggestions from a wide range of inter-
ested parties, including best-selling author Jim Webb and the actor,
Jimmy Stewart, who had been a World War II bomber pilot. General
William Westmoreland had to be asked, of course, and he suggested

"They gave their lives for a noble cause." Cooper offered several possibilities about where the words might be placed . . . on a ground-level plaque, for example, or in a prologue and epilogue for the timeline at the foot of the wall. Jan Scruggs and the organizers finally came up with draft language and clearly imagined it writ large and bold, in the most prominent place possible.

Aesthetically, the apex of the two walls of the chevron was the strongest point of the design. At the top and bottom of the juncture the years 1959 and 1975 were to be cut large and bold, designating the duration of the war. That seemed like the best place for the inscription consistent with the idea of prologue and epilogue. For these two prominent places Scruggs and company came up with two epigrams: *These were the names of those who gave their lives in the Vietnam War. Our nation honors the courage, sacrifice and devotion to duty and country of its Vietnam veteran.*

On October 28, the VVMF held another press conference to announce what would be inscribed on the wall.

Now it was Maya Lin's time to make her presence felt. This was the moment to push back against the military men and seasoned architects who had been so condescending toward her. Minutes before the occasion began, she turned up with a miniature Styrofoam model of the wall with the VVMF draft inscriptions indeed next to the years 1959 and 1975, but etched in the same, diminutive size as the sea of names all around it. If she had to acquiesce in allowing two patriotic inscriptions, let them be small in size. It was, as if she were remembering the words of her mentor, César Pelli: "You might not win, but fight as hard as you can!" The organizers were shocked and dismayed. But this was a design question. And in this case the designer won out. It was to be Maya Lin's only compromise.

Once the memorial was built, both inscriptions were overlooked for all but the most limber and keen sighted. Unless one knew they were there, they were easily missed. The one at the top required at least a squint, and the one at the bottom required a stoop. Still, Lin had satisfied the demand of the veterans . . . technically, while at the same time making the evocative statements nearly indecipherable. By downplaying the theme of glory, she implicitly acknowledged the sensitivities of those who hated the war, had resisted it, had protested against it, and had avoided it.

Always not far beneath the surface was the rift between those who had served in the war and those who had evaded service.

—

At the fundraising gala with Senator Warner, Elizabeth Taylor, and General William Westmoreland back in October 1980, the ex-Marine turned author, Jim Webb, had maintained a jolly camaraderie with his fellow veterans. It was not to last. He had agreed to be an original member of the VVMF's National Sponsoring Committee. In his current job as a minority counsel for the Veterans Affairs Committee in the US House of Representatives, he had worked hard to sign up congressmen as sponsors for S.Res 119. But now, a year later, he had much else to concern him, and he had only fleeting contact with the memorial staff.

Before the competition reached its remarkable conclusion, Webb had, however, sent a clipping from the March issue of *Texas Monthly* to the staff about the troubled effort in Austin to build a fitting memorial to the Vietnam dead of Travis County. Webb could not know that the Austin brouhaha prefigured the national controversy in which he was about to become a central player. An Austin sculpture committee had chosen a design by a University of Texas art professor of Thai origin, Thana Lauhakaikul, who proposed to mount a field of ninety-eight concrete eggs, each egg three feet tall, on a metal grid. According to the sculptor, the symbolism of egg shells suggested the fragility of life and the egg shape, in Christian thought, represented the resurrection. In the midst of his egg field, he had left two spaces for grass and shrubs, and this was to suggest "the infinity of life." Inevitably, the military community, which had imaged a traditional artwork, howled and demanded something more like an obelisk or a sculpture of a soldier. The arts community responded with scorn at these "philistine Archie Bunkers" who could not appreciate postmodernist art, nor could they understand the importance of respecting the integrity of a juried artistic competition. Predictably, this fierce conflict between artists and veterans became too intense, and the whole idea of an art contest was scrapped.

Thana Lauhakaikul with his "egg carton" design for a
Vietnam Memorial in Austin, Texas

In his note to the VVMF staff, Webb quipped, "We're not going to get an egg carton, are we?"

When he saw Lin's design, his ire knew no bounds. They had ended up not with an egg carton but with a mass grave, he thought. He immediately let John Wheeler III, a top official at the Fund, know his disgust. Wheeler did his best to calm down the dissenter, protesting that Lin's design was high art, akin to the Eiffel Tower. This highfalutin argument was met with guffaws. Black was black, and white was white. There was no American flag; no inscription about a soldier's valor; not even the word Vietnam on the "grave." Wheeler pleaded for time. Couldn't Webb delay going public with his disenchantment for at least a month, giving everyone time for reflection? Webb took this to mean that the VVMF itself was reconsidering, and so for a time he held his fire.

Through the late spring in his capacity with the House Veterans Committee, Webb met often with veterans groups, and by his account, the consensus was that Lin's design was dreadful, only slightly better than no memorial at all. As the month for reflection grew into several months with no word about reconsideration, and as the design sailed

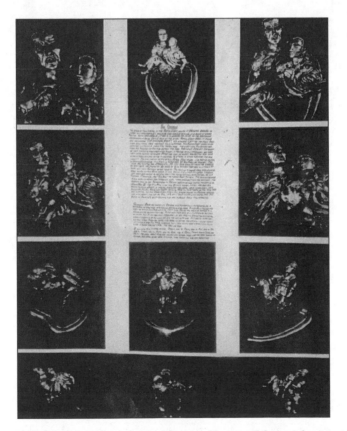

Tom Carhart's design entry for the Vietnam Veterans Memorial competition

through the July meeting of the US Commission of Fine Arts, Webb's fury grew. He found a kindred soul in another veteran and West Point graduate, Tom Carhart. Carhart had been an infantry platoon leader in Vietnam and had received two Purple Hearts. As it turned out, he had submitted his own design to the memorial contest—a statue of a grieving Army officer holding the body of a slain comrade, eyes lifted skyward toward a medical evacuation helicopter, standing on a base in the shape of a purple heart and waves suggestive of a rice paddy. He did not expect to win the competition, he insisted—it was his first effort ever at sculpture—but he wanted to participate in the process. He despised Lin's design.

The final straw for Carhart was the winner herself. When he was first asked about what inscription should go on the wall, he suggested "designed by a gook." It would not be long before this slur was taken up by a set of like-minded veterans, and the phrase became not just a gook but a "fucking gook."

In September 1981, the blowback began in earnest with Webb and Carhart leading the charge. But first Webb headed north. In mid-month veterans dedicated a Vietnam War memorial in the Irish working-class neighborhood of South Boston, and Webb was the honored guest. Ironically, the memorial was a stark cenotaph of black granite, the very color that Webb held in such contempt as evocative of shame and defeat. The names of twenty-five Southies—fifteen of them Marines—who had died were etched in white on its curved, black surface and bordered by the seals of the four military services. Below their names was the inscription:

"If you forget my death, then I died in vain."

While the occasion featured the usual assortment of bands and babies, flags and old men in lawn chairs, there were complaints that the politicians droned on too long. But there were no complaints about combat veteran Webb. He smiled his way through the ceremony, as he was made an honorary member of the South Boston Veterans Brigade and accepted the traditional Irish claddagh ring with hands clasped around a heart. When he took the microphone, he was quick to point out that if the ratio of war dead in South Boston was true of the country as a whole, the national casualty rate would have been three times as high. He took the opportunity to draw attention to the rift between the working-class boys of South Boston who had answered the call and the upper-class Bostonians across the river who had gone to Andover and Harvard and had avoided the unpleasantness altogether. In the four brutal years of the Vietnam buildup, 1965–68, out of nearly five thousand Harvard students, ten died in Vietnam.

Webb spoke eloquently about the Irish boys who had been in his company.

"I can see them now on the ridges and in the pockets of raw earth they had scraped away to make fighting holes," he said. "We roamed like nomads through villages and mountains; we ripped the earth with our bombs. We stained it with our blood. When we left a part of us stayed forever focused in the stench and dread of combat and at the same time, those who made it back . . . part of it clings to us forever. It becomes an inseparable part of us, like a burden few of our countrymen seem willing to share. Giving your life in a war is the ultimate, irretrievable gift to your culture. The manner in which we as a people and community express our thanks for that gift is the ultimate judgment of our values."

A few days later, the conservative magazine *National Review* weighed in with a withering critique of Lin's design. It objected to the black color, the listing of the names by date, and even to its V shape, which suggested the reviled peace symbol. The editors fumed: "If the current model has to be built, stick it off in some tidal flat, and let it memorialize Jane Fonda's contribution to ensuring that our soldiers died in vain." But the most memorable line was: "Our objection to this Orwellian glop does not issue from any philistine objection to new conceptions in art. It is based on the clear political message of this design." The phrase "Orwellian glop" stuck.

The next important meeting of the US Commission of Fine Arts loomed on October 13. Carhart let it be known that he and Webb planned to be at the session to raise a little hell. The VVMF's efforts to dissuade them from attending failed. That there would be no backing down was clear when Webb wrote a formal letter of objection to the commission that he wanted put in the record. It was dated the day before the hearing opened.

Webb's letter listed three central objections. First, the entire concept suggested a black hole or "cave." Far from the requirement that the contest entries be apolitical, Lin's design was implicitly "a very strong nihilistic statement" regarding the war. Second, the design contained no implements of war. "This sort of artistic denial . . . when so many carry around [the war's] scars, is one of the purest forms of denigration imaginable." And third, there had been no Vietnam veterans on the jury.

In a perfect world, Webb wrote, this horrible design would be scrapped and a new competition opened. But this, he acknowledged, would terminate the entire enterprise, and that was not his purpose. And so, he proposed four modifications to the memorial. An American flag should be placed prominently at the apex of the wall (even though in the original competition a flag was discouraged, lest it compete with the circle of flags that surrounded the Washington Monument); an inspiring inscription about the duty and sacrifice of the veteran should be etched boldly on the surface; the memorial should be raised above ground or the stone color changed from black to white; and the listing of names by date of death should be altered or abandoned.

The fat, as the saying goes, was in the fire.

At its decorous offices on Lafayette Park across from the White House, the commission's deliberations began with Kent Cooper reviewing the status of the project. For construction to stay on schedule, the immediate need was for the commission to approve the stone. Maya Lin had specified polished black granite with no veining, and she had approved a sample from Sweden. Swedish black granite was the finest in the world, Cooper said, and there was no equivalent in the United States. But since Sweden (along with Canada) had been the prime destination for draft evaders, Swedish granite was out. The next best choice was granite from India. (A few months later, when the memorial was debated in Congress, Representative Larry McDonald of Georgia picked up on the Indian granite theme and labeled the wall "the black hole of Calcutta.")

And then Carhart was recognized. A long, loud, and angry rant followed, and it might not have occurred to him that with his oversized square glasses, brush mustache, slicked-down hair, and bombastic delivery he was presenting the very image of the marginalized and hysterical Vietnam veteran that, to many, had become an unflattering stereotype. He began with Robert E. Lee's invocation that to be called to service in a time of war was the highest calling of all. He cited Ronald Reagan's reference to Vietnam as "a noble cause," a sentiment, he said blithely, that was shared by virtually all Vietnam veterans. He was stunned at the winning design, that "black gash of shame and sorrow," and found it to be "intentionally insulting" to all who had served. He spoke movingly about being spat on upon his return—like a spear passing through him—and said he was tired of being considered a loser. Lin's concept made him feel dishonored, and if it was built, it would be seen in the future as commemorating an "ugly, dirty experience of which we are all ashamed." He would not apologize for his service to America, he said, fist clenched. The commission should reopen the competition and appoint a jury comprising only Vietnam veterans. He hoped for something white and graceful.

As counterpoint, Jan Scruggs, the father of the whole endeavor, was recognized. He pointed out that the detractors were a small group, well-connected perhaps, but scarcely representative of the veteran community at large. By way of contrast, he spoke of the American Legion's support for the design. The Legion, the largest of all the service organizations, had contributed $1 million to the memorial, and the Veterans of Foreign Wars, another major service group, had contributed $180,000. The Vietnam Veterans Against the War (VVAW) also supported Lin's design. Thousands had seen the model of the memorial at recent veterans' conventions, and they overwhelmingly accepted it as a beautiful tribute. Given the height of the wall at ten feet, veterans told Scruggs that the design made them feel ten feet tall.

Nevertheless, Carhart's indignation and overheated rhetoric could not be ignored, and it succeeded in planting a notion that would stick: the black gash of shame and sorrow.

It was left to the chairman, J. Carter Brown, to lower the temperature and restore a sober tone to the proceedings. It was not the purview of the commission to reopen the competition, he said, and its purpose that day was only to approve or reject the granite material. But he also underscored the consensus of the commission that Maya Lin's design possessed an "extraordinary sense of dignity and nobility" precisely because of its simplicity. It had not evoked any "corny" references that might seem briefly satisfying. He was sure that the design would call up in the visitor's heart tremendous admiration and gratitude for the sacrifice of soldiers. The trend in building memorials was to get away from "bits of whipped cream" on fancy pedestals. The commission had voted unanimously that this was the kind of memorial that would do honor to the people it memorialized.

Carhart insisted on responding. Not surprisingly, he rose to the bait of "corny" and "whipped cream." It may be "that the new direction in artistic monuments is correct," he said, "Rather than bits of whipped cream we will have solemn low-key monuments. . . . It may be that you are right, that this is the new wave. . . . But the problem is that you are wrong. There is too much political baggage associated with Vietnam to take a chance on it. There are too many people whose hearts are torn apart. . . . I will never take my children to the black hole. I will go across the river to the Arlington Cemetery where there are monuments of heroes that I can be proud of, not spat upon."

Minutes after the hearing ended, the veterans turned on one another viciously. On the steps outside the commission's offices, Scruggs accosted Carhart, calling him a traitor and asking if they taught disloyalty at West Point. Another memorial organizer, John Wheeler III, called Webb at home and allowed that Carhart must be suffering from post-traumatic stress syndrome. Aspersions were cast on Carhart's medals. Webb, in turn, was later to make fun of Wheeler's rearguard tour at a desk job at Long Binh, when because of an Article 15 citation (one step lower than a court-martial) he had not even received an end-of-tour medal. Later, Webb would also scoff at Scruggs' receipt of an Army commendation medal with V for valor, calling it "the Army's lowest award for valor." Webb called Scruggs "pathetic," and Scruggs called Webb "a cocky platoon leader."

"As for your comment regarding 'cocky platoon leaders,'" Webb responded, "I know that you have often publicly expressed your hatred for your officers, but that is your own problem. My men nominated me for every award I received. . . . If platoon commanders . . . were cocky in the right way, they saved lives." (Webb had been awarded the Navy Cross, a Silver Star, two Bronze Stars, and two Purple Hearts.)

For now, Webb drew two lessons from the exchange. "If you didn't support the memorial you were crazy," and "if you spoke up against it, you could expect a barrage of hateful innuendo."

Nevertheless, Webb and Carhart could be pleased at the firestorm they had sparked. In the weeks ahead, both published op-ed pieces in the *Washington Post* and *Wall Street Journal* with Webb fashioning a new slogan. The wall would be "a wailing wall for future anti-draft and anti-nuclear demonstrators," and then he raised the ante further by likening the memorial to "the ovens at Dachau." Meanwhile, Carhart, obsessed with his cause célèbre and his vendetta, began to lobby congressmen. In Don Bailey, a Pennsylvania congressman, he found an especially receptive ear. Bailey would soon cause considerable mischief.

In good tried-and-true Washington fashion, and with a whiff of the old red-baiting of the 1950s, the opponents searched for ulterior, anti-war motives among the distinguished jury members. Four of the eight jurors had military experience, and three of them—Clay, Belluschi, and Weese—had served in combat. One had overtly supported the war; others had quietly been against the war but said nothing publicly. Richard Hunt, an African-American sculptor, had participated in civil rights sit-ins, but there was no evidence of anti-war activities.

And then there was juror Garrett Eckbo. A towering figure in the world of landscape architecture whose projects dotted the globe, he had taught at "radical" UC Berkeley, where he had been chairman of the landscape architecture department. One of his most famous former students was superstar Frank Gehry. Detractors focused on Eckbo's career, which showed that he was drawn emotionally to projects involving low-cost housing and had even designed camps for migrant workers in the Central Valley. Carhart began to circulate the rumor that there had been a "Commie" on the jury.

In a transcript of the 1957 House Un-American Activities Committee hearings, Eckbo's name did, indeed, appear in the an investigation of Communist Party members in the arts, but nothing more than the name. In fact, he had never been a member of the party, but in the 1940s he had been involved in labor union activity against fascism. And then, no doubt to Carhart's delight, it came out that Eckbo was a signatory to a full-page ad against the Vietnam War that appeared in the *San Francisco Chronicle*. And in 1968 he had signed on to something called the "Berkeley Vietnam Commencement," which stated, "I pledge to support [refusers of military induction] with encouragement, counsel, and financial aid."

The smear was on. In the debate that followed, Eckbo's anti-war position would be recast as active support for "the pro–Viet Cong movement from his Berkeley, California sanctuary."

Simultaneously, Webb floated the rumor that no one by the name of Grady Clay (the chairman of the jury) had served in the US Army before 1947. Thus, Webb publicly implied that Clay had embellished his resume. Clay was quick to refute to this slander. He had, indeed, been an artillery officer in the Italian campaign in World War II and had been wounded in Anzio. Webb was forced to apologize.

Others waded in behind the dissidents. Admiral James Stockdale, one of three American prisoners of war from the Vietnam War period to be awarded the Congressional Medal of Honor, resigned from the Memorial Fund. The Marine Corps League expressed its dismay. And conservative columnist Patrick Buchanan called Lin's design a mockery. Ross Perot, who in May had told the Fund he was "folding his tent," now said he grew angrier about the memorial with every passing day. The veterans he talked to regarded the Lin design as an apology, not a memorial, he told the press. He offered to fund a new competition with a jury of only Vietnam veterans. He also announced that he would finance a poll of veterans on their attitudes toward the memorial. Soon enough, Perot would charge financial irregularities in the VVMF and demand an independent audit.

Of all the back-and-forth on the editorial pages during the fall, there were some surprises. Few commentators felt comfortable addressing the issue as a purely aesthetic question, except perhaps the *Cleveland Plain Dealer*. In a November editorial, the paper wrote, "We could argue aesthetics forever. Beauty speaks softly into each individual's ear. If you don't hear, then you don't, and that which may exist for others is lost to you." In the *Washington Post* William Greider eloquently made the point that the war did not include any suitable heroic images that an artist might transform into stone or bronze and therefore the committee had chosen a "neutral and soft-spoken monument." Ironically, next to Greider's article were three iconic images: the Vietnamese police chief holding a pistol to the head of a Viet Cong and shooting him dead; the naked Vietnamese girl fleeing an American napalm attack; and the helicopter on the roof of an apartment tower evacuating the last Americans from Saigon at the end.

But perhaps the most surprising article showed that the divide on the memorial did not necessarily fall along liberal-conservative lines. It came from the dean of all conservative commentators, James J. Kilpatrick. A one-time segregationist and editor of the *Richmond News Leader*, Kilpatrick was a familiar figure in American political culture during the early 1980s. Beyond his syndicated column, "A Conservative View," he was a weekly fixture on the CBS television program *60 Minutes* as the conservative pundit against sharp-tongued liberals Nicholas Von Hoffman and Shana Alexander in a segment called "Point-Counterpoint." In an October 16 letter to the editor responding to the *National Review* slam, Kilpatrick wrote, "Far from being an 'outrage,' the winning design approaches a level of architectural genius. It promises to be the most moving war memorial ever constructed." Then in his keen debating style, he set up his straw man.

"You would prefer a piece of 'suitable sculpture,' on the model of memorials to Gettysburg or Appomattox. Bosh! Such memorials gather moss in every village square from Mobile to Manchester. Washington is full of suitable sculptures, and with perhaps a half a dozen exceptions they are dreadful. . . . [They] arouse no emotion whatever. The proposed Vietnam memorial, believe me, will pack an unforgettable wallop." Three weeks later, Kilpatrick wrote: "This will be the most moving war memorial ever erected."

Through all of this, Maya Lin tried to hold onto her equanimity. Her journal entry on November 22 revealed her anguish. "Beginning to vanquish the devils. A silly way to put what is within me, but for months it has been getting darker and colder inside. The memorial [design details are] nearing completion, the AIA reception was crazy, a mixture of elation and anorexia nervosa, had forgotten to eat for days, and then the eyes and whispers she's the one . . . the little girl, the child, praise and awe, i felt like a prize, yet so small, not me but the competition was on parade, i was just a victim of it, you would be grateful of the compliments only if you knew who was being sincere."

But the torrent of passionate dispute was becoming overwhelming. The Fund offices were besieged with letters. Why had there been no Vietnam veterans on the jury? What was wrong with an American flagpole at the site? What about the war's survivors?

The memorial's organizers were forced into crisis mode. If they could weather the flood of mail and the negative press, opposition in Congress was an entirely different matter. The biggest blow came at the end of 1981 when a powerful congressman, Henry Hyde of Illinois, sent a devastating letter to all his Republican colleagues in the House. It alerted them to the fast-approaching March 1 groundbreaking date for the memorial. This runaway train had to be stopped. He mocked a statement by Paul Spreiregen, the competition administrator, who had said that, "In a city of white memorials rising, this will be a dark memorial receding." How does a "dark memorial receding" honor the memory of those who served? Hyde wanted to know. He quoted Webb's line about the "wailing wall" and directed them to Patrick Buchanan's column that repeated the canard of a "Communist" on the jury. Shame, not honor, was the message of the memorial, and that violated the intent and spirit of the congressional authorizing legislation.

In the early days of the new year, the Illinois Republican sent a letter to President Reagan signed by thirty fellow congressmen demanding that Lin's design be scrapped and a new selection process undertaken. It asked Reagan to direct his secretary of the Interior, James Watt, the official with authority over the National Mall, to withhold permission to break ground on March 1.

"War memorials may be too important to leave simply to artists and architects," Hyde would write.

This initiative clearly had the power to scuttle the entire effort of the past three years. Jan Scruggs and the other organizers saw now that they were in big trouble. They had already raised three million dollars out of the seven million that was needed, and suddenly it looked as if the massive effort might all be for naught.

It was time to think about a compromise.

Chapter Seven

EX NIHILO

I f Maya Lin's arrival on the national stage at such an early age was dramatic and rare, the trajectory of Frederick Hart's early career as an artist was nearly as remarkable. He came from a family of tragedy. An older brother had died as an infant. His mother contracted scarlet fever and died when Hart was sixteen months old. And a half-sister named Chesley, with whom he was especially close, died of leukemia when she was only sixteen. These tragedies would later have a profound impact on his work. Raised by his aunt, Essie, in Conway, South Carolina, he had a turbulent youth. There were a few encounters with the police that would label him a juvenile delinquent, and he was kicked out of school. But after performing brilliantly on the Scholastic Aptitude Test, he catapulted from the ninth grade into the University of South Carolina at the age of fifteen, only to become caught up in the civil rights movement and once again find himself in trouble with the law. For his activism, he was arrested, jailed, and thrown out of school. When he heard that the Ku Klux Klan was looking to kill him, he fled to Washington, DC.

Once safely ensconced in his new city, Hart gravitated to the art world and found his calling in a sculpture class at the Corcoran Gallery of Art. His talents were quickly noticed. His interest was in representational sculpture, for he had developed a strong distaste for modernist and postmodernist abstraction, regarding it as a dead end. The American sculptors Augustus Saint-Gaudens and Daniel Chester French were his heroes, and he briefly apprenticed with Felix de Weldon, whose most famous work is the US Marine Corps War Memorial across the Potomac River from Washington in Arlington, Virginia. Importantly, de Weldon's heroic figures raising the American flag on Iwo Jima are perched on a black granite base.

Because realistic work was so out of fashion at the time, Hart found it difficult to get instruction in figurative sculpture. Eventually, he wangled a job as a stone carver at the Washington National Cathedral, the last great gothic cathedral to be built, where gargoyles and bosses and label terminations still had to be fashioned. There, working with meticulous Italian stone carvers and under the influence of master carver Roger Morigi, he flourished. To Hart the cathedral was a magical place. "[It] was the best experience of my learning life," he would say. "It taught me 'how' to work. I wanted to know and feel the discipline—the mastery of stone carving—and I learned that in the hours of working up on the scaffolding in the heat of summer and through the winter."

Hart's early years at the Episcopalian cathedral occurred as the Vietnam War escalated to its most violent crescendo and when every young adult American male was subject to conscription. Far from being a gung-ho soldier, Hart joined the thousands of his generation protesting against the war. Considering what was to happen to him later, the picture of him demonstrating is startling. Perhaps partly because of his anti-war activities, but more significantly, the trauma over his sister's death, he was in need of psychiatric counseling. As a result, the Selective Service conferred a 4 F deferment on him. In truth, such a designation, for a certain set of young Americans, was not, in those days, so difficult to get. The irony is enduring. The artist who would be so embraced by those fervently opposed to the Maya Lin design, who put himself to the task of imagining the bravery, the camaraderie, and the

Frederick Hart, right, protests the Vietnam War on the National Mall, 1971

sense of duty of the Vietnam soldier, was himself an anti-war protester and the beneficiary of a free pass out of military service.

In the mid-1970s, after ninety years in construction, the great cathedral of Washington was nearing completion. The last part to be finished was the prominent west entrance, the building's face to the Wisconsin Avenue thoroughfare. Cathedral officials agreed that the theme of the grand entrance should be the world's creation, a theme that, most memorably, had been imagined by Michelangelo in the Sistine Chapel in Rome. What artwork should grace the tympanum— the triangular space over the central doors? And what sculptor should be commissioned?

An open, anonymous design competition, such as would be conducted for the Vietnam Memorial, was thought to be beyond the cathedral's resources. And so, cathedral officials invited five sculptors to submit designs. Four of the five were luminaries in the art world, men whose works graced a number of important historic spaces from Omaha Beach in Normandy to the Cathedral of St. John the Divine in New York, and who in equally prominent places had depicted such statesmen as Winston Churchill and Abraham Lincoln. After Hart had sculpted a lovely statue of Erasmus for the cathedral's south nave, church officials invited him to be the fifth competitor in a courtly gesture to the promising young man in their midst.

To the surprise of all, the young upstart won the contest with a concept he would call *Ex Nihilo* ("from nothingness"). His design portrayed eight nude figures (four males, four females) that appear to be emerging from the maelstrom of cosmic chaos at the creation of the world.

The writhing, sensual figures, chiseled in high relief, eyes still closed to evoke a feeling of becoming, and bodies still unformed, are springing from what Hart would call a "primordial cloud." In niches between the three main doors are Hart's sculptures of St. Peter, Adam, and St. Paul. Of these figures, Hart would say, "I don't think of myself as an architectural sculptor but as a sculptor using architecture as a medium . . . and a structure like the cathedral is the finest medium there is. Sculpture should not just be *viewed*; it should be *experienced* by the audience."

Hart found his antecedents in the Renaissance, but his *Ex Nihilo* reminded some of the work by the symbolist artist Jean Delville, whose painting, *Satan's Treasures*, also had figures emerging from the cosmic churn in a similar composition, albeit writhing in hell rather than heaven. The sculptor was also influenced by the creation myth of Pierre Teilhard de Chardin about the world constantly in the state of becoming. Hart had studied de Chardin, the controversial Jesuit priest, in his research for the creation piece.

Indeed, it was in the very process of researching his sacred commission that Frederick Hart had a religious awakening, and he converted to Roman Catholicism. His guide was theologian Stephen Happel. (Twenty-five years later, Reverend Happel would deliver the eulogy for Hart at a packed funeral mass at the Cathedral of St. Matthew the Apostle in Washington.) His conversion imparted a deeply spiritual quality to all his subsequent work. Spiritualism would become his signature.

It would take the artist eight years to bring his moving masterwork at the cathedral to its splendid realization. By the spring of 1979, he had finished the modeling of *Ex Nihilo*, and the work had been cast into plaster. He began looking for his next big project. That summer he noticed a letter in the *Washington Star* by Jan Scruggs about his campaign to build a Vietnam War memorial. Given the sculptor's unexpected triumph at the cathedral, he had the bravado to believe that he could capture the plum assignment of a Vietnam commemorative statue as well. He contacted Scruggs.

Scruggs embraced him, as did the others in the memorial campaign. They had found their sculptor! In succeeding months, Hart was taken in by the veterans, including Jim Webb. Two avid sportsmen, they quickly bonded over hunting and fishing at Hart's cabin in West

Frederick Hart with Ex Nihilo, *destined for the front of Washington National Cathedral*

Virginia. And the veteran and patrons must have been doubly pleased as the publicity grew for Hart's extraordinary tympanum. *National Geographic* magazine would publish a long article on the cathedral, and in it there was a moody picture of Hart posing in front of a full-size plaster model of *Ex Nihilo*. The picture covered a two-page spread. They had found their sculptor all right.

And then in July 1979 came the dinner at the home of the *Washington Post*'s Wolf Von Eckhart, where the architecture critic reacted in horror and disbelief at hearing that the veterans had simply crowned their favorite sculptor with the prize of building a memorial on the National Mall. When the idea of a national competition took hold, Hart felt the commission had been snatched away from him. With his soaring reputation, he never imagined that he would have to compete with hundreds of other applicants. Grudgingly, he teamed up with notable landscape architect Joseph E. Brown and together they mounted the very strong submission that ultimately took third place.

But in the fall of 1981, when Webb and Carhart launched their ferocious attack on Maya Lin's design and a powerful group of congressmen joined in opposition, Hart felt there just might be a way to get back in the game. Webb and his cohorts were insisting that a figurative sculpture be added to Lin's wall, and the Hart/Brown submission was the only finalist with representational work. Who better than he? He had the inside track once again. Among Hart's many attributes as an artist was his skill as a dogged in-fighter.

In 1982, the year that the fate of the Maya Lin design would ultimately be decided, the first days began with the deafening sound of contention. The press was rife with overheated diatribes on both sides; furtive meetings were held in Congressional back rooms, in the White House, in the offices of the organizers and of the architects. Both sides were blustering about filing respective lawsuits, as opponents argued that the Lin design violated the essence of the Congressional resolution S.Res 119, while Lin's lawyers argued that her winning design was being butchered in violation of the competition rules.

On January 3, the *Washington Post* raised the temperature substantially with a sweeping profile of Maya Lin that focused on her Asian lineage and her artistic development. With refreshing openness, she spoke about her disconnection from current affairs, her fascination with death, and her disinterest in world affairs. She told of how she lived entirely within her own head and in her imagination. She did not read newspapers, she boasted. She just ignored the world.

"It's like everything is up in my head [with] no real, concrete experiential reality," she said. "It's all what I feel."

She also tossed off a few lines that might have been endearing in the halls of Yale but sent shivers through her sponsors now. "Everyone thinks I'm morbid. . . . I've always been the little kid," she said in good dorm room parlance, and "Everyone has always told me to grow up. I don't know if I ever will, whatever that is. If I do, I don't think I could design. I've seen people grow up and lose it and spend lots of time trying to get back down to it." A photograph accompanying the article pictured her wearing a porkpie hat. It would become something of a signature. Well-enough known now, she made appearances in Washington gossip columns, hanging out in raucous Georgetown bars. She seemed to have no sense that she had become a public figure who ought to watch her step. At a Washington party with the town's cultural elite, a man commented on her outfit, wondering if her look was "strategic"?

"i knew what he meant at the time," she wrote in her journal. "Is it an act? no, just me, and to think i thought i was being subtle? do they think i wear jeans? hah. i guess my pinafores and jumpers are too foreign to their age and class."

All this made fine sense for an artist, and especially a young artist, to say, but building the memorial had become an intense political drama now, played out at the highest levels, and her comments did not serve her cause well. Her VVMF patrons cringed at the reporter's line about "an Asian artist for an Asian war," at her open disinterest in the war, and at her emphasis only on her internal artistic sensibility.

If many readers were smitten, finding her both flighty and endearing, the veterans behind the memorial began to wonder if they shouldn't have insisted on a clause in her contract about their right to control her interviews with the press.

In the following days, as the date for groundbreaking loomed, editorial pages across the country from Charleston to Palm Springs to Baltimore carried opinions that spanned the gamut of emotion. The issue was no longer who was right and who was wrong, but the sheer noise of dissension was dragging the whole project down. Rather than the memorial being a catalyst for healing, the debate was reawakening all the passionate, divisive arguments of the war years themselves. It was becoming like a giant Rorschach test on what anyone felt about the war. For many it became impossible to separate one's opinion of Lin's design from one's opinion about the war. And Lin herself was suddenly either a subversive radical or an artistic genius. Was her design a catalyst for healing or an icon for pacifism? It could be interpreted both ways. Of his side, Jim Webb would say: "We were like scorpions in a jar, with the rest of the country shaking it."

Political cartoon by Jeff MacNelly

Conservative columnists were especially vocal. Phyllis Schlafly joined others in labeling the design an insult and a tribute to Jane Fonda, while James J. Kilpatrick took the opposite view and berated Buchanan for taking cheap shots. Meanwhile, Carhart and Webb plied the corridors of Congress, closeting themselves with Congressman Henry Hyde and his supporters and girding for battle ahead. Perhaps most surprising of all, General William Westmoreland issued a stern rebuke to Webb.

"[The memorial] is in no way a 'trench'," he wrote. "Black polished granite is far more handsome than any other possible stone, the chronological listing of names is not inappropriate, the structure reflects dignity and good taste and blends in aesthetically [with] that beautiful area of the Mall." The ex-commander-in-chief was promising to donate all future royalties from his book, *A Soldier Reports* (1976), to the Memorial Fund.

Ross Perot may have been the most strident dissenter of all. He was moving forward with his poll of Vietnam veterans on the design. First, he polled those who had been prisoners of war, then he broadened it to a larger sample of veterans. Given Perot's well-publicized opposition, the survey's outcome was a foregone conclusion. When the results came in, two-thirds of the 587 POWs questioned disliked the Lin design. Seventy percent thought the color should be white. Ninety-six percent said there should be a flagpole, and 82 percent said it should be above ground. Scruggs responded that the questions were loaded.

Simultaneously, Perot began to question the finances of the Memorial Fund, suggesting shenanigans with his generous $160,000 contribution, and demanding an audit conducted by his own auditor. He blasted the black color of the granite once again, and when he was told it was already bought and on its way from India, he offered to buy it from the Fund. A few days later, he softened his stance, acquiescing to the color, if the design would only move above ground. He came to Washington with military officers in tow to view the scurrilous design housed in the Fund's basement. On one of those visits, Maya Lin was working upstairs. When she heard that her most shrill critic was below, she went down to confront him, and the two went toe to toe for more than fifteen minutes, with the twenty-two-year-old holding her own against the high-pitched diatribe of the Texas billionaire.

Meanwhile, the matter was taken up at the highest levels of the White House, and ultimately, almost all the senior staff was involved in the discussions. Even the national security adviser, Judge William Clark, became embroiled. Deputy Chief of Staff Michael Deaver was charged with monitoring the debate over the memorial, and intense discussions about what the administration should do took place within the domestic policy staff. In a memo to senior staff, Deaver favored a change of stone color to white. But more senior members of the inner circle, principally Chief of Staff James Baker, Edwin Meese, and Richard Darman thought some compromise that would respect the winning design was possible. Above all, a January 28 National Security Council (NSC) memo stated, "A role other than that of a 'fair arbiter' by the Executive Branch in the controversy is likely to be a no-win move—inviting attack from either side."

The White House asked to see the design model, and it was set up in the West Wing's Roosevelt Room a few doors from the Oval Office. Jan Scruggs would later describe the reaction of White House aides, which reflected the advice of the NSC memo: "Some liked it. Some did not. No one wanted to kill it. And no one wanted to defend it. They seemed to view the whole issue as a problem that would not go away."

At the same time, conservative voices in Congress were doing their best to pressure the White House. Congressman John Ashbrook (Ohio) wrote to Reagan that the Vietnam War was a noble cause that was fought "to save a people from the slavery that is communism." He advocated for a new design, "ennobling, bold, and bright." A new memorial "will help redirect the nation's view of that war and its meaning. It will assist in instilling the belief in our youth that fighting for freedom is indeed a high calling of an American."

At this critical juncture, the memorial's best friend remained Senator John Warner, and it fell to him in mid-January to arrange a grand meeting of the contending parties in an effort to salvage the project. The point man for the Reagan administration was the abrasive secretary of the Interior, James Watt. The Mall was his dominion, and, therefore, the right of final approval rested in his hands. His distaste for Lin's design was palpable, as was his inclination to scuttle the project altogether. Before he even saw Lin's wall, he proclaimed it "an act of treason."

But Watt was under pressure from the White House to find a compromise if at all possible. He acted like an angry parent, knocking heads together and brandishing ultimatums. The loud controversy had to end, he told the organizers. Unless each side bent a little, he would refuse outright to grant a permit to build. There would be no groundbreaking on March 1, as was scheduled. Indeed, there might never be a groundbreaking.

On the afternoon of January 27, Warner's meeting convened in a hearing room in the Russell Senate Office Building, across from the Capitol. A square table was set up as if for a diplomatic summit between major powers. At the head of the table, Warner was joined by Senator Jeremiah Denton of Alabama, a former Navy pilot who had been shot down and imprisoned for nearly eight years in North Vietnam; Representative Don Bailey of Pennsylvania, a recipient of Silver and Bronze Stars as a member of the 101st Airborne Division in Vietnam; and Representative Philip Crane of Illinois, a conservative stalwart who was also an Army veteran. It was as if they were serving as a four-judge panel. At the appointed time Ross Perot stormed in, followed by an army of supporters, perhaps forty of them, that he had flown in for the event. Except for Webb and Lin, the usual players were present. Supporters of the winning design were outnumbered five to one. Several legislators were also in attendance.

With Senator Warner hovering paternalistically, the proceedings lasted a highly charged, grueling five hours. As the hours ticked away, smoke filled the room and jackets were discarded. The proponents put on a slide show that displayed Lin's design and praised the open competition. The opponents delivered their demands. Change the color to white. Move the memorial above ground. Add a flag, and a patriotic inscription about duty and honor. During the presentation, an image of Carhart's kitschy fallen-warrior design popped up. Carhart himself delivered his familiar diatribe. Scruggs referred to "my memorial." Perot orchestrated a show of opposition as his followers each stood and read a prepared statement from a 3 x 5 index card. One dissatisfied veteran asserted that dealing with the memorial organizers was "a pissing match with skunks." Congressman Bailey insisted that the inscription declare the Vietnam War a noble endeavor, while Senator Denton spoke eloquently of his ordeal as a POW. He expressed his distaste for the design, but thought there was room for compromise. Afterward, he broke down in tears.

The issue boiled down to either "fixing" the memorial or "starting over." In the spirit of giving a little, the proponents offered to add a flagpole and think about "strengthening" the inscription. Several suggestions for a more glorified inscription would be offered. One suggestion was: "We are honored to have had the opportunity to serve our country under difficult circumstances. God Bless America." And more ponderous was: "For those who fought for it, freedom has a flavor the protected will never know."

And then came the flashpoint: the color black. After the usual assertion that black denoted disgrace and humiliation, Brigadier General George B. Price, an African-American officer with twenty-eight years of service in the Army, stood up, and a hush fell over the room.

"I am sick and tired of hearing black called a color of shame," he said. "If I hear this from anybody again, he can answer to me!" No one took him up on it. "Color meant nothing on the battlefields of Korea and Vietnam. . . . Color should mean nothing now."

Eventually, as the sun began to set, a four-star general took the floor. He was Michael S. Davison, who had been the commander-in-chief of the US Army in both Europe and the Pacific. A more daunting figure could scarcely have been imagined, and in what he would say there was a whiff of orchestration. Retain the Lin memorial, he suggested, but add a statue of a fighting man, something like the twelve-foot figure of the heroic soldier at Fort Benning, Georgia, shouting "Follow Me" to his men. Others suggested the Green Beret statue at Fort Bragg that conveyed the bravery, toughness, and inspiration of the commando, or the William Leftwich statue at Quantico, Virginia—Leftwich had been Perot's roommate at the Naval Academy—that honored the Marine lieutenant colonel who had participated in twenty-seven operations against the Viet Cong.

"Yeah, a statue for the living and a wall for the dead," Ross Perot cheered.

Follow Me *(1960), by PFC Manfred Bass, Fort Benning, Georgia*

Scruggs and his colleagues had been outmaneuvered; others felt betrayed; and still others dirtied. To them, at first blush, Davison's proposal was as bizarre as it was horrifying. A heroic figure at the base of the wall? A flagpole atop the vertex? An inscription proclaiming the nobility of the Vietnam War? A greater violation of the integrity of their non-political, juried competition and its requirement to be "reflective and contemplative" could hardly be conceived. Nevertheless, they acquiesced, confident that subsequent rounds, especially those with the Commission of Fine Arts, would torpedo so preposterous a notion as this.

Proudly, Senator Warner proclaimed victory. A compromise had been achieved. Hurrah! It was a triumph of the proverbial smoke-filled room. Secretary Watt and the White House would be mollified. The wall could go forward with these "refinements." Proceed with the groundbreaking! The whole scheme had been fixed, and the opponents of the wall were jubilant. Warner's office issued a self-congratulatory press release about the compromise. All had agreed, it suggested, that the flagpole would be placed at the apex of the wall, and the statue immediately in front of the wall. No such promise had been made at all, and in any case, this ad hoc meeting carried no authority to require anything.

Meanwhile, Maya Lin huddled with her architect, Kent Cooper. Both were livid and on the verge of resigning. Cooper was adamant. Lin's wall did not need to be "[adorned] . . . with patriotic claptrap." Their patrons pleaded with them to stay and persevere for the good of the memorial. Without them things could only get worse. Wolf Von Eckardt joined the conversation. They should move forward with the groundbreaking, he counseled, or it might never happen. While the Warner compromise authorized the Fund to select three artists for the proposed sculpture, Von Eckardt promised to advocate for another national competition to choose the sculptor through the good offices of the National Sculpture Society. To Lin and Cooper that was cold comfort.

"Aesthetically, the design does not need a statue," Scruggs told Lin, "but politically it does."

Chapter Eight

HOW CHINESE ARE YOU?

The art world was not about to lie down and accept a political invasion into its sacrosanct dominion. What did politicians and veterans know about high art anyway? They were trampling on the time-honored process of a juried competition. They understood nothing of the inviolable sanctity of an artist's work. A member of the Fine Arts Commission that would soon consider the additions called them "maudlin" changes to the "most sublime monument Washington has received in a long time." Harry Weese, the architect for the Washington subway and a jury member, was even more blunt. "Putting those elements in that design is a spoiled brat approach—if you can't kill it, adulterate it." The *Washington Post* critic, Benjamin Forgey, called the additions a "monumental absurdity" and a disastrous decision that would "muck up an extraordinary work of memorial art." The *Boston Globe* put the situation succinctly: "Commemorating the war in Vietnam is likely to prove no simpler than fighting it."

The criticisms of the purists, however, overlooked the fact that this was not pure art but public art, and the memorial would be installed in a very prominent place on public land in the most precious political landscape in America. The public was entitled to its say in the matter.

Meanwhile, Maya Lin's architect-collaborator, Kent Cooper, had grudgingly and reluctantly agreed to stay on as an adviser. But he was deeply unhappy about the violation of Lin's design. A statue with the wall "tends to weaken the powerful formality—the necessary inhumanity—of the memorial," he said. "It's going to be a long summer."

The Warner compromise had specified that the VVMF patrons should nominate three prominent sculptors, and that they should submit their concepts for review. But the patrons had no appetite for another grand, costly, and contentious competition that would further postpone execution of the memorial. More delay would only encourage more hurdles. Though he was now tentatively on board, Secretary Watt continued to play hardball. He would not authorize ground to be broken until "better and proper language" to honor the 2.7 million Vietnam veterans was found, and the plans for the flagpole and the statue were settled. And he would not approve a dedication date for the memorial in November—as the veterans wanted—until the "refinements" were in place. As a result of Watt's resistance, groundbreaking was delayed three weeks.

Meanwhile, politics interceded in choosing the actual sculptor. In a genuflection to the concern that no Vietnam veterans had been on the original jury, this time the four judges of the "Sculpture Panel" had all served in Vietnam; two favored the Lin design and two opposed it. But it was scarcely an even divide, since the elephant on the panel was Jim Webb. (Carhart, by this time, was regarded as a loose cannon.) Another panelist, Bill Jayne, an ex-Marine and Lin supporter, defined their challenge: to find a sculpture that would be "prideful, but not glorify the war." The other premise for debate was how the sculpture should interact with the wall. There should be "artistic tension" between the three elements, it was supposed, but they should act in concert as a single memorial. The wall was not to be simply a backdrop for the sculpture, nor should the sculpture be relegated to the sidelines.

For the lucky or unlucky artist who got the nod, successfully navigating these issues made for a tall order.

In fact, there was no sculpture contest. Frederick Hart had always been the favorite of the patrons, and his growing stature made an open competition unnecessary. By 1982 he was better known in the art world than Maya Lin by virtue of his masterwork at the National Cathedral. He was a consummate professional, renowned for the virtuosity of his exacting technique in the classical mode, even though many in the arts considered him something of a throwback. His attention to detail was unparalleled. The spiritualism of his previous work was also a plus, as he perceived the challenge of his commission to be spiritual. And unlike Lin's artistic remove, Hart had read deeply about the war. He had interviewed scores of veterans for his entry, and he had carefully nurtured his relationship with the key players in the drama, especially Webb. Indeed, he may have been aware that, during the autumn of discontent, Webb and Carhart had conspired to get the first and second place finishers thrown out in favor of the third place entry.

In late April, the panel began discussions with Hart. He would be the only sculptor to be considered. So much for Von Eckardt's idea of another national contest. Rather quickly all agreed that a single figure would be too forlorn and lonely and have trouble interacting with Lin's wall. To his credit, Hart rejected outright the idea of a triumphal macho hero commanding his troops to charge up a hill, like the Fort Benning and Fort Bragg statues. That, in relation to the wall, would leave the macabre impression of a leader summoning his troops into the swamp of sure death. Three figures would work better, Hart felt. Their pose should indeed suggest bravery, but also youth and vulnerability, and project the camaraderie and the wariness that defined the lot of the Vietnam soldier. With three servicemen, the triad could also present the racial diversity of the American armed forces. After his first meeting with the committee, the sculptor repaired immediately to his studio and began working on a "clay sketch." He would tell his patrons later that he imagined his concept almost immediately and that the model almost sculpted itself.

A month later, Hart met with Cooper to describe the evolution of his thinking. By Cooper's description the sculptor imagined three fully equipped and armed GIs on patrol. "They emerge from a thicket and freeze in surprise as they behold the wall of the memorial." The grouping should be close-knit, fully realistic, with their clothing accurate in every detail, and multiracial. Cooper continued to believe that the addition of a statue was unnecessary, but if politics required it to save the entire enterprise, he could think of no better solution to the unpleasant dilemma. Perhaps, he thought, if Hart could produce something reminiscent of Auguste Rodin's *Burghers of Calais*, the country might end up with two superb works side-by-side. But how side-by-side? Cooper thought the statue should be placed at the tree line well south of the wall. In that he expected a fight. A full-sized mockup should be fashioned and then moved around on wheels at the site to determine the best spot.

Placement now emerged as the most heated point of contention. Webb had a very different idea. He believed, incorrectly, that the Warner compromise had specifically authorized placing a flagpole on the high ground thirteen yards directly behind the apex of the wall and positioning the sculpture in the open ground on the knoll about fifty-five yards in front of the apex. The politicians would soon jump in to demand that the statue go immediately in front of the vertex.

A meeting of the Commission of Fine Arts was set for October to sort all this out.

In July, Maya Lin had had enough and went public. The time had come for her to clear her conscience. In an interview with the *Washington Post*, she weighed in with a devastating critique. "This farce has gone on too long," she fumed. "Past a certain point, it's not worth compromising. It [the memorial] becomes nothing—even if it's a 250-foot-long nothing." Invoking the famous desecration of the *Mona Lisa*, she charged Hart with drawing mustaches on other people's portraits. "Artists don't go around scabbing on other artists' work." Hart's sculpture would create the feeling that the visitor is being watched.

Worse, "I don't want it to appear they're going to shoot you when you start walking down toward the walls."

A week later she went on NPR and NBC's *Today Show*. When an interviewer asserted that unspecified veterans groups were complaining that her design was not heroic enough, Lin replied, "It's a question of who 'they' are, and I say the people that dislike it are a very small few, and they happen to be very traditional artistically." Referencing the Washington Monument, an abstract simple conceptual work of art, she noted that "You have people, the same sort of 'they,' complaining that we need a statue of George Washington on top of it before it is a memorial."

With all this contention, she was asked, had she lost all the satisfaction of her achievement? Concern rather than satisfaction was her emotion now, she replied.

Then for the first time she gave voice to the universal reach of the memorial. It was far broader in scope and significance than a mere veterans memorial. "I designed something—it's not mine—I designed it for not only for the Vietnam veterans but for the country, for people one hundred years from now. . . . It's not an object to be owned by anyone." She was trying to fight for a "very pure thought."

Would she attend the dedication in the fall?

"Probably not," she snapped, for the break with Memorial Fund was complete. "I don't believe that what is happening is very ethical. . . . I sort of want to stand away from it."

She was now represented by a lawyer from a major New York firm, and he put the Memorial Fund on notice that according to the rules of the competition no feature that was not part of the winning design could be added without the express consent of the winner. To do so would be a "material breach" of the rules. Until his client agreed to an addition, no modification to the original design should be submitted to any commission.

The reaction was intense. Jan Scruggs, the man in the middle, seemed to retract his previous support of Lin. Hart's statue will make the memorial "one hundred percent better," Scruggs said now. To Lin it was a straightforward betrayal. The sharp-tongued juror Harry Weese came to her defense, putting his contempt for the political interference on display. "It's as if Michelangelo had the secretary of the Interior climb up on the scaffold and muck around with his work."

Four days later, passionate letters appeared in the *Washington Post*. One saw Secretary Watt's compromise as glorifying war and debasing Lin's design. Another picked up the theme. "Instead of a daringly simple memorial to honor those who served, which is intended to inspire peaceful contemplation . . . a statue and poor Old Glory are, once again, demanded, on center, to shout, 'Our country, right or wrong.' Why?" Five days later another batch of letters appeared. A Vietnam veteran expressed his anger that the controversy "is a memorial to the indecision, political meddling, and lack of principle and conviction that marked the war," while another argued that, if anything had to be added to the wall, let it be a grove of weeping willows.

Inevitably, this batch of letters contained the obligatory slur on the wall itself. The Maya Lin design, wrote a veteran, was "a great privy, an outside urinal of German beer garden design."

The press picked up the phrase that an "Art War" was now under way.

In August, Robert Lawrence, the president of the American Institute of Architects, denounced the additions as "ill-conceived" and a "breach of faith" that would cut the soul out of Maya Lin's design. He called on architects across the country to lobby against them. And Paul Spreiregen, still intent to highlight the grandeur and fairness of his competition, called the addition of a sculpture "an outrageous desecration," pointing out that no bronze sculpture of soldiers existed in the Arlington National Cemetery.

Nevertheless, the construction process was moving forward. Ground had been broken on March 26. By late summer granite panels were being set in place, one by one. Lin visited the site and expressed her satisfaction. "It really fits in. It slides right into the ground." In the coming weeks others visited, including Secretary Watt. Kent Cooper, representing Maya Lin, and Joseph Brown, representing Frederick Hart, visited the site together and wrangled over the placement of the flag and the Hart statues. Cooper argued for the tree line, while Brown kept pushing the maquette closer and closer to the wall. Theirs was a testy relationship.

As the wall neared completion, the most noteworthy visitor was the conservative columnist James J. Kilpatrick. In a piece the following day, Kilpatrick wrote of being reduced to tears. As the memorial came into view, "nothing I had heard or written had prepared me for the moment. I could not speak. I wept. . . . This memorial has a pile driver's impact. No politics. No recriminations. . . . The memorial carries a message for all ages: This is what war is all about."

As the public controversy grew more and more intense during the summer, Frederick Hart quietly moved from a rough clay "sketch" to a clay model. On July 1, the "Sculpture Panel" announced to the press his selection as sculptor, and contract negotiations commenced. Hart asserted that it would take him two years to complete the final statue. For his work, he asked for a handsome fee of $330,000, more than sixteen times what Maya Lin had received. At this early stage he adopted a conciliatory tone toward her. "I realize," he said, "that there is an existing design and that the integrity of the design should be maintained." With time his language would become far more pointed and combative.

Through the summer, efforts to bring Lin and Hart together were unsuccessful. She did not see Hart's maquette until September 17, and she said nothing as she viewed it sullenly.

Three days later an elaborate public viewing of Hart's figures took place in the Great Hall of the Pension Building in downtown Washington. Dwarfed by the building's massive Corinthian columns, the clay soldiers were set on a table, and Hart stepped forward to describe his concept. Bowing to the "elegant simplicity and austerity of the existing design by Maya Lin," he hoped for a "unified totality." Of the emotion he wished to evoke, he said, "The gesture and expression of the figures are directed to the Wall, effecting an interplay between image and metaphor. The tension between the two elements creates a resonance that echoes from one to the other. . . . I see the Wall as a kind of ocean, a sea of sacrifice that is overwhelming and nearly incomprehensible in its sweep of names. I place these figures upon the shore of that sea gazing upon it, standing vigil before it, reflecting the human face of it, the human heart."

The press reaction was mixed. The contrast between the two works was hard to fathom; it was an artistic collision, a radical edge, a tortured response to Modernism that would fade in significance with time. But could the collision be made to work? One juror of the original competition, the distinguished landscape architect Hideo Sasaki, thought so. If the Hart statue was placed at some distance from the "visual mass" of the wall and in opposition to it, it could work. "Often works of other artists, if sensitively done, enhance the totality of the design. I hope this latter is true." Fellow juror Harry Weese was not moved. "I view the adulteration of Maya Lin's design by any dissident group as arbitrary, capricious and destructive and the approval [of the additions] is irresponsible and beyond the pale. . . Art is uncompromisable."

Nor had Paul Goldberger, the architecture critic of the *New York Times*, embraced the compromise, feeling that the statue and the flagpole would destroy the beauty of Maya Lin's mystical space. "It tries also to shift this memorial away from its focus on the dead and toward a kind of literal interpretation of heroism and patriotism that ultimately treats the war dead in the most simplistic of terms."

Goldberger defined the issue thus: With the addition of the statue and the flagpole, Scruggs and company hoped to convert "a superb design into something that speaks of heroism and absolute moral certainty. But there could be no such literalism and no such certainty where Vietnam is concerned," he wrote. "To try to represent a period of anguish and complexity in our history with a simple statue of armed soldiers is to misunderstand all that has happened, and to suggest that no lessons have been learned at all from the experience of Vietnam."

As for Lin, she shot back her response through her lawyers. Expressing her disapproval of the proposed additions and denouncing the "enhancements" as a violation of her concept, she seemed especially incensed at the notion that her design lacked humanity. "As each person enters the memorial, seeing his face reflected amongst the names, can the human element escape him? Surely seeing himself and the surroundings reflected within the memorial is a more moving and personal experience than any one artist's figurative or allegorical interpretation could engender." The proposed sculpture and flagpole "splits the Memorial at its focal point," she wrote. The intrusion undercut the circular concept of the names and their timeline and "destroys the meaning of the design."

The animus between Lin and Hart grew worse by the day. While she seethed at the "immoral" intrusion of another artist on her work, he pouted about operating largely in her shadow. When his magnificent work, *Ex Nihilo*, was finally dedicated at the National Cathedral on October 2, the event was completely ignored in both the popular and the art press, and the audience was small (although it did include Prince Philip of Great Britain). These snubs, no doubt, thickened his competitive juices.

On October 10, the CBS News program *60 Minutes* ran an extensive segment on the controversy. The dramatic triangle of Perot, Lin, and Scruggs was the centerpiece. And for the first time publicly, the question of Maya Lin's race was put up in lights.

"They sort of lump us all together," Lin said in response to a question about her Asian ancestry. "I first heard [the term] two years ago. It's called a gook." Hearing the word come out of her own mouth, she emitted a nervous laugh. And then she became diplomatic. "If you were being rational and logical, there would be some people who fought in that war who would really hate the idea that someone of my descent would have designed [the Vietnam memorial]."

"How Chinese are you?" Morley Safer asked.

"As apple pie." (This time the interviewer laughed.) "Born and raised in the Midwest, surrounded by non-Chinese people, I just really never looked at myself as a minority. I looked at myself as just any other kid."

Cut to Scruggs. Had an Anglo-Saxon male designed the memorial, "I think the difficulties that we had would have been considerably less."

And then to Perot's bluster. What if the Fine Arts Commission says, yes, you can have the flag and statue, he was asked, "but not right in front?"

"If anybody ever even raises that point . . . it is the worst kind of bad faith, the worst kind of double-dealing," he responded. "If that should even begin to occur, I will intend to spend whatever time, money and energy is necessary to see that people keep their words, because we owe that to the Vietnam veterans. And I'm going to have a lot of powerful allies."

As the meeting of the Commission of Fine Arts loomed, the Art War was hurtling toward its Stalingrad.

Chapter Nine

A BREACH OF FAITH

O n the morning of the climactic day in the brawl over Vietnam memory, with jangled nerves on all sides, when the fate of Frederick Hart's traditional soldiers would face off against Maya Lin's abstract wall, the *Washington Post* did an extraordinary thing. Having been reasonably evenhanded in its coverage of the controversy up until this point, the paper turned over three pages of its Style section to gadfly Tom Wolfe to fulminate over "The Tribute to Jane Fonda" that the Lin design was to him. With florid, overheated prose, and a few *bon mots*, Wolfe's interminable, over-the-top essay was replete with long, ponderous passages about the contempt of the contemporary art elite for the "bourgeois" creations of the classical past. The essay, which chronicled how the Vietnam Veterans Memorial went awry, embraced the Webb/Carhart/Perot position, including Perot's silly poll about veteran attitudes, and put forward examples of what he regarded as other failed efforts at public art. Why, other than vanity, Wolfe felt compelled to inject himself into this fraught debate, at this time, is a mystery, as is why the *Washington Post* decided to accord him a measure of credibility on the issue. The essay was inflammatory and rekindled passions, possibly making compromise even harder.

Tom Wolfe's essay was mainly about Tom Wolfe and his theories about the poverty of modern art, taken from his book called *The Painted Word* (1975). The disaster of Lin's "banal" design—he would later call it "skill-proof"—was the fault of the competition's jury, Wolfe supposed. Its members were tired old men, creators of boring, unadorned glass boxes, who celebrated public artworks that "baffled" and "annoyed" the public, who hailed from a "world as bizarre and totally removed from the rest of American life as anything any soldier had ever run into in Vietnam." (How Wolfe would know this is a puzzlement, since he came of age during the Korean War, when, while others fought, he was in Yale graduate school preoccupied with his thesis on the Red baiting of American writers.) According to him, the mission of the cognoscenti was to bring abstract modernist works out of the galleries and into the streets. He regarded the eight jurors of the Vietnam competition as among the "Mullahs of Modernism," by which he meant not only wrong-headed but orthodox and inflexible.

With its anticlassical bent, the art establishment had lost interest in human anatomy, Wolfe averred. The mullahs felt that to draw or sculpt the human body would "retard imagination," and they did not want their students to be bothered and burdened by the "dead hand of the past." To sculpt realistic works of the human body was bourgeois, but to sculpt a realistic figure of a heroic soldier was the most bourgeois thing of all to do. In a later essay, Wolfe would quote playwright Tom Stoppard from his play *Artist Descending a Staircase*, "Imagination without skill gives us contemporary art."

Meanwhile, according to Wolfe, all the forlorn and unappreciated Vietnam veteran ever wanted out of this memorial was to remove the accusing finger of shame that unfairly blamed the warrior rather than the decision maker or the malingerer or the protester for the worst defeat in American history. Glibly, he asserted that "the unspeakable and inconfessional (*sic*) goal of the New Left on the campuses had been to transform the shame of the fearful into the guilt of the courageous." This was an original thought. In this construct, Lyndon Johnson,

Richard Nixon, and their Washington warriors were absent from the passion of the protester.

In Frederick Hart, Wolfe had found his rebel against this disastrous and tyrannical vogue of modernism. Here was a figurative artist of consummate technical skill who saw the human body as God-given. Hart's hardscrabble early life, Wolfe thought, was akin to that of Giotto di Bondone in the thirteenth century who, like Hart, had been discovered at a tender age. If Giorgio Vasari, the author of the seminal Renaissance book, *Lives of the Artists*, were still living, Wolfe suggested, Frederick Hart would have an honored place in his collection. Wolfe proclaimed Hart to be the avatar of a movement to restore a concept of classical beauty to modern works and to reverse this most "ludicrous" collapse of good taste in the history of American art. Through him the beauty of the human form would be rediscovered.

Portlandia *(1985), by Raymond John Kaskey, Portland, Oregon*

He would be joined by three other notable sculptors with realistic masterworks: Raymond Kaskey (*Portlandia* in Portland, Oregon), Eric Parks (*Elvis* in Memphis), and Audrey Flack (a grouping of four Classical goddesses called *Civitas* in Rock Hill, South Carolina). Through them the Giotto tradition of fine art would make a comeback.

Within hours, these weighty, self-absorbed musings were quickly forgotten, as the pivotal hearing of the Commission of Fine Arts convened. But Wolfe would not give up the cause. He became Hart's friend and chief booster, later declaring him to be America's most popular sculptor whom the critics, in their ignorance and arrogance, consistently ignored.

—

Over the proceedings hovered the mood of A. E. Housman's poem:

> Here dead we lie
> Because we did not choose
> To live and shame the land
> From which we sprung.
>
> Life, to be sure,
> Is nothing much to lose,
> But young men think it is,
> And we were young.

The US Commission of Fine Arts convened at 12:37 p.m. on October 13 and settled in for a long afternoon in the pivotal showdown. Because of the intense press interest in a possible ceasefire in the Art War, the proceedings were held in the cavernous, two-story Cash Room in the US Treasury Building next to the White House. Dating back to 1869, the Victorian-era room featured three enormous brass chandeliers, large, light-blue marble panels, and elaborate floral grill work over the radiators. Even if the event would deal with recent history, the grandeur of the nineteenth-century décor might well have pleased the aesthete who was the commission's worldly, old-fashioned chairman, J. Carter Brown.

The witness list featured five lead-off speakers. Frederick Hart was accorded the honor of speaking in this first group, bracketed by Jim Webb, Jan Scruggs, and the two architects, Kent Cooper and Joseph Brown. Twenty-nine speakers for the additions followed, and then ten against, including Maya Lin herself. When the opponents finished making their case, the commissioners would vote, and Carter Brown would announce their decision.

Since the purpose of the meeting was to consider compromise, Hart was diplomatic and respectful, eloquent and brief in his presentation. He described his creation as both unity and contrast to the wall. He wished to preserve the austerity of Maya Lin's design with a grouping of realistic soldiers that would be understated and removed some distance from the wall, so that it did not "intrude or obstruct" or "compete or dominate." His soldiers would be quite small, slightly larger than life-size. There would be an artistic tension between the elements where one would echo the other. His figures would project youth and innocence and vulnerability, and they would be clothed in combat garb and armed with the weapons of war. He repeated his metaphor of the wall as an ocean.

Menace was quickly evident. The first speaker for the additions, Deputy Secretary of Interior Donald Hodel, speaking for his boss, James Watt, led off with a threat. The secretary had been under considerable pressure to disapprove the original design totally, to modify it radically, or insist that the design process be started all over again. A fragile compromise had been reached. But the Department of the Interior would allow the dedication of the memorial to go forward, even before the statue and the flagpole were in place, *only if* the design refinements were approved by the commission. "To permit dedication of the memorial to proceed if the flag and sculpture have not yet been approved would be to break faith with all who have negotiated in good faith."

In their testimony the architects, Cooper and Joseph Brown, presented a plan to place the sculpture and the flagpole at a tree line of red maples and sweet gums about sixty yards from the vertex of the wall. These elements would form an "entrance experience." At this juncture, the two estimable professionals acted as a team in service of the compromise, even though their relationship had been anything but harmonious.

Cooper defined the question with which they had wrangled in the previous weeks. Could aesthetics be separated from message? What defined "non-political" and what satisfied "appropriate patriotic content"? To this point Cooper spoke forcefully. "Aesthetics in itself is an important component message and cannot be separated out." Where to place the flag then? It was "a powerful symbolic element" in itself and should not be placed within the composition "without extreme care."

The architects had found this problem of location especially vexing. If the flagpole was seen anywhere within the panoramic sweep of the horizontal wall, it would completely destroy the mood of contemplation that Maya Lin intended. If the flagpole were placed at the apex of the wall, as Webb and company insisted, the horizontal thrust of the wall would be "resolved" upward as a distraction, said Cooper. If it were placed behind or to the side, it would convey the impression of a golf hole. The architects were leaving the problem to the commission to settle.

There followed a parade of witnesses for the additions that included the now-familiar rant from Tom Carhart and an appearance by the two generals, Price and Davison. Most of the witnesses hailed from military service organizations that espoused support for the additions in the flat tones of corporate spokesmen. Conspicuously absent from the group was H. Ross Perot. But his influence was felt, and he was not finished. Congressman Donald Bailey, who had been a constant thorn in the side of the entire enterprise, *was* on hand. A decorated veteran of the 101st Airborne Division, he was one of the few Vietnam veterans in Congress. As it happened, he was on the verge of electoral defeat after his Pennsylvania district had been gerrymandered into the larger district of Congressional titan John Murtha. But the memorial would be Bailey's swan song, and now, among all supporting testimonies, his raw authenticity was the most moving.

"One question that still clouds the entire issue, that question whether or not [the veterans] fought for a proper reason . . . That is what carries the message of an insult. . . Allow us, please," he pleaded, "to carry a message of honor and respect and recognition for the reasons why that war was fought. . . . When your face is dirty and a friend is dead, and you haven't bathed in a long time, and you are hungry, and you are surrounded, and you don't know if you are going to live or die, there is an issue of pride that keeps you pursuing what you believe in."

Maya Lin led off the opposition with a forceful defense of her accomplishment. She appealed to the "artistic conscience of the Nation," whatever persuasiveness that might have in the face of the powerful political forces arrayed against her. She spoke of her creation as a "living park," symbolic of life that left the visitor the freedom of contemplation. It was not a memorial to politics or war or controversy. She scorned the proposal that would harm her work "visually by the abrupt verticality of a flagpole or conceptually by a sculpture that forces a specific interpretation."

But the thrust of her testimony dealt mainly with the incongruity of the two works. What was being proposed was not one memorial but two. "To make a 'unified totality' out of two different works of art fails," she said. Worse: "These 'intrusions' which treat the original work of art as no more than an architectural backdrop reflect an insensitivity to the original design's subtle spatial eloquence." Under the proposal her wall would become nothing more than a "retaining wall." The sculpture and the flagpole desecrated the artistic integrity of her concept. "It violates a basic principle of design in trying to juxtapose incongruous elements."

The most extensive testimony in opposition to the additions, however, was delivered by Paul Spreiregen, the patriarch of the original competition. While he had no role in this advanced stage of the memorial's development, he came now to express his passionate alarm at the damage that had been done to his beloved contest by relatively few outspoken veterans and to defend the integrity and authenticity of the process that had chosen Lin's design.

It is a design, he told the commission, "which operates fully only when it is unencumbered."

In his lengthy discourse that was by turns eloquent and ponderous—the proposed additions were "an insult to the aesthetic spiritual sensibility of Americans"—Spreiregen was at his most effective when he asked the commission to imagine Arlington National Cemetery if in each grouping for America's past wars there was a larger-than-life statuary of soldiers in historical combat garb or imagine if at the base of the Washington Monument there was a large statue of a fife player and a drummer boy or imagine the Lincoln Memorial with brigades of Union soldiers traipsing through the trees around the Reflecting Pool. That, he said, would occasion a mediocre joke, worthy only of *Saturday Night Live*.

"A great work of art doesn't tell you what to think, it makes you think," he said.

After the witnesses finished, the commission recessed to visit the site. When it reconvened, Carter Brown spoke for all the members. His ambivalence about the compromise was clear enough. Picking up on Spreiregen's metaphor, he too imagined the horror of a statue of Washington crossing the Delaware being placed at the foot of the Washington Monument, or a replica of a rocking chair next to the eternal flame at Kennedy's gravesite. On the one hand, a flagpole was a wonderful idea, and at the same time, a dangerous precedent, for he did not approve of flags proliferating throughout the National Mall. And he gave a bland endorsement of Hart's maquette: the muddy faces and simple clothing of the soldiers were promising as far as they went, he allowed, but the commission reserved the right to approve the final product. At this point Hart's figures scarcely looked like a great work of art in the making. The two works of art, Carter Brown said, were as different as opera and country music.

But the shocking aspect of the proposed additions, at least to their opponents, had to do with location. The commissioners agreed that the flagpole and the statuary should be moved far back from the wall to form an "entrance experience" to the memorial.

With that, the commission's proceedings were concluded.

It would be said later, most significantly by Carter Brown himself, that Frederick Hart's deferential, accommodating tone at the hearing and his willingness to separate his soldiers at some distance from the wall had saved the Vietnam Veterans Memorial. That is not how the detractors saw it. They cried foul betrayal, and this time, it was they who had been outmaneuvered.

—

It was time to exhale, it seemed. A truce in the Art War had been declared. The "refinements" had been certified, if not exactly validated, and the peacemakers, especially J. Carter Brown, congratulated themselves on their navigation through a bitter, nasty fight. *U.S. News and World Report* carried the headline: PEACE AT LAST. "The last battle of the Vietnam War ended on October 13," said the magazine. The last major hurdle was cleared for the memorial to be dedicated in three weeks. Late the following evening, *Nightline* with Ted Koppel devoted its entire telecast to the compromise. It became another installment of the Lin/Perot/Scruggs triangle with Maya Lin in Boston, Ross Perot in Dallas, and Jan Scruggs in Washington. Had the show been given a title, it might have been: "Burying the Hatchet?" Koppel began with a mention of the astonishing fact that for the dedication of the great Vietnam Veterans Memorial, its designer had not even been invited to the gala. Why was that? At first, he directed the question to the wrong person.

"It could arise from a certain amount of compromise that has gone down," Lin answered blandly.

"Would you like to be there?"

"I would very much like to be there."

Moving around the triangle, Koppel asked Scruggs, the Great Compromiser of the piece, if the agreement was satisfactory.

"We're very happy with the approval of the flag and the statue," he answered. Everyone liked the statue. "We're certainly hoping Ms. Lin will join the team again."

"When did she jump off?" Koppel asked.

"I guess when we were essentially maneuvered into a position in which we had to make a compromise over her design." This was a concession.

Then to Perot. Was he satisfied?

"Well, if the veterans like the memorial and the compromise, as far as I'm concerned it is [okay]," he replied. "Our nation lost its will for the war, and yet didn't have the courage to stop it; so, we left them on the battlefield, we left the men in the prisoner-of-war camps. . . . We brought these men home not as heroes, as they should have been brought home, but we neglected them and abused them after we brought them home." The Vietnam veteran deserved a great memorial.

Cut to Scruggs: "The veterans need this memorial, and I don't mind putting up with a little more baloney to get the job done."

When the caviling was nearly over, Koppel gave Lin the chance to elevate the discourse. What, he asked, did she think the veterans would feel in three weeks when they actually saw the finished memorial?

"I think for each and every individual they will feel a different thing," she replied. "There will be a sense of sadness, a sense of sacrifice, a sense of loss; but also, a sense of life, a sense of a park, a sense of the memory—if you're a veteran returning, you will see yourself reflected within the names of friends, friends will be linked together in time, and it will be very moving. And I would hope each individual who comes and visits that site will come out of it a little bit more at peace, a little bit more resolved, in a sense, within himself."

Several days later the *Washington Post* ran a long excerpt of Carter Brown's final, decisive statement at the October 13 meeting, immediately after the commissioners had returned from the memorial site. "One can visualize what the final effect will be," he had said. "It is extraordinarily moving. I think the litany of names [of Americans dead in Vietnam] is enough to bring enormous emotions to everyone's heart, emotions of pride and of honor in the sacrifices that have been made in serving this country." The ground upon which the memorial rested was prime real estate, and that alone spoke to the country's pride in the people who were being memorialized. It was true that the commission had vetoed the proposal to put Hart's statues on the knoll directly above the axis of the wall. "If the sculpture is allowed to shiver naked out there in the field, to be an episodic element that is not integrated," he said, "[the elements] will not combine to have the critical mass and impact that those elements deserve."

The commissioners, said the chairman, wanted to be part of the healing.

Not so fast.

The political backlash to the commission's aesthetic decision about positioning began immediately. Art and Politics were conjoined as never before in American history. Within two days of the proceedings, three senators and four congressmen delivered a letter of protest to Secretary Watt, expressing strong opposition to the commission's decision to place the additions "outside the memorial wall area" and insisting on the "integration" of the statue and the flagpole within the span of the wall itself. *Integration* was the new code word for an intimate, contiguous arrangement of all three disparate elements. The lawmakers urged the secretary not to allow the memorial's dedication until the location of the modifications was settled "in conformance" with the compromise reached with the veterans. Unstated was the fact that *conformance* referred to the meeting with Ross Perot and his

Gallery of Selected Entries Submitted to the Vietnam Veterans Memorial Competition,

with samples showing the variety of design styles

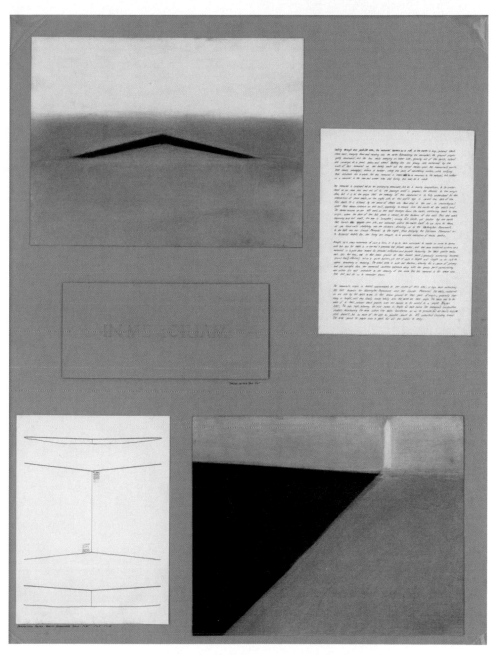

This page and the verso: Two entry panels by Maya Lin

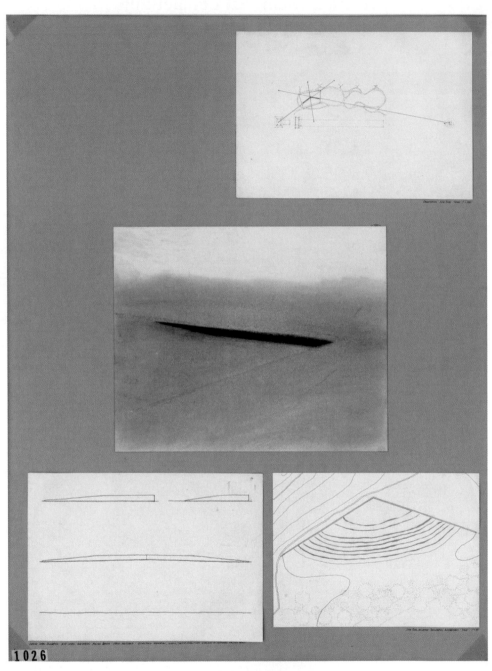

A second panel by Maya Lin

Raymond Scott McCord, team leader

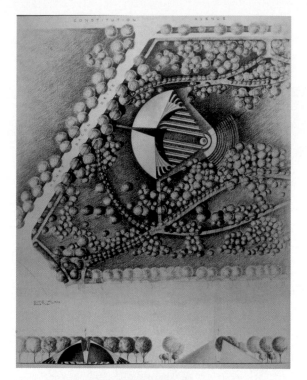

Armand P. Avakian

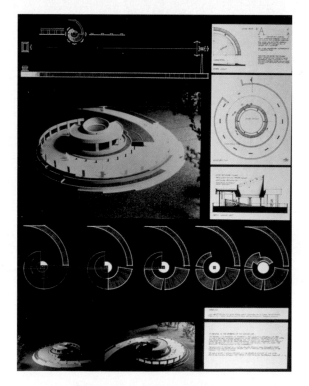

Bruce Northwood White

Garth E. Bute

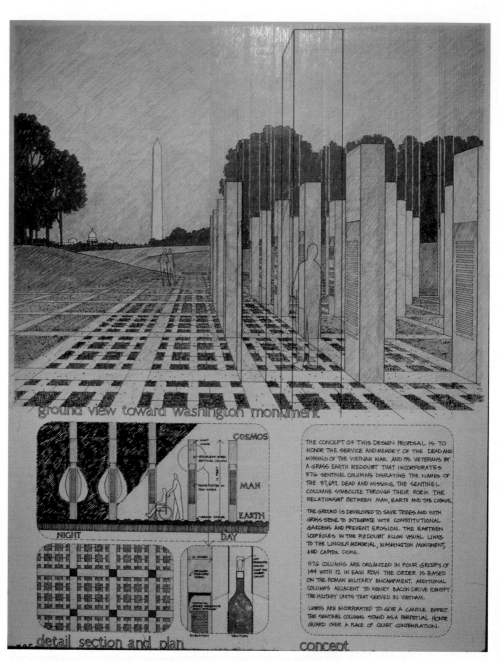

ground view toward washington monument

detail section and plan

concept

Duane Thorbeck, team leader, Inter Design Inc.

THE VIETNAM VETERANS MEMORIAL DESIGN COMPETITION - 1

Byron Rosenbaum, team leader

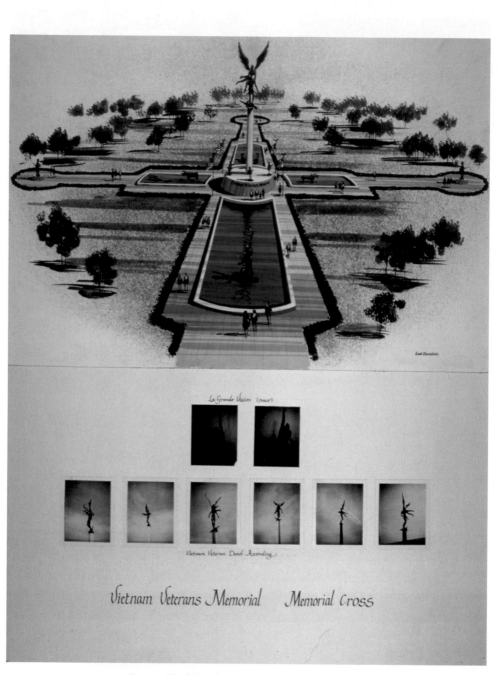

James Earl Reid, team leader, The Studio

Raymond John Kaskey

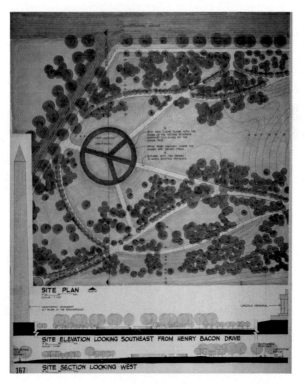

J. Stuart Pettitt

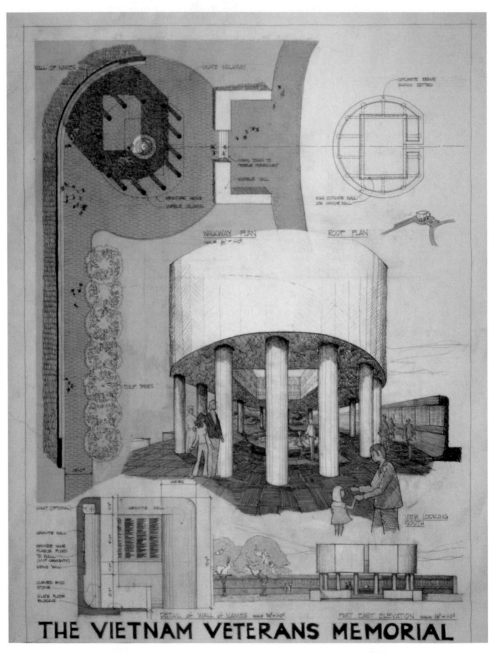

THE VIETNAM VETERANS MEMORIAL

Fred D. Ordway

Daniel C. Osborn, team leader

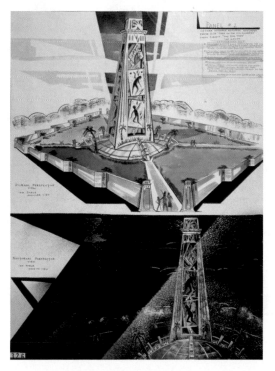

Gabriel P. Cartwright

Willard Milton Pounds, Jr., team leader

Max Balassiano

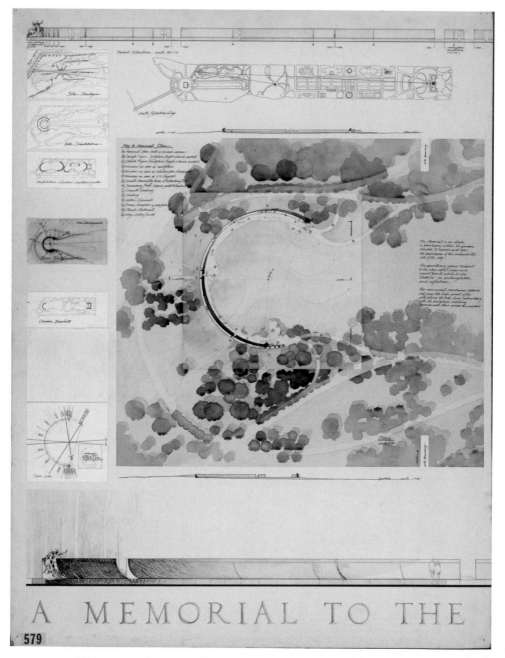

This page and opposite: Design entry panels by Joseph E. Brown
and featuring sculpture designs by Frederick Hart

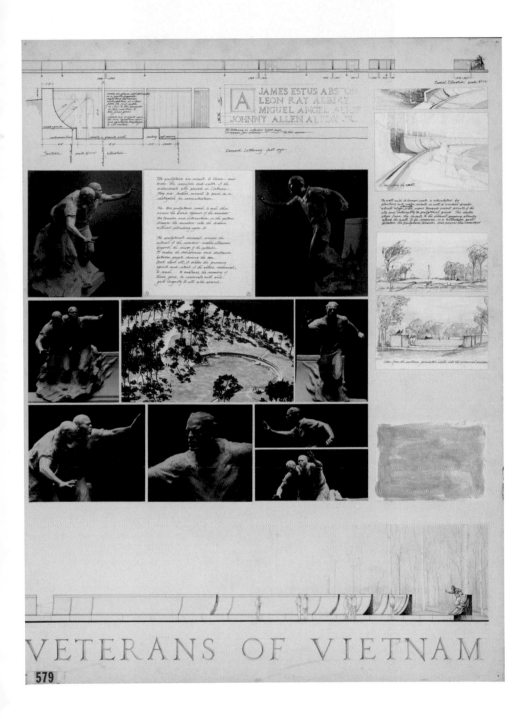

VETERANS OF VIETNAM

Karole Lee Warren

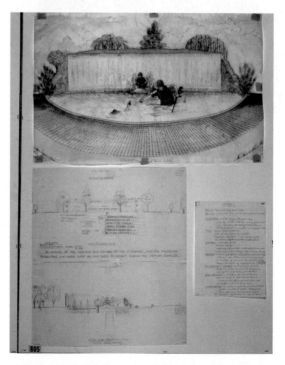

Michael D. Rich, team leader, Rich Designs

posse the previous March in which there was a show of hands from his supporters.

It was left to Robert Lawrence, the president of the American Institute of Architects, to stand up for the artistic side. In a letter of support to Carter Brown five days later, Lawrence praised the commission for "rejecting the 'compromise' plan" proposed by Secretary Watt. "By recommending a complete separation of the disparate design elements the commission has preserved the integrity of Maya Lin's award-winning design," Lawrence wrote. "An admirable balance has thus been struck between a recognition of service and comradeship as well as an acknowledgment of sacrifice."

But the artistic world was not entirely of one mind about swallowing the horror of the additions. In the just-published November issue of a professional journal called *Design Action*, there was this comment: "Maya Lin's idea is no longer hers. It has a life of its own. Now broader interests have been brought to bear on that life, ignoring her and her supporters. Her idea still has enormous strength and clarity. It can easily survive the additions proposed. Indeed, they may give it a richness it needs."

The Washington political process was now operating at full steam. J. Carter Brown's card was the official decision of his duly constituted commission; Secretary Watt's card was his authority to cancel the dedication on Veterans Day with all the consequences that might portend; Jim Webb and Tom Carhart had convinced official Washington that they spoke for all veterans as they worked effectively behind the scenes; and Jan Scruggs & Company had seen their memorial realized but stood in the strong countervailing winds, just hoping that the storm would not further damage and tarnish their dream.

On October 19 Brown and Watt met. Brown held to the commission's decision for an "entrance experience" but fudged on the exact, final location of the additions, while he reassured Watt that the sculpture and flagpole would indeed "complement" the wall and not be "shunted off out of view" in the trees. Moreover, he offered the carrot that for the dedication ceremony a temporary, removable flag-pole could be raised above the wall. Watt, in turn, promised to continue working with the commission toward an acceptable solution. A few days after that, Brown met as well with Webb, and no doubt, reaffirmed in soft, dulcet, but firm tones that his commission had received its mandate from Congress in 1910. It was then given the sole authority to advise and consent to artists' selection, to judge the quality and appropriateness of their models, and to determine the location of all statues, fountains, and monuments in the public spaces of the nation's capital. No patched-together *ad hoc* meeting in a congressional conference room had any such authority whatever.

On November 4, Webb, Carhart, and Congressman Bailey called a press conference to make their last stand. Having come very close to scuttling Maya Lin's design altogether, and now having succeeded in imposing the refinements on the composition, they greeted the commission's decision as a betrayal. Bailey came armed with threats. He would urge President Reagan to command, by fiat, the location of the additions in close proximity to the wall. If that didn't work, he promised to spearhead a congressional resolution to legislate proximity. And if those measures failed, and the wall stood alone as built, he would support an effort to find an alternate site on the Mall for a second Vietnam memorial.

"We fear that the black wall will be left on the field," Carhart added wanly. "We've been driven off the field in a breach of faith."

The press conference was their last gasp, for their objections were soon to be swamped by much more profound events. Still, Webb made the most of his final bow. This eighteen-month brawl was not just about a wall. "Like Moby Dick," he said, "this is more than a story about a whale." It was about art and history, but also about politics. He was someone who knew something about all three, he said, for he was "an artist of the written word." As such he knew a bit about metaphors, about choosing "symbolic events to tell a story larger than your plot or canvas or figures." Public art about a political event like Vietnam was

unavoidably political, he said. Even Plato had said so, when he wrote
"art is politics." But Lin's design was not even art; it was merely two
walls stuck together whose effect was "incomplete, negative, nihilistic, sad." When one visits the Washington Monument or the Lincoln
Memorial, one was supposed to be uplifted. Lin's place, by contrast, was
not a place for celebration, but only a place "to go and be depressed."

He took his swipes and a few cheap shots. He couldn't resist invoking Maya Lin's overgenerous grade in Professor Burr's architecture
course at Yale. Of the open competition that chose Lin, Paul Spreiregen was its "Svengali." Spreiregen was right to say that there were
no sculptures in Arlington National Cemetery, but so too there were,
until now, no tombs on the National Mall. He heaped contempt on
that splinter group called Vietnam Veterans Against the War that had
supported Maya Lin. And as for J. Carter Brown and his remark about
the Hart statues being placed prominently out in the open, "shivering
nakedly in the cold," these were "blowsy words." The true purpose of
the Hart statues was to change the metaphor and remove the nihilism
of the wall.

His last hurrah was well-crafted and powerful. He had fought a
good fight, and his advocacy for the bravery and heroism of the American soldier in a difficult time would be well-remembered. He had lost
this battle, he acknowledged; it was a fight that was won by the high
priests of American culture. But his forceful efforts would propel him
to an appointment as the assistant secretary of Defense for Reserve
Affairs two years later, then as secretary of the Navy, to his election as
a United States senator from Virginia in 2006. In that vigorous sen-
atorial campaign, he toured the state with his Vietnamese-American
wife, Hong Le, at his side and in the combat boots of his son, Jimmy,
who served in Iraq in the Marines. It was a tribute, he would say, to
"all the people sent into harm's way." Finally, though briefly, he was a
Democratic candidate for president in 2015.

Ironically, years later, Maya Lin would find some common ground
with Webb's discourse on the political nature of memorials. "The

choice to make an apolitical memorial was in itself political to those who felt only a positive statement about the war would make up for the earlier anti-war days," she wrote. "It was extremely naïve of me to think that I could produce a neutral statement that would not become politically controversial simply because it chose not take sides."

Chapter Ten

DEDICATION

M aya Lin flew in from Boston several days before the dedication, having finally been invited as something of an afterthought following the *60 Minutes* embarrassment. She was given no special role nor was she publicly recognized or thanked. Grady Clay, the gracious Kentucky gentleman who had chaired the competition jury, met her at the airport, and they went immediately to the memorial for a quiet stroll and for official photographs. For the first time, she could see all the panels in place with the landscaping and the lighting finished. After all the wrangling over the inscriptions, she could read them in their final form:

> *In honor of the men and women of the Armed Forces of the United States who served in the Vietnam War. The names of those who gave their lives and of those who remain missing are inscribed in the order in which they were taken from us. Our nation honors the courage, sacrifice, and devotion to duty and country of its Vietnam veterans.*

To see the cobblestone walkway complete, grandstands and the podium in place, was deeply affecting. It terrified her, in fact. "It was a strange feeling, to have had an idea that was totally yours be no longer a part of your mind but totally public, no longer yours."

Even though a dune fence still surrounded the memorial, making it off-limits for another day, veterans were already walking the wall. When a few of them recognized her, they gathered around her emotionally and tearfully to convey their gratitude and congratulations. From the drawings and the gossip, they had been initially skeptical. "Is this the best they can do?" one veteran remembered thinking beforehand. Now, they were elated.

When Lin and Clay arrived at the apex, a tall, red-haired veteran, his Purple Heart pinned to his fatigue jacket, burst from the scrum and accosted her aggressively. "Why did you do such a thing?" he shrieked. "This memorial is to you, not to us!" He towered over her, his mere physical presence overwhelming and intimidating. "Why didn't you put in a flag?" he snarled close in her face. "Why did you try to bury us?"

Deeply shaken, she cowered beneath his hulk. Clay tried to interpose himself, but the veteran was overpowering and swatted him aside, continuing his rant until, finally, three vets in green berets rescued her and told the angry assailant to cool it and get lost. It was one thing to face off in professional settings against the likes of Ross Perot or Tom Carhart in defense of her art. Or even over the past eighteen months to hear remotely the multiple personal slurs about her in the press. But this was different, deeply personal and upsetting. Had it all come down to this? Could she expect a lot more of it when the hordes gathered for the dedication? What had she unleashed? Why had she come? She left hurriedly for her hotel room, where she dissolved into sobs.

Meanwhile, at the tony Cosmos Club, near Dupont Circle where he had once protested against the war, Frederick Hart celebrated. Secure now with his handsome commission, he hosted a dinner for his boosters, Tom Carhart and Milton Copulos, to thank them for all their help. Copulos, a disabled veteran who served in Vietnam from 1967 to 1969, was drawn into the memorial movement by negative portrayals in the national media of Vietnam veterans as drug addicts, alcoholics, and wife beaters. A militant anti-Communist and a passionately anti-Lin member of the shadow "Sculpture Panel" that had conferred the prize on Hart, he had just finished writing an op-ed piece for the *Washington Times* calling the memorial "an effort to victimize Vietnam veterans one last time." He began telling people that Lin's wall would not exist in another year. He knew a group of vets who planned to blow it up. In fact, on the day before the dedication, a call came into the offices of the VVMF.

"We're going to blow up the memorial," the voice growled.

Robert Doubek, the executive director of the VVMF, later recalled that Carhart made a similar threat that if the Fund did not add the statue to the wall, "they'd show us what they had learned from the Viet Cong about explosives."

The dedication of the Vietnam Veterans Memorial on November 13, 1982, was the culmination of a five-day salute to the Vietnam veteran, a week replete with seminars and musical events, full-throated renditions of the "Battle Hymn of the Republic," "When Johnny Comes Marching Home Again," and "America the Beautiful." Occasionally, as wistful counterpoint, sung somewhat more softly, the strains of Pete Seeger's song "Where Have all the Flowers Gone?" could be heard, with its plaintive line, "When will they ever learn?" There were readings by actors Jimmy Stewart and Brian Dennehy. A headline event for the week was a ninety-minute concert by Mr. Las Vegas, Wayne Newton. The Washington National Cathedral held a vigil in which all the names on the wall were read straight through, taking fifty-six hours. For that somber reading, President Reagan and the First Lady stopped by for five minutes. Afterward he repeated his shop-worn lines that the fallen had died for a "just cause" and that they were asked to fight and die for a cause that their country was "unwilling to win."

The night before Veterans Day, two inches of rain had fallen, and the morning broke cold and cloudy, in the forties with a strong wind. While the ground was soggy, the weather cleared somewhat, with a few rays of sunshine breaking through by afternoon. It was an entirely appropriate weather pattern for the spirit of the day. Mary McGrory, the crusty columnist for the *Washington Post*, saw shadings of gray in the dedication. The event was, she thought, worthy of Dante.

"The dark majesty of a wall [is] constructed to bear the unbearable grief and pain of the only war in our history where men who fled it were more honored than those who fought it."

In the heat of their combat, as Ross Perot had done his best to undermine Maya Lin, the Texan baited her with the question: Didn't she really think that the veterans would much prefer just a parade instead of her memorial, something happy and uplifting? Pondering the question later, she thought in response that "a parade would not, in the long term, help them overcome the enormous trauma of the politics of that war." They needed both.

The grand parade down Constitution Avenue began at the National Gallery of Art on 7th Street and ended ten blocks away at the memorial. Fifteen thousand marchers—people from every state—were involved. General William Westmoreland, in a trench coat, led a company of veterans. (He was then in the midst of his $120 million lawsuit against CBS for a program alleging that he had manipulated intelligence about enemy strength before the Tet Offensive to create the false impression of progress.)

The parade had the air of a 1960s happening. Veterans dressed in various relics of their service kibitzed amiably with clapping spectators. Many had amazed looks on their faces, for they had never been applauded before. Predictably, an effigy of Jane Fonda was burned to the raucous approval of the crowd. Flags and banners of military units festooned every contingent, and there were a fair number of burly, bearded men wearing bush hats. One exuberant, disabled veteran did joyous wheelies in his wheelchair. If the flags bespoke pride and patriotism, more signs than not evinced bitterness and anger. "No More Wars. No More Lies. No more Stone Memorials" read one; "We killed. We bled. We died for worse than nothing," read another;

"57,000 killed in vain, shame, horror, deceit, treachery" read a third. This was scarcely the image of the mystical, idealized soldier of Frederick Hart's vision, nor did these angry marchers comport with the vainglorious image of the American soldier promoted by the super patriots.

Once the parade reached the memorial, the dedication ceremony began. It featured the usual fare of patriotic speeches by dignitaries. Jan Scruggs was introduced as the biggest hero of them all, and the crowd serenaded him with the song "To Dream the Impossible Dream" from the Broadway hit, *Man of La Mancha*. Senator John Warner was accorded the honor of keynote speaker, after President Reagan declined the offer. Indeed, ranking members of the Reagan administration were conspicuously absent. (The highest-ranking official present was the deputy administrator of the Veterans Administration.) The US Marine Band, the president's own, was on hand. But the veterans were the focus. This was about them and for them.

After the speeches, after the flyby of F-4 jets and Army helicopters, after the honor guard cased their trumpets and the colors were retired, the veterans swarmed the wall. There were men in tattered fatigue jackets, some with battle medals pinned to their chests, and men with hooks for hands. There were fathers with their young sons solemnly pointing to a name, as if to touch a name was to ignite a magical response, in the manner of the character ET. One curly-haired veteran was photographed, hands and forehead to the wall in an unknowable dreamlike state. There were awe-struck teenagers with blank faces, walking in stunned silence, and widows and gold star mothers in white uniforms with flowers. There were a lot of hugs between old friends and strangers.

"Who were you with?" was a common question. "And what year?"

"Remember Bu Dop?" "My God! *Bu Dop!* Man, I've thought about that place. I've daydreamed a lot about Bu Dop."

The sky had cleared, and the low November sun now made the reflection off the wall more vivid. Around that portion of the wall that displayed the names of the fallen from the bloodiest battles, there was a

A veteran at the wall

noticeable crush: the battle to recapture the city of Hue and the battle of Khe Sanh a month later, where hundreds of Americans were killed and thousands wounded before the base was abandoned as no longer strategic. In one private scene after another, the effect of the wall was evident and overwhelming. In such a moment two veterans stood in front of the panel that listed the names of those at Hue, where 1,609 American soldiers had been wounded and 216 had been killed, including an Army intelligence officer named Ronald Ray.

"So many guys on the same day, it's incredible," one said in disbelief.

"What difference does it make if you find one name?" replied his friend, sweeping his hand across the wall. "Look at all of the names." And then he collapsed on his friend's shoulder.

"Some of them are special to you," the other said consolingly. "Others are special to other people." What was one to say?

There was bravado as well. There's Richard Housh, "a real good lieutenant," said a beefy guy. "I saw him jump up with his pump gun one time and blow away four guys coming at us. He was something else, one good lieutenant."

The throng stretched far up the grassy knoll all the way to the tree line, and a few brave hearts had climbed trees to get a better look across the expanse. Someone left a pair of combat boots with a small American flag. It began an artifact collection that in the years since has filled a warehouse in a Washington suburb. The size of the crowd was later estimated at about 150,000.

Maya Lin stood above the apex of the wall. She was just one of the crowd now, with no special notice accorded, looking down on the thousands and pondering what she had wrought. A picture taken of her that day displayed no sense of triumph or accomplishment. If anything, her jaw seemed to be set in a mix of determination and wariness. Perhaps she feared another veteran might burst from the crowd, accost, and humiliate her yet again.

Maya Lin at the dedication of the Vietnam Veterans Memorial,
Washington, DC, November 13, 1982

Because this was America, where free speech matters, there were also grumblers and naysayers, voices that were not moved by the spectacle of grieving veterans or impressed by fighter planes flying over. A group called About Face distributed flyers along the parade route with a message from a veteran: "Buttering up Vietnam veterans as 'forgotten heroes' is a slap in the face directed at millions in the country who resisted the war." Meanwhile, as downtown hotels cleaned up the broken beer bottles and the cigarette burns on their lobby carpets, the *Philadelphia Inquirer* wondered how many alcoholics and drug addicts this war had produced. And Richard Cohen, a columnist for the *Washington Post*, expressed his relief that the memorial contained no equestrian statue, "no paean to heroism, no attempt to make something wonderful out of something tragic."

"It is nice just for once to remember that wars kill kids," he wrote.

The next day a very different throng, better dressed and better behaved, passed through the main door of the cathedral, high above the city, beneath Frederick Hart's magnificent *Ex Nihilo*, for a commemorative service. Reverend Theodore H. Evans, Jr., who had been a minister at the Episcopal Congregation of Saigon in the mid-1960s, delivered the sermon. He began by remarking that this was "Remembrance Sunday" in the Anglican calendar, the Sunday closest to November 11, the end of World War I. "For us at this time in our history," he said, "it means that we have to pull a painful memory from the recesses of our collective memories, to look at it, to understand it, to begin to reconcile it as an important and tragic part of our national life, but one with power to heal and make us whole again."

First impressions of the memorial were duly noted in the press. These included the reaction of a refugee from Vietnam named Nguyen Ngoc Loan, who had arrived in the United States in April 1975 and who now owned a pizza parlor called *Les Trois Continents* in the northern Virginia town of Burke. He thought the memorial was quite beautiful. But sometime later Loan abruptly gave up his business when someone scrawled on his restaurant's wall, "We know who you are, fucker," and his past was revealed. Nguyen Ngoc Loan was a former general of the South Vietnam Army and police chief, famously photographed executing a Viet Cong prisoner with a pistol shot to the temple.

The dedication would become an occasion for some very fine writing. In an essay in *The Nation*, the irrepressible contrarian Christopher Hitchens weighed in with a characteristically entertaining brew of insight and wrong-headed cynicism. The Maya Lin design was "rather mediocre," he groused, and one could almost hear him drawing out the syllables contemptuously in his upper-crust Oxford English. Her wall was "a travesty" delivered by jurors who were going for the "lowest common denominator." The design could never have been satisfactory to any party, Hitchens wrote. "If it had incorporated a frieze of tiger-cages, napalm shells, air strikes accidentally blowing up American troops, officers shot by their own men, peasant casualties and Lazy Dog bombs, it would never have had a prayer." As an Englishman whose reference was Europe, Hitchens wrote that in the first days of the Battle of the Somme in World War I, just as many men were lost as in the entire Vietnam War. He gravitated to the poem of Wilfred Owen in speaking to the pro-war enthusiasts.

> My friend, you would not tell with such high zest
> To Children ardent for some desperate glory,
> The old Lie: *Dulce et decorum est*
> *Pro patria mori.*

But, in stating the obvious, Hitchens was right about one thing: the dedication "has done nothing to banish the arguments or still the controversy. This is as it should be."

Among the best writing was that of William Broyles, Jr., then the editor-in-chief of *Newsweek* magazine, who had been a Marine lieutenant in Vietnam in the dire years of 1969 to 1970, when it was already clear that the war had been lost. Echoing the thoughts of Maya

Lin, Broyles viewed the memorial as merely about the cost of war. It was, he wrote, a "bill of sale."

"Our only stated objectives were meaningless bits of territory we would fight over and abandon."

Their sole mission was to survive. Only one's buddies mattered. Broyles had attended the reading of names at the cathedral, able to chortle over the readers' difficulty in pronouncing tongue-twisting Polish, Polynesian, and Russian names, names that "reach deep into the heart of America."

"To my knowledge there are no names of any sons or grandsons of the policymakers who plotted the war or the congressmen who voted the appropriations to keep it going. They weren't there. The war divided America, most of all by driving a wedge between those who went and those who didn't."

And Robert Kaiser, the associate editor of the *Washington Post* who had covered the war from Saigon in 1969 to 1970, picked up on the theme of catharsis. Maya Lin had said you had to experience the pain and face it and only then could healing begin. But Kaiser made the distinction between individual catharsis and collective catharsis. "It would do no real honor to the Vietnam veterans to confuse their personal and deserved catharsis and the sort of genuine national catharsis we have never had," he wrote. "The Vietnam monster has not been buried under those granite panels on the mall. It is still hiding under the rug where we stashed it years ago. . . . Hiding it does not disguise what the war in Vietnam really was: a terrible betrayal of the American people by their elected rulers."

Whatever the shortcomings of the wall might be to Hitchens, Broyles, and Kaiser, to its diehard detractors, to the veterans in attendance or the millions elsewhere, or to the other millions who protested and avoided the ugly business altogether, November 13, 1982, proved that the wall worked. It had become a place of national pilgrimage for veterans and pacifists alike, therapeutic for some but not comforting for anybody. It advanced only a tentative reconciliation but never a completion or an end. If it represented a rift in the land and a rift in the generation, it was a wound that would never heal completely.

Yet, it worked on the three separate levels that counted: the emotions, the aesthetics, and the symbolism. Its very existence alone was a miracle; that it was consummated in less than four years was part of the miracle.

Poets confirmed its triumph. A Bronze Star veteran named Yusef Komunyakaa, among others, certified the triumph with his poem "Facing It."

> My black face fades,
> hiding inside the black granite.
> I said I wouldn't
> dammit: No tears.
> I'm stone. I'm flesh.
> My clouded reflection eyes me
> like a bird of prey, the profile of night
> slanted against morning. I turn
> this way—the stone lets me go.
> I turn that way—I'm inside
> the Vietnam Veterans Memorial
> again, depending on the light
> to make a difference.
> I go down the 58,022 names,
> half-expecting to find
> my own in letters like smoke.
> I touch the name Andrew Johnson;
> I see the booby trap's white flash.
> Names shimmer on a woman's blouse
> but when she walks away
> the names stay on the wall.

Brushstrokes flash, a red bird's
wings cutting across my stare.
The sky. A plane in the sky.
A white vet's image floats
closer to me, then his pale eyes
look through mine. I'm a window.
He's lost his right arm
inside the stone. In the black mirror
a woman's trying to erase names:
No, she's brushing a boy's hair.

Chapter Eleven

A KIND OF OCEAN

After Frederick Hart was commissioned to provide a suitable sculpture to complement Maya Lin's wall, he would muse to his wife and model, Lindy, about his dreams for the work. The Renaissance was his ideal, as much for the philosophy of the artists as for their virtuosity of technique. Then, unlike now, he felt, art was not an end in itself but a form of service. The art that graced the plazas and the churches of sixteenth-century Italy embraced the values of the common man, as well as his religious beliefs, history, and ideals. Sculpture was, in Dante's words, "visible speech," and the artist's dedication to service gave art its "moral authority." In ancient Greece as well, Hart believed, there was no distinction between aesthetics and ethics.

"Works of art achieved greatness by embodying great ideas," he would write later.

For the uniforms of his soldiers, he planned to emulate the exacting detail of the Italian Baroque master Gian Lorenzo Bernini, especially the flowing drapery of Bernini's alabaster angels that grace the Ponte Sant'Angelo in Rome.

"I want to make Bernini's angels weep," he told Lindy.

With so lofty an idea of his calling, the sculptor found himself somewhat paralyzed at first, when, amid the nasty contention and the notoriety Maya Lin was enduring through the spring and summer of 1982, he contemplated the task ahead. By midsummer, however, he finally got under way. At this point he did not resent all the attention accorded to Lin, nor did he mind that his work was being labeled as "the compromise statue," for he needed quiet space to work and concentrate. In visualizing his three soldiers he first needed to imagine the composition and proportions of the grouping. The easy part was the correctness: a Hispanic machine gunner, an African-American infantryman, and a white platoon leader with his men. Then the mood: camaraderie, youth, vulnerability, wariness, exhaustion, dirt, sweat, and amazement as the figures gazed upon the magnitude of loss spread out before them. Then the gear and the garments in the style of Bernini. But the faces would be everything. He would reach for expressions that would make the viewer wonder what each soldier was thinking, so that the veteran could associate his own experiences in Vietnam with the figures. The goal would be for the surviving veteran to enter himself into the sculpture itself.

Quietly turning aside the pressure for a heroic sculpture, a mantra developed in his imagination: his soldiers were not fighting for their country but for each other.

In early September, two months before Maya Lin's wall was dedicated, Hart invited his patrons to view his progress. As Jan Scruggs and the board members of the Fund arrived at his studio, their eyes fell first on Hart's larger plaster works: the figure of Adam that was headed for a prominent niche at the Washington National Cathedral, an unfinished sculpture of St. Peter, and a triangular scale model of *Ex Nihilo*. In the middle of the floor was a headless mannequin dressed in full combat gear. As they entered, Scruggs's group was gossiping. Was Maya Lin really going to sue the Fund for breach of contract?

"I don't think she'll sue," one of the veterans was saying. "It would be a very bad step for her professionally. And we could bring a lot of heat on her if she did." It was clear now whose side they were on. They chortled when someone remarked on what a difficult person Lin was. She was not accustomed to "assertive restraining," someone quipped.

They then approached Hart's clay model for their first look. In Hart's view, he was presenting a sketch, a first draft. The maquette stood only 17 1/2 inches tall, and the visitors had to imagine what it would look like when it was larger than life, at about seven feet tall. Hart was still struggling with certain aspects of the piece, especially the face of the black figure. When his agent admired the angry expression on that soldier, Hart scowled. He was going for anguish, not anger. The body was okay. He had used a regular at his favorite Dupont Circle bar, Childe Harold, as the model. But the face was wrong. A few days later he would slice off the angry visage completely and start over. The face of the Hispanic soldier was more satisfactory. Beneath a bush hat, that soldier carried a machine gun on his shoulders, and now Hart told his guests:

"I always thought of a machine gunner as a tough, bulky, rough-and-tumble type. But I wanted to make this figure the youngest-looking and most innocent, so you get the contrast between his youthfulness and the ferocity of the weaponry. In the juxtaposition of those two extremes, you get some poetry."

The session showed how comfortable the artist had become in the company of veterans, and how much, by this time, he identified with their experiences, despite his 4 F deferment and his time on the protest lines. His patrons loved his concentration on the details, the veins in the hands, the bullets in the bandolier, the multiple canteens they carried, the towel over the neck of the black soldier, carrying his helmet behind him.

"That's a guy I've met," said one of the veterans.

"You wonder what he's thinking, what he's seeing," said another. "You're invited to make up a story that fits with him, and that's what makes it a work of art."

Still another noticed that Hart had placed a dog tag on the boot of one figure, and this led to a discourse on dog tags in general, how they were often taped over when the soldier went into combat, and how sometimes platoon sergeants suggested to his troopers that they duplicate the tags in both boots. If his head was blown off, the sergeant advised drolly, the tags might be lost, but the odds were less that both feet would be blown off at once.

Couldn't the sculptor put a serial number on the tag? someone asked.

"I'm not that good," Hart chuckled.

"Then what about blood type?"

In the days that followed, the problem of the black soldier's unsatisfying expression was solved in a fortuitous way. In a waiting room of a hospital where Hart had gone to visit a sick friend, he encountered an African-American mother with her seventeen-year-old son. With his full forehead and dreamy expression, the teenager had just the face he wanted. That was it! Hart recruited the boy to be his model.

—

As the Art War over Vietnam memorialization moved into its fifth year, it appeared in the early days of 1983 that there was peace at last. Maya Lin's wall was built and dedicated. The Commission of Fine Arts had accepted a compromise to add a sculpture and a flagpole to the memorial. Suitable language had been found for an inscription that honored veterans without glorifying them or their war. Frederick Hart's statuary had been conceived, and a model had been found worthy. In its October 13 meeting the previous fall, the Commission of Fine Arts had settled on the placement of the statue and the flag as an "entrance experience." It remained only for the statue to be finished, approved, and installed.

Hold on.

When Congress came back into session in January, the efforts of ex-Congressman Don Bailey to legislate the location of the flag—immediately above the junction of the walls and to place the Hart statue directly in front of the vertex—acquired new life. This became known as the "Bailey option" even though he was no longer in Congress. A congressman from California, Duncan Hunter, who had served in the 75th Rangers in Vietnam, took over the mission and urged the public to pressure the commission. Of course, any new legislation that might be introduced would require time-consuming congressional hearings. That, wrote *Washington Post* columnist Philip Geyelin, was likely to rekindle the war "in a mindless and impassioned way."

The Bailey Option

Jan Scruggs and his cohorts reacted in horror. By this point the aesthetic arguments exhausted them, and they were ready to go with virtually any option for the placement of the flag and sculpture, so long as there was no further delay in completing the memorial. Indeed, by this time, it seemed as if only the commission still cared about aesthetics . . . and it was the commission that would have the final say.

Inspired by the diehards in Congress, Secretary James Watt jumped back into the fray with full-throated support for the golf hole alternative. "This so-called Bailey option for placement of the statue and flag staff fully meets the commitment we made to reach a compromise on this issue," he wrote in a letter to the relevant government agencies.

In a speech to the US Chamber of Commerce, Watt threatened to stall the completion of the memorial until a consensus developed on the location issue. That could take up to a year. "It's a memorial and a monument to those who lived and died for America, and it's a political expression," Watt told the chamber. "It's not an expression just of the arts community, although it includes them, and so I would expect that [the matter] will be resolved within the next twelve to fifteen months." The Memorial Fund expressed its shock at this renewed interference from the political world. Philip Geyelin wrote that if Watt did what he said he was going to do, the rift over Maya Lin's design would make the wounds of Vietnam even worse.

The next meeting of the Commission of Fine Arts was scheduled for February 8, and as the date got closer, Secretary Watt seemed to relent slightly, acknowledging the commission's authority, dropping his threat of delay, and expressing the lame hope that the commission would "not overlook the feelings of the Vietnam veterans in consideration of aesthetic and architectural concerns." All hoped that the commission would lay this last issue to rest. The political noise in advance of the meeting did not quiet, however. Congressman Hunter released a statement denouncing Kent Cooper's characterization of the flagpole as a "long stringy object." Said Representative Hunter: "The veterans never considered the flag 'a long stringy object,' and I can guarantee that the families of the individuals whose names are inscribed on the memorial walls don't think the flag is a long stringy object."

And yet, as the commission convened before a packed crowd the following day, when a scale model of a fifty-foot flagpole was placed immediately above a scale model of the wall, it did, indeed, look like a long stringy object. The proximity of flagpole and wall was palpably absurd, which was appreciated by all except Hunter and Bailey. "Pure aesthetics" is not the only consideration, Hunter complained, and rested his case for the Bailey option, producing a threadbare press release from the Warner meeting that seemed to support his apex positioning. Very quickly, J. Carter Brown pointed out that the commission was not a party to that compromise, and only it could make the aesthetic determination. No ad hoc congressional gathering held any sway here. He was very glad, the chairman said, that the country was "governed by laws and not by press releases."

The usual suspects testified in the usual way that day, and there was the familiar bickering back and forth about the flag and the Hart sculpture. "This baloney has gone on long enough," Jan Scruggs groused. By this time, he had come to view his fiercest opponents, Webb, Carhart, Copulos, and company, as "evil" men. "The Vietnam Veterans Memorial was a Rorschach inkblot," Scruggs would write later. "Right-wing Vietnam War Defenders saw the Hand of Satan emerging as a two-finger peace sign on the Mall dishonoring America's sacred dead as it honored communist victory."

It was left to Hart himself to make the convincing and conclusive case. The artist had acquiesced in the idea that his prized statue would be placed at the tree line, not exposed and lonely in the open ground of the knoll across from the wall. A careful plan had been worked out between himself, his landscaping colleague, Joseph Brown, and Cooper, the architect of record, that treated Maya Lin's design with "the utmost reverence" while providing emphasis, coherence, and prominence to each of the elements. The commission should vote for it.

After the vote, J. Carter Brown announced the verdict. By placing the statue and the flag at the intersection of pathways as an entrance experience in a copse of trees, the plan would give "maximal prominence" to the American flag. It would be a "rallying point" for visitors who came to visit the wall. Positioning the statue away from the wall would make it stand alone—he did not use the word "naked" this time—and complement rather than compete with the wall. The landscaper Brown put the concept differently. This final design would create a soft, ushering outdoor room.

Still, something was left to Lin's opponents. On the flagpole pedestal, the inscription read: "This flag represents the service rendered to our country by the veterans of the Vietnam War. The flag affirms the principles of freedom for which they fought and their pride in having served under difficult circumstances."

There was a footnote to this denouement of the Art War. Toward the end, there was a surprising witness who was not there to talk about flagpoles, inscriptions, or statues. Historian and psychologist Dr. Steven M. Silver was treating veterans suffering from PTSD. He had been a Marine fighter pilot in Vietnam, flying numerous combat missions in 1969 to 1970.

Straying from the specific issue at hand, Dr. Silver told the commission of the value in taking his patients to visit the wall. Nine years after the end of active combat, he said, "It is virtually a cliché to state that the American people have gone through a period of repressing their country's Vietnam experience. . . . In their agony and trauma, the people of this country tried to ignore reminders of the war. . . . We are beginning to see an end to this repression. . . . As the repression ends, the buried thoughts and feelings come boiling, sometimes exploding, to the surface. Whether taking place on the individual or the national level, such surfacing can be painful, terrifying, exciting, joyous, or cathartic—above all, it is necessary."

Dr. Silver did not choose sides between Lin and Hart but applauded both for their value to the tormented Vietnam generation. Lin's design was effective in eliciting these buried feelings, not only for his PTSD patients but for all Vietnam veterans as well as the dissenters, precisely because the wall did not interpose an image on the viewer. And Hart's soldiers were important for those veterans in need of "specificity."

However, something he wrote beforehand to the Memorial Fund was far more memorable than his psychologizing. He proposed a Constitutional amendment that would read: "Before any President may commit American forces to combat, and before any member of Congress may vote on a declaration of war, said President or member is required to read aloud the names on the Vietnam Veterans Memorial."

After the commission's decision, Frederick Hart separated himself from the turmoil. He had hit his stride. He knew what he was doing and where he was going. He had heard the slurs: his work was trite or stale, his figures mere cartoon characters, reminiscent of a Hallmark card or GI Joe toys. Much of the criticism came from people who had only seen pictures of his sketch. When they saw the finished product, he was sure, he would be vindicated.

Frederick Hart with the maquette for The Three Soldiers

An armature had been built for each figure, and a seven-foot-long block of clay stood before him. Marines from the Capitol Hill barracks were serving as models. It was time to give the faces of his soldiers life and character. The real sculpting had begun. As his wife Lindy would say, it was time for the poetry and the music. It was time to make them sing.

Chapter Twelve

THE TROUBLED MARRIAGE
OF TRUE MINDS

"Great minds against themselves conspire
And shun the cure they most desire."
—*Dido and Aeneas*, Henry Purcell

I n the spring of 1983 there was no love lost between the true minds
that had been thrown together in this shotgun marriage. The enmity
between Lin and Hart, smoldering for so long, burst now into full
flame. When two artists go after one another, trashing each other's
work, blood is sure to be everywhere. "You can always tell a serious
artist by his teeth" was the byword of the Alliance of Figurative Artists,
a group that met every Friday in a basement on the Lower East Side of
New York, where artists paid $1.50 to attack one another's work and
sometimes one another. At these rowdy sessions, the unkindest cut
of all was to dismiss an artist as merely an "illustrator." To describe
another artist's work as a *depiction* was an insult. Of course, Lin and
Hart had taken their random shots before. But in an article in the April
issue of *Art in America*, their anger toward one another reached a new
level.

Overall, "The Tale of Two Memorials," a long article by Elizabeth Hess was a fine piece of work, comprehensively reprising the past four years of the Art War. But Hess also touched a raw nerve. If Lin's memorial was a tribute to Jane Fonda, she wrote loosely, Hart's was a tribute to John Wayne.

Her feminist slant on the saga was especially incendiary, as the author suggested a sexual connotation to the Lin design in juxtaposition to the Washington Monument. The Hess article was not the first to enter this dangerous turf. A year earlier *The Spotlight*, a fringe publication quoted a critic as saying that "The subliminal sexual overtones of the Washington Monument reflecting or casting a shadow onto the polished Black V-shaped memorial are disgusting. It is unfit for the capital of a Christian nation."

Picking up on this theme, Hess wrote, "To add insult to injury the eight male jurors had chosen a memorial with a distinctly female character, placing at the base of Washington's giant phallus a wide V-shape surrounded by a grassy mound. . . . It could indeed be read . . . as the expression of a female sensibility. The vast number of names inscribed on the wall comes across as powerful anti-war statement. As a woman standing in front of the memorial remarked, 'What an unbelievable waste.'"

Hess's take encouraged Maya Lin to cast the entire Art War saga as a struggle between men and women, or more precisely between a young woman and old white men. At last, she gave full bore to her frustrations at the Washington male establishment, and by extension, Hart himself, that had so tormented her. Hart, in turn, would label this tack as female bias, sheer idiocy, and an act of opportunism that was an "exercise in ideological squatters' rights."

The article contained interviews with both Lin and Hart. Prodded by Hess, Lin uncharacteristically veered into sexual imagery. The Vietnam War was different from all other wars, she said, because "the veterans got screwed." Quoting a vice president of the Fund, she said that the Hart addition amounted to a "rape" of her design. The veterans of the Fund saw her as "a female, as a child. Their attitude was—OK, you did a good job, but we're going to hire some big boys—boys—to take care of it." With her bitterness showing through, she added, "I gave them the design, and they could do what they wanted with it. They expected me to take the money and run." As for her upbringing, her Asian heritage and her femaleness had never been important, but when she got to Washington, "my biggest shock was that no one would listen to me, because I had no power—no masculinity." And finally, on the counterpoint of phallic versus vagina symbolism and whether her design evinced a female sensibility, Lin responded: "In a world of phallic memorials that rise upwards, it certainly does. I didn't set out to conquer the earth or overpower it, the way Western man usually does." She had not created a "passive piece," but neither was it a paean to macho warfare.

This theme of male/female duality would be picked up a month later by writer Michael Sorkin in an article in *Vogue*. "That a woman—the ultimate outsider—should have won the commission was the final affront, absolute confirmation that the war was to be remembered differently, a monument emasculated," he wrote. "It had to be an anti-monument."

And in her memorable 1985 novel *In Country*, about "Sam," the daughter of Vietnam casualty, and "Emmett," her quirky, debilitated uncle who survives Vietnam but suffers from Agent Orange, Bobbie Ann Mason also picks up on this theme of a sexual juxtaposition between the wall and the Washington Monument. The novel ends with Sam and Emmett traveling from Kentucky to Washington to visit the wall. An installation by Christo, the artist of colossal works who in 1983 had surrounded islands in Biscayne Bay with pink polypropylene fabric, occurs to Sam. She thinks Christo's next project should be to cover the Washington Monument with a giant condom.

"The Washington Monument rises up out of the earth, proud and tall," Sam imagines. "She once heard someone say the U.S.A. goes around fucking the world."

In this clash of swords with Frederick Hart, Maya Lin held a distinct advantage. Her memorial had been open to the public for five months, and it had been warmly embraced, as visitors flocked to see the wall. As Christopher Knight, the art critic for the *Los Angeles Times* later wrote, the memorial was on its way to being recognized as "the greatest aesthetic achievement in an American public monument in the twentieth century." And the apologies began to roll in. Even Paul Gapp, the Chicago architecture critic who had been such a fierce detractor, apologized. "I'm really sorry," he wrote Lin. "I made a mistake."

Meanwhile, Hart's soldiers were still a work in progress. Therefore, opinions about the figures were forming and hardening in a void. His patrons had hoped that his statues could be finished and installed only months after the dedication of the wall. But the sculptor was way behind schedule.

Nevertheless, Hart found time to defend himself, and he could wield a mean scalpel. His contempt for modernist, non-representational art was profound. As he would later write, "Once, under the banner of beauty and order, art was a rich and meaningful embellishment of life, embracing—not desecrating—its ideals, its aspirations, and its values. Not so today." Do people today really care if art lives or dies? he would ask rhetorically. "Of course, they don't, but why? Because today's art has given them nothing, nothing that bears the slightest resemblance to their own lives, that touches their fears or cares, that evokes their dreams or gives hope to the darkness. It has, in short, become an irrelevant pursuit."

Was Lin's wall just art for art's sake? Hess asked him.

"I don't like blank canvasses," he replied tartly. "Lin's memorial is intentionally not meaningful. . . . I don't like art that is contemptuous of life."

For her part, Lin had confessed to know little about the Vietnam War itself. To her, ignorance of the war was an artistic plus. Hart, by contrast, was proud of all the research he had done and of how close he had become with veterans in order to understand them.

If Lin's wall is political, as he had suggested, wasn't his also? Hess asked.

"Yes, but it's different," Hart replied. "My position is humanist, not militaristic. . . . Lin's piece is a serene exercise in contemporary art done in a vacuum with no knowledge of the subject. It's nihilistic—that's its appeal." Later he elaborated on this point: "Lin's design is elitist and mine is populist. People say you can bring what you want to Lin's memorial. But I call that brown bag aesthetics. I mean you better bring something because there ain't nothing being served."

The realism of his sculpture, Hart argued, was meant to confer dignity on the nineteen-year-olds who had actually fought the war and to accentuate their youth and innocence. His statue, he said, was meant to humanize Lin's design . . . and to save it.

Things were getting very personal indeed. Lin called Hart's sculpture "trite." As she explained, "Three men standing there before the world. . . . It's a generalization, a simplification. Hart gives you an image—he's illustrating a book." Hart was merely mercenary, she charged, surmising that he had thought long and hard about taking the commission, since it wasn't necessarily "going to be good for his reputation, but the price was right."

Wasn't it true, Hess persisted, that veterans could relate more to his work than hers? She denied it. "I don't think the veterans are as unintelligent as some people would like to judge them."

In his response, Hart was dismissive, as if rattled by all the attention she was getting, and suggesting that if she had been "a professional" her design would have been summarily discarded. "Everybody is worked up about this poor little girl who is getting kicked around by the secretary of the Interior," he said. Reporters had romanticized her as a Cinderella.

"There is nothing more powerful than an ingénue."

—

Was there ever an attempt at reconciliation between the two artists? And did the two artists ever confront one another directly? Two of the principals in this story said no.

In an "appreciation" of Frederick Hart in the *New York Times Magazine* in January 2000, only months after the sculptor died, Tom Wolfe reported that a meeting between the two had indeed taken place in the summer of 1984 in Plainview, New York, as a Long Island foundry was completing the statue of the three soldiers. By Wolfe's account, based purportedly on a conversation he had had with Hart himself, Lin asked Hart if his models had ever felt any pain when the plaster casts were removed from their face and arms. On its face, this would be a blistering affront, implying that Hart possessed no skill whatever, that his work was merely a technical gimmick, lacking in artistic imagination. In this purported conversation, Wolfe suggested that Lin might have been referencing the sculptor George Segal, for Segal (who died in 2000) had pioneered a process whereby plaster bandages were wrapped around his models and allowed to harden. Then the gauze strips were removed in sections, and reassembled to create a hollow shell, from which a bronze figure was cast. Lin was saying Hart probably had done the same. Wolfe, Hart's great booster and Lin's detractor, wrote, "No artist of her generation . . . could even conceive of a sculptor starting out solely with a picture in his head, a stylus, a brick of moist clay and some armature wire. No artist of her generation dared even speculate about . . . skill."

Neither Maya Lin nor Hart's widow, Lindy, nor the owner of the Plainview foundry say this "make-peace-get-together" ever took place. This disinformation was yet another example of the bad faith that had characterized the entire art war.

In a *Smithsonian Magazine* interview two years later, Lin expanded on her conflict with Hart. "Hart looked me straight in the face and said, 'My statue is going to improve your memorial.' . . . At this time, the statue would have gone at the apex, and their heads would have stood above the wall." This meant that Hart's statue would have been over eleven feet tall. And in an interview with Bill Moyers on PBS a year later, Lin took her assertion one step further, saying that Hart wanted his soldiers "right there at the apex," in so gigantic a size that their heads would poke above her wall.

"Obviously, it was very traumatic and upsetting," she told Moyers, "but I didn't take it personally. I felt that everyone's entitled to their opinion." That Hart had consistently conceived of his final rendering as seven feet in height, just larger than life size, and had argued forcefully in pivotal Commission of Fine Arts sessions for the statues to be set apart in the nearby trees went unmentioned.

Of course, Frederick Hart was no longer around to confirm Wolfe's story or to deny Lin's assertion.

—

In the early months of 1984, as emotional scenes were played out at the wall every day, as artifacts by the hundreds—combat boots, family photos, military patches, and even medals—piled up to be collected, catalogued, and stored by the Park Service, Frederick Hart worked quietly on his grouping. His patrons understood that their artist could not be rushed. Veterans Day 1984 was set as the time for the grand unveiling.

Hart's Marine Corps models came regularly to his F Street studio to sit for the sculptor, their military discipline tested as they sat still and rigid for hours. Their bodies and their body language were useful. With scalpel and calipers he sculpted the three figures naked from the waist up to get the proportions right before he fashioned their Bernini-like "drapery." But the expressions of his figures were everything. They had to come from the artist's imagination, and there would be a number of do-overs where he was dissatisfied with the result, cutting the face off entirely and starting over. The model for the middle figure was Corporal Jim Connell, a soldier so handsome that Hart at first rejected him. Decades later, the ex-Marine remembered how slow and meticulous Hart was in his work. And Corporal Connell could be wry in recalling his experience. After months of modeling he was impressed at how Hart had captured perfectly every vein in his "veiny hands and arms." The sculptor could spend hours and sometimes days

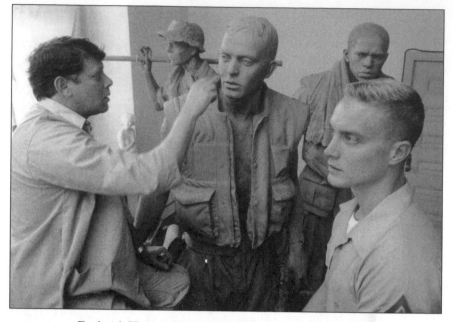

Frederick Hart with one of his models, Corporal Jim Connell

on the smallest detail like an eye or an eyebrow and then wipe it away
and start over. Hart had instructed his model to have no expression
whatever, but just to stare straight ahead. Connell came to think of
that as his "thousand-yard stare."

Then one day some vets came to his studio to see his progress.
Most of them were smoking, and by the time they left, Hart's big
studio was enveloped in a gray haze. "My eyes always had trouble
with smoke," Connell said, "and they became very red and irritated.
When we got back to work, Rick began working feverishly. It was
one of those 'in the zone' moments. It was the look he kept on the
statue."

Early in 1984 the foundry of Joel Meisner of Plainview, New York,
was chosen to execute the final statue. For Hart, this association would
require a number of trips north, sometimes meeting Meisner employees midway on the New Jersey Turnpike. By late spring the clay model
was finished. The next step was a coating of hard, dental-quality plaster

over the clay, called the "negative mold." With that completed, the clay model was destroyed.

In the world of sculpture, the mantra is: "The clay model is the birth. The plaster mold is the death. The bronze cast is the resurrection." Hart would say he was looking forward to the Easter of his work.

Once the plaster mold arrived in Plainview, the Hart family moved to Southhampton for the summer, so that the artist could watch over the process. From plaster, a rubber mold was made. That was then covered with molten wax, then coated in ceramic. The wax inside the mold was then replaced with molten bronze. There would a number

Frederick Hart at work on The Three Soldiers

of dippings and coolings. With the deadline looming, the foundry worked long hours on its rendering. As the word got out about the project, veterans and family members of the fallen came calling.

"We could have patinated the piece with tears," Joel Meisner would say. One of those visitors, a Marine, had written to Hart after seeing the model.

"You have captured the dignity and individuality of the uniforms that allows us, the Vietnam veterans, to say with pride, 'yes, that is us, that is how we went into battle.'" Of the figures, he continued, "I have the eerie feeling they are searching for their own names among the mortally wounded."

The patina was the last step. For that Hart wanted a luminous caramel brown color, though he insisted that the surface of the clothing be slightly different in hue from that of the skin. This would pose additional technical problems, requiring a different chemical mix to be painted on the model before the surface was hardened with a blowtorch. As his sculpture was to last for all time, it did not bother Hart that age and the pelting of acid rain might turn the patina green and splotchy. He trusted the Park Service to clean the work regularly and occasionally subject it to a new coat of wax.

In late October, the press got its first look at the finished product, and Frederick Hart began his campaign to influence how his soldiers were viewed. When they had been seen alone, he argued, the controversy about them was a mix of contradictions, with one group finding his rendering too militaristic, while the "neo-Iwo Jima" crowd found it not militaristic enough. But he never thought of his statue as "a thing in itself." With his "humanistically oriented" creation, he thought he had found just the right balance between the poles. But he was naïve, he confessed.

"Nobody was happy," he told the *New York Times*. "The right wing didn't like the ambivalence . . . and the left wing . . . treat[ed] it as if it were an Iwo Jima thing even if it wasn't. People were dug into their positions . . . so they just continued to throw rocks." The final test would come in a few days when the two elements were seen together. He wanted to create the feeling that the soldiers had come unexpectedly upon the wall "as a kind of vision or a metaphor for the war itself."

View of Frederick Hart's detailed work depicting the soldiers' gear and clothing

The viewer might feel that the figures were about to whisper to one another about what they were seeing. They were meant to represent "a brooding, unknowing, unknowable tragic presence."

In this final culmination, he could be forgiven for his pride in his creation. Without invoking the name of Gian Lorenzo Bernini, he told the *Washington Post* that he would put "the folds of those fatigue jackets and pants up against the folds of any [carved] medieval angel you can find." The night before the dedication of his work on Veterans Day, he hosted a black-tie dinner for his friends at the Cosmos Club. At the event, Jim Webb presented the sculptor with a Marine Corps sword.

A few days earlier, Webb's right-hand man, Tom Carhart, delivered his own Parthian shot. In an interview with the *Washington Post*, he spoke forthrightly of the exhilaration and the savagery of the combat soldier. "I killed people. I watched men die. I wept," he said. "But I would be lying to you if I didn't say it was the most thrilling thing I ever did." It was a rush. "It was like I was high. I had never felt so elated. But that's life. That's war. . . . I killed—and I enjoyed it."

The reaction was horror and disgust. So, these were the people who wanted their actions to be honored and celebrated as heroic? It was as if Carhart had defined precisely the stereotype of the Vietnam soldier that he himself had fought so hard to debunk. And yet, if it was bad public relations, there was a brutal honesty about his statement. It spoke to the dilemma of all soldiers in all wars.

In a letter to the *Washington Post* that appeared after the dedication, Carhart seemed to appreciate the damage he had done to the cause. He had no regrets about fighting against the Maya Lin design as the only physical remembrance of Vietnam, he said. "Because I and others spoke out against the original design, we have attained the addition of a powerful statue, an American flag, and a fitting inscription to our memorial. Now it is a beautiful and complete memorial, and I believe that we Vietnam veterans can all agree on that."

—

As it had been exactly two years previously for the dedication of the wall, the day for the dedication of Hart's soldiers and the formal acceptance of the complete Vietnam Memorial was gray and blustery. Likewise, the throng was huge, estimated to be about 150,000 people. Unlike on the first occasion when no senior officials attended, this time the president of the United States was present. It was as if the administration was giving its blessing to the three soldiers, having withheld it from the wall. Now only five days after his landslide reelection, Reagan was accompanied by other senior members of his cabinet. Among them was a new secretary of the Interior, since James Watt, having become a political liability, had been forced to resign following a series of ill-considered remarks.

The security was extremely tight that day. Indeed, a forty-foot ply-wood tunnel had been built so that the president and the First Lady could walk safely and unnoticed from their limousine to the dais. Long lines of well-wishers stretched toward the Lincoln Memorial, as people inched forward to pass through metal detectors and were then corralled so far away from the stage that the president could scarcely be seen, much less heard.

Reagan spoke in a subdued voice, befitting the gravity of the occasion, almost in a stage whisper. This time he did not repeat his evocation of the Vietnam War as a noble cause. Rather he spoke of provisional healing. "I do not know if perfect healing ever occurs," he said. But he did know that a broken bone, when healed, could sometimes be stronger than it was before. He gave Hart's statue a

Frederick Hart's The Three Soldiers *(1984)*

cursory mention. "The fighting men depicted in the statue we dedicate today . . . are individual only in their battle dress," he said. "All are as one, with eyes fixed upon the memorial bearing the names of their brothers in arms. On their youthful faces . . . we see expressions of loneliness and profound love and a fierce determination never to forget." Gnarled veterans looked on skeptically. It was a day for the politicians, not the artist of the three soldiers. Hart was somewhere hidden in the back rows behind the president.

In the days that followed, the sculptor waited expectantly for the critics to have their say. Would he receive the recognition he craved—denied to him when *Ex Nihilo* was unveiled two years earlier at the cathedral? Benjamin Forgey, who had succeeded Wolf Von Eckardt as the architecture critic of the *Washington Post*, was the first to assess. Acknowledging that he had opposed the additions initially and that their inclusion was clearly a political rather than an aesthetic necessity, he wrote, "Only time will tell if these radically different solutions to the same problem, this forced joining of the particular and the universal, will grow together as a strong expressive whole. But time, I strongly feel, is on their side."

Beyond Forgey there was basically silence. With time the contention faded but did not disappear. Five years later a dismissive letter to the *Post* would say, "Perhaps Hart should visit the Vietnam Veterans Memorial and try to fathom why Maya Lin's contribution to it is becoming acknowledged as a masterwork of contemporary art, humbling to us all, and his is not." By contrast, six years after that, the novelist Mark Helprin would write to Hart, "The soldiers are so moving. I've been a soldier: I know: I stood like that once. They are absolutely true. I read Maya Lin's comment, and what that little fluffball doesn't understand is that you pulled her chestnuts out of the fire and gave meaning to her otherwise cynical gravestone. I think that without your three soldiers the monument would have been nothing but the last Vietnam war protest. The fifty thousand dead and the rest of the country owe you a great debt."

But perhaps the most fulsome praise for the three soldiers came from Donald Kuspit, a professor of art history and philosophy at the State University of New York at Stony Brook. In a 2007 essay entitled "Tragic Beauty and Human Wholeness; Frederick Hart's Reparation of the Figure," published eight years after Hart's death, Kuspit described the three soldiers as men facing their fate unflinchingly, knowing what was coming, anticipating their doom, pausing in "midstride" to get their bearings and to take stock of their situation. "They are under stress, but they show no distress. *The Three Soldiers* is about a state of mind."

By contrast, he found Lin's wall dismaying. "In my opinion the wall is better understood as an example of vainglorious art than as an homage to the war dead and an acknowledgement of the emotional and physical suffering caused by war."

—

Performance artist Kim Jones, a former marine, dressed as the "Mud Man," at the wall, 1994

It has become a welcoming place for reflection and even a bit of whimsy. In 1994, an ex-Marine and combat veteran named Kim Jones had become a performance artist who also wrote staccato lines in the occasional poem:

> vietnam dong ha marines its summer time 125 degrees sweat like pigs
> work like dogs live like rats red dust covered everything.

Covering himself with red mud, he called his act "Mud Man." What better backdrop was there for his performance than the Vietnam Wall?

And so, a rarefied debate continues, but only within a small coterie of art historians concerned with esoteric and dated considerations. Meanwhile, the Vietnam Memorial lives on vibrantly for the millions who visit yearly even as the war and the rift in the Vietnam generation recedes farther and farther from memory.

THE NOISE OF YOUR SONGS

"Nothing sublimely artistic has ever arisen out of mere art, any more than anything essentially reasonable has ever arisen out of pure reason. There must always be a rich moral soil for any great aesthetic growth."

G. K. Chesterton

The careers of Maya Lin and Frederick Hart continued to soar after the Art War, but no matter what fine, memorable work they produced in the coming decades, their reputations would forever be defined by their struggle to design and to consummate a national memorial for the Vietnam War. It may have been harder for Lin than for Hart to overcome the shadow, since her astonishing achievement in Washington had come such an early age. How was she ever to top that? Her situation reminded me of the remark that Russell Baker, the wise and witty *New York Times* columnist, gave to me when I published my first book, a Vietnam-generation novel titled *To Defend, To Destroy*, in 1971: "I wish you success, but not too much."

After graduating from Yale, Lin pursued a master's degree in architecture at Harvard University, splitting her time between her studies, her often contentious consultations with Kent Cooper, and her gritty public defense of her masterwork. The stress of balancing these daunting challenges took its toll, as she was briefly hospitalized in Boston with nervous exhaustion. It was said that at Harvard she became more open to criticism, and in her public appearances, she had visibly matured. If she was often in the library, she was also frequently on national television. She was fast becoming one of the most admired women in America. She completed her master's degree in architecture back at Yale, where in 1987 she was awarded an honorary doctorate.

She went on to design other memorials, two of which were, for more discrete audiences, just as important, as elegant, and as moving as the Vietnam Memorial. The first was her commission to design a civil rights memorial in Montgomery, Alabama. This time there would be no competition, for the driving force behind the idea was the dynamic founder and director of the Southern Poverty Law Center, Morris Dees. Eddie Ashworth, a colleague of Dees at the center, simply called her up and gave her the job.

As with the Vietnam War, Lin had scant knowledge of the civil rights struggle of the 1950s and '60s. She was too young to know about the movement that transformed America; that history was barely mentioned in her cloistered schooling in Athens, Ohio. This ignorance did not bother Dees and Ashworth. They too were operating on instinct. By this time her artist's creative process was clear in her mind. She needed to define for herself what the essence of the entire historical saga was, to strip it bare of its details and noise, and get to the heart of the revolution. Only then could she begin to design a concept. But what was the essence?

Lin took three months to research the history, but it was only on the plane ride down to Alabama that she read Martin Luther King, Jr.'s "I have a dream" speech and came upon King's invocation of the biblical passage from the book of Amos, which reads in full:

Take away from me the noise of your songs;
to the melody of your harps I will not listen.

But let justice roll down like waters,
and righteousness like a mighty stream.

She knew instantly that the memorial had to have water as its central, unifying element, water that could bind together the events of the movement and the forty martyrs of the struggle like Emmett Till, Medgar Evers, and Jimmie Lee Jackson, whose names were to be carved on the monument. The names had to be joined to the events in which they were involved, as cause and effect, creating a timeline of the movement, to show how these lost heroes of the struggle helped to change history.

The result was a circular black granite table—black again—from whose center a thin veneer of water flows evenly across the surface. From the center, lines are carved in the stone to radiate outward as names and seminal events were intertwined. Like the Vietnam Memorial, the visiting pilgrims could touch the names and the events and feel the water that binds everything together. For the participants in the struggle, like the veterans of the Vietnam War, the mere touching was meant to trigger memories and bring the monument alive. At the 1989 dedication of the monument, Rosa Parks touched her name and watched how that touch changed the flow of the water, as if somehow her story might have been different. Behind the table as its backdrop is a high black granite wall in which a portion of the line from King's speech is carved in large bold letters (unlike the nearly invisible epigraph at the Vietnam Memorial). King's words paraphrased and embroidered the Amos passage:

We will not be satisfied until justice rolls down like waters and righteousness
like a mighty stream.

As if she was channeling her Vietnam Wall experience, Lin would describe her vision of the plaza as "a contemplative area — a place to remember the Civil Rights Movement, to honor those killed during the struggle, to appreciate how far the country has come in its quest for equality, and to consider how far it has to go."

Maya Lin at the dedication of the Civil Rights Memorial,
Montgomery, Alabama, 1989

Her second significant memorial was her *Women's Table* (1993) that the president of Yale University commissioned her to design in commemoration of the twentieth anniversary of coeducation at her alma mater. Again, as Lin contemplated the essence, she enlarged the idea and came up with the unexpected. What emerged was an egg-shaped granite table with a fountainhead at the center from which, like the civil rights memorial, a thin layer of water flows across the surface. Spiraling outward from the center, nautilus-like, lines denoting years were cut in the surface, not starting in the celebratory year of 1969, but rather in 1701, the year the university was founded. At the end of the lines near the edge, simple digits denote the number of female students at the school. From 1701 to 1873 the number is zero. From 1873, the numbers are low for the few female students who were allowed into the nursing program or the School of Fine Arts. This implied criticism of the way in which women were barred from higher education for 265 years at one of the country's most prestigious institutions did not sit well with everyone. A feminist scholar likened the structure's womb-like shape as well as its sense of procreative flowing water.

After 1995 Lin made the environment her passion as she considered how people view landscapes and relate to the natural world. In her environmental installations, she was driven, she would say, by "a simple desire to make people aware of their surroundings, not just the physical world but also the psychological world we live in." After cutting a rift in the earth that symbolized the rift in the Vietnam Generation, she has produced a number of environmental earthworks that shape and mold the landscape in startling ways. The job of the artist, she professes, is to say something new and not quite familiar. Among those works are her aerodynamic wave fields in Ann Arbor, Michigan, and Storm King Mountain in New York, where man-made, parallel earth mounds suggest ocean waves . . . or piles of glass beads shaped to suggest mountains or the Chesapeake Bay. There have been more strictly architectural projects as well, including the Langston Hughes Library and Riggio-Lynch Chapel in Clinton, Tennessee, the Weber House in Williamstown, Massachusetts, with its wavy roof that mimics the hills in the distance, and a renovation of the Smith College library.

The artist wanted to counter the fixed notion of a memorial as a mark on the ground. She founded a memorial that was to be without form. Called "What Is Missing?" it is a Web-based celebration of the natural world: what it is now, what it used to be, how wonderful the things are that remain, and how many wonders have been lost. Employing videos in an interactive multimedia format, the cyber-memorial is meant to be an "ecological history of the planet," paying special attention to extinct species and disappearing places in what is called the "extinction crisis."

In 2000 Lin published her first book, *Boundaries*. "I feel I exist on the boundaries somewhere between science and art, art and architecture, public and private, east and west," she wrote. "I am always trying to find a balance between these opposing forces, finding the place where opposites meet." In 2009, she was given the highest American award an artist can receive, the National Medal of Arts. And in November 2016 President Barack Obama presented her with the country's highest civilian award, the Presidential Medal of Freedom. She looked a

Maya Lin receives the Presidential Medal of Freedom from President Barack Obama at the White House, November 22, 2016

bit sheepish next to two other recipients, Kareem Abdul Jabbar and Michael Jordan. Obama invoked Lin's own phrase, "physical acts of poetry," adding that her work reminds us "that the most important element of art and architecture is human emotion." When the president mentioned the B+ she had received in Andrus Barr's architecture class at Yale, laughter filled the room. What must be the most famous undergraduate grade in the history of higher education had finally become the grist for a presidential joke.

Through these decades of immensely productive and varied work in architecture, art, and landscape design, Lin has grown weary of talking about the Vietnam Veterans Memorial, afraid of the age-old curse of being typecast. (She would turn aside a number of requests to build other monuments, not wanting to be known as a memorial "specialist.") Routinely, she explains to interviewers that she will not discuss that painful yet triumphant chapter of her life. But the shadow will not go away. In a conversation with a Xin Wu, a professor of art history at William and Mary University, she was asked about her activism in the environmental movement and more broadly about her attitude toward the artist's role in world affairs.

"I supposed it has changed quite a bit since the Vietnam Veterans Memorial twenty-seven years ago, now that you are more mature and certain of yourself," Dr. Wu prodded.

"I think I was less mature but more sure of myself then," Lin replied. "As you get older, you get more reflective and possibly question more. What protects you when you are young is the belief that you are right. There is a naivety of youth. One loses that naïve certainty when getting older. You understand that life is more complicated."

After the terrorist attacks of September 11, 2001, the largest commission in history for a memorial followed, and in the opinion of Martin Filler, the distinguished historian of architecture, Lin could have had for the asking the job to design it. Instead, she agreed only to be on the jury which, in the end, would consider 5,201 entries, more than four times the number of submissions as the Vietnam memorial jury had judged. The eventual winner of the World Trade Center memorial competition, Michael Arad, was a thirty-four-year-old junior employee in a New York City municipal office, and like Lin, Arad had an enormous amount of success at a very young age. His original concept called for two gigantic sunken pools whose measurements comported to the footprints of the fallen twin towers; to complete the emotion of grief and identification, visitors would be allowed to descend into the abyss below the cascading water. But in the contentious eight years it took to realize the memorial, the possibility of descent below the waters had to be scrapped. Once again, the essence of the final design was the combination of victims' names engraved in black granite and a non-representative work of art where the emotional reaction to the piece was left to the individual viewer. To Filler, Arad's work reaffirmed Maya Lin's "radical reconception" of memorialization with her Vietnam wall.

"The test of time has already proven the validity of Maya Lin's insights into the wellsprings of mourning in the modern age," he wrote.

The Vietnam Women's Memorial (1993) by Glenna Goodacre

—

The 1990s was a political period for Frederick Hart, when he was at the peak of his international fame and the controversy over his soldiers had largely subsided. He sculpted figures that drew upon his Southern roots and his political proclivities. His statue of former US president and Georgia governor Jimmy Carter had been placed on the grounds of the state capital in Atlanta. His stolid rendition of Richard Russell, the Georgia senator and towering legislative hawk of the 1960s, graced in the grand rotunda of the Russell Senate Office Building in Washington, DC. He had completed his head-tilting, smiling bust of the ferocious segregationist icon, Strom Thurmond, for the Strom Thurmond Room in the US Capitol and finished a bland bust of former vice president Dan Quayle.

Much more important at this time, though, were his purely artistic sculptures that reflected his range, his imagination, and his spiritual longings, which did far more to burnish his reputation as an important American artist. His bronze and Lucite pieces in limited editions made him a wealthy man. Through the 1990s the sculptor had developed a unique process of transforming a clay model into an ethereal image that would be embedded in clear acrylic resin or Lucite. He called his first efforts in this new medium his "creation series" and his "dream series"; memorable in this collection was an unrealized piece, *Heroic Spirit* that was proposed for the 1996 Summer Olympics in Atlanta. In 1997, he finished his extraordinary *Cross of the Millennium*. Commissioned by St. Vincent de Paul Catholic Church in Andover, Kansas, the altarpiece featured the willowy, other-worldly figure of Jesus Christ appearing to float within the plastic cross. Lit with soft light from below, Hart called it "sculpting with light." In May of that year when he presented the cross to Pope John Paul II at a Vatican ceremony, the pontiff said to him, "You have created a profound theological statement for our day."

But perhaps his most impressive work during this period was his *Daughters of Odessa*, depicting the four Romanov daughters of the last

Chesley, the Virginia country estate of Frederick Hart

Russian czar, Nicholas II, who were assassinated in 1918. This lovely, sensual grouping of youthful, energetic figures, draped in willowy gossamer gowns, reflected his fascination with Russian history. He called it an allegorical work, "an elegy in bronze which is dedicated to the memory of all the innocent victims of the twentieth century." A bronze of this moving work ended up in the private garden of the Prince of Wales at Highgrove House, England, along with his bronze bas-relief of Lord Mountbatten that Prince Charles had commissioned.

Unapologetically, the artist reveled in his reputation as a "classicist," even as a segment of the modern art world continued to heap scorn on his work. A former New York museum director would call him an "art fascist," and a critic for *Art in America*—a sculptor himself—labeled Hart's commercial pieces as "kitsch." "Everything is so conventionally handled—I find them appalling," he complained. Resentment abounded at his financial success, his sophisticated marketing acumen, and his lavish, country squire lifestyle. If his antebellum mansion, Chesley, was a throwback to a prior century, Hart embraced the feeling. A love of grandeur reflected a "sense of the heroic," he remarked. "The idea of the heroic life, especially in artistic terms, has always been one of my personal myths." Wryly, he described Chesley as a "revival of a Beaux Arts Revival of Greek Revival" and a "landmark of reactionary architecture." It was there, he said, that "I'm doing things that just haven't been done in a hundred years, like using huge amounts of highly ornamented plaster, lots of faux marble, the statuary and the big murals—Who else does that kind of thing?"

During this high-flying period, however, trouble emerged. In October 1997, Warner Brothers released *Devil's Advocate*, a big-budget movie starring Al Pacino as a sleazy New York lawyer who is supposed to be Satan himself. The climactic scene ushered the viewer into the devil's chamber, decorated as if it were a New York penthouse, with cathedral ceilings, heavy wood paneling, panoramic windows, and a huge platform desk. This becomes the tableaux for a crude sex scene and gory suicide. Behind the desk a huge white frieze featured naturalistic naked, marbled figures, frozen in the maw, the maw of creation. The action gets hot and heavy when the devil tries to force his son (Keanu Reeves) to have sex with a temptress (Connie Nielson)—her name is Christa Bella, a play on the words beautiful Christ—in order to create the Antichrist. During the devil's pitch, the naked figures in the frieze behind him come alive and begin to writhe lasciviously, erotically toward one other.

The frieze was Hart's *Ex Nihilo*.

This scurrilous debasement of religious art into profane art was astonishing, and it soon became clear that the filmmakers had simply placed *Ex Nihilo* on a computer template, removed one figure, and then manipulated the figures into suggestive motion. That a work of sacred art could be so blatantly misappropriated, vulgarized, and transformed into pornography without consequence was totally unacceptable. It raised the question, ironically similar to the complaint of Maya Lin with the Vietnam Veterans Memorial, about the inviolability of an artist's work and that artist's moral rights to protect the work from infringement.

Within days the National Cathedral joined Hart in a lawsuit against Warner Brothers for copyright infringement. In a statement the cathedral hierarchy said that it "considers all objects of art and iconography depicted on or in the cathedral as sacred objects intended to convey God's immanence and presence in the world." In short, the west entrance of the cathedral had been debased and demonized.

During sessions at US Federal Court over the case that winter, the strain on Hart was wincingly visible as he obsessed over the details, even as the case seemed to be going his way. Early in 1998, the presiding judge warned Warner Brothers that if the studio did not settle the case promptly, he would immediately halt the distribution of 400,000 videotapes of the movie. At this, the studio collapsed, agreeing to pay several million dollars in damages, to turn the faux Hart backdrop to white spaghetti in future syndications of the film, and to attach a disclaimer to the cassettes or pay-for-view screenings disclaiming any relationship to *Ex Nihilo*.

As the case took a turn toward Hart's favor, he had a stroke that impaired the right side of his brain, paralyzed his left hand, and defeated any effort to sketch or even to stabilize his clay. Nevertheless, he would drag himself to the Vietnam Veterans Memorial one last time on May 31, 1999—Memorial Day—for his last words on the controversy. "Public art can serve no higher purpose than to reveal and embody the nobility of the human spirit such as that exemplified by the Vietnam veteran's dedicated service to his country." He died ten weeks later. He was fifty-six.

On August 18, 1999, a celebration of his life and work was held at the imposing cathedral of St. Matthew the Apostle in downtown Washington. On the altar, bathed in light, was his luminous *Cross of the Millennium*. Among the formal celebrants were two individuals who had been central to his spiritual life and his artistic success. One was Reverend Stephen Happel, who had shepherded him through his conversion to Catholicism in the 1970s. The other was J. Carter Brown, the former director of the National Gallery of Art and chairman of the Commission of Fine Arts. It was Brown, more than anyone, who brokered the deal to join Maya Lin's wall with Hart's three soldiers.

In 2004 President George W. Bush presented the National Medal of Arts to Frederick Hart's widow, six years before Maya Lin received the same medal.

The artist surely knew that his legacy would not be his luminous acrylic cross or his *Ex Nihilo* or his *Daughters of Odessa*. It would rest on his three soldiers. Massive reproductions of their faces embellish the sides of tourist buses that roam Washington's memorial-filled center city. There is often a clutch of people who gather around the Hart soldiers with its exquisite detail before they enter the pathway to the wall and join the others who are contemplating the enormity of the Vietnam conflict.

—

Of the other players in this saga, Maya Lin's chief antagonists—Jim Webb and Tom Carhart—spurned repeated invitations to reflect on their campaign against the wall, especially as to whether, in light of the memorial's universal acceptance, they had any regrets. From their silence, we are left to draw our own conclusions. The guru of the grand competition, Paul Spreiregen, would, by contrast, continue to think and write extensively of his pride in the fairness and professionalism of the competition he ran and his joy in the final result. "To put art in the service of memory," he wrote, "is an ancient ritual of the tributary giving of its most valuable resource, thus its highest honor." He also wrote of his disappointments. With a competition so emotional and fragile, he felt that both Lin and her opponents came very close to undermining the entire enterprise. The veterans' opposition was at times vicious and underhanded, and at other times, highly effective. It nearly succeeded. But years later he still harbored a special resentment for Lin. He deplored the mythology that he felt had grown up around her. He had found her naïve and antagonistic behavior destructive from the start, and he kept detailed notes on her incessant complaining, which he saw as subversive. To his credit, however, despite his personal animus, he unfailingly supported her design as the best and wisest choice. He had fought bravely and eloquently for its integrity. "If the flagpole and the statue were to disappear this afternoon," he wrote, "the [memorial] would not lose an iota of its power." If he had any qualms at all about the design, he wished that the memorial had been more constructive and "life-giving."

"I wish the effort had been to make a better plowshare rather than to bury a sword."

—

For me, like so many others, that walk down the cobblestone pathway is personal. Down the slope, my image is reflected in the blizzard of names, past the low point at the vertex and then up the slope to Panel 35E where the name of my one comrade in arms is etched.

US postage stamp issued January 12, 2000

AUTHOR'S REFLECTION

I was one of those who took advantage of a loophole in the early years of the Vietnam conflict. The US secretary of the Interior, Stewart Udall, had hired me straight out of college as a researcher for his seminal book about the history of American conservation called *The Quiet Crisis*. Eventually, I became his speech writer and remained with him in a singularly blessed association for fifteen months. During that period, the secretary had protected me from being drafted by writing to my draft board and asking that I be deferred because of important government work. I left him in September 1964 to take a job as a reporter for the *Chicago Daily News*. Like so many guardians of Vietnam-era youth who professed reasons to keep young men out of harm's way, Udall renewed his request for my deferment, claiming that he needed to use my services in connection with "a number of vital problems in the field of conservation." Of course, this was a lie. And so, for more than a year as the Vietnam conflict began to heat up, I lived my own quiet crisis of guilt over my fake deferment.

On July 28, 1965, at a news conference in the East Room of the White House, after he committed the first American combat units to the Vietnam conflict, President Lyndon Johnson announced an immediate increase in troop strength from 75,000 to 125,000 and doubled the monthly draft call to 35,000. "This is a different kind of war," the president said. "There are no marching armies or solemn declarations. . . . But we must not let this mask the central fact that this is really war. It is guided by North Vietnam, and it is spurred by Communist China. Its goal is to conquer the South, to defeat American power, and to extend the Asiatic dominion of Communism. There are great stakes in the balance."

Conscience-stricken, I felt I could no longer hide behind Udall's largesse and my own hypocrisy. I was not truly or sincerely a conscientious objector. For better or for worse, I wanted to participate fully in the experience of my generation and succumbed to the infectious allure of national service and masculine testing. On September 27, 1965, I enlisted for a three-year hitch in US Army Intelligence. And that led to a different quiet crisis. As the war raced toward its peak of violence, I was deployed first to Baltimore for intelligence training, then to Monterey, California, for a year of Japanese language training, and finally, to an Intelligence Headquarters Unit in Hawaii. Conflicted between joyful relief and a tinge of regret, I was missing out on the war.

Things could have gone very differently for me. On Maya Lin's wall, I have one friend. His fate does have something to do with a battle and even a war, won or lost.

Ronald E. Ray

His name was Ronald Edwin Ray, but in Vietnam his cover name was Mr. Reynolds. He was a stocky, jovial, athletic native of Spokane, Washington, American to the core, a football player and class president in high school, an indifferent political science major at Washington State University, for whom military service afterward was just the next natural step. He was neither for nor against the war. I can't recall ever having a political discussion with him when we bunked next to one another at Fort Holabird, Maryland. Unlike me, he had no thoughts about the dilemma of his generation or about the question of engagement or detachment from his country's cause. Nor was he a romantic like me. He was a genuine, uncritical friend, and I liked him immensely. He covered for me at morning musters when I slipped away overnight to Washington, DC, against regulations.

Like me he had volunteered for army intelligence. By opting for an extra year in the service, we thought we could exercise some measure of control over how we "served our country." By agreeing to that third year we made an honorable contract with our government—a notion so alien for a later generation of soldiers that endured multiple deployments to Iraq and Afghanistan—and avoided the fate of the draftee on the front lines. We could also focus on the somewhat glamorous training for recruiting foreign agents for dangerous missions. If, God forbid, we were sent to Vietnam, by law the tour could last for only one year.

After our training in Baltimore, as I went off to California, he was ordered to a small headquarters unit on Ford Island at Pearl Harbor. A year later, I too got orders to the same unit in Hawaii and was stunned to hear that Ron had left and was in Vietnam. What had happened? I wondered. Why on earth . . . ?

—

It was a perfect afternoon for a parade in the fall of 1983 when I left the Vietnam Veterans Memorial and crossed the Potomac River to

Arlington National Cemetery. The air was crisp and clear, after a morning rain, and the white marble of the amphitheater sliced across the dazzling blue of the sky. The Veterans Day ceremony was to be held in a copse of dogwoods. Already the Air Force band had assembled, lounging about, flaccid, middle-aged musicians poured into ill-fitting costumes. The honor guard was rehearsing its slow approach to the viewing stand.

I was early, and Ron's mother still had not arrived, so I wandered away, down Sherman Drive to McPherson Drive. It was a strange way to get to a Confederate monument. Moses Ezekiel, a Virginian who fought in the Battle of New Market in 1863, had sculpted the Southern tribute, a gift of the United Daughters of the Confederacy, as a testament to the Lost Cause and to the sacrifice of the Southern soldier. Towering high upon a circular pedestal, there upon the back ridge of the vast cemetery, thirty-two feet in height, crowned with olive garlands, the heroic figure of a woman looks down sorrowfully on the Southern graves. Facing south, she holds out a laurel wreath in love and resignation. Below her a circular bronze frieze depicts poignant scenes. Strapping men comfort hoop-skirted ladies on their departure, and harried, plainly dressed women comfort raggedy men on their return. Time had poured green rivulets from the bronze over the stained white marble. Time would not corrode black marble, I thought.

Back at the amphitheater Mrs. "Reynolds" broke away from a covey of care-worn ladies. The day before, when she wore a black sweat shirt, sequined with a sparkling American eagle clutching a Star-Spangled Banner above the words "Vietnam Heroes," she had given me a copy of Ron's Bronze Star citation. Now she was resplendent in white, her immaculate wool suit and white military cap held perfectly in place with bobby pins. In the lapel of her jacket a lovely piece of jewelry, a demure gold star set upon a blue background, completed her look.

She gave me a program, and we chatted about her week in Washington. She was a woman of few words, and they were delivered in the smoky flat tones of the Arkansas rice country from which she hailed. She had been cautious with me. Her volunteer work in veterans' hospitals embraced her son's heroism. She harbored no bitterness, although she had encountered the bitterness of other Gold Star mothers countless times. Once in Spokane, she had invited forty-three mothers to tea, and no one accepted.

"Why be bitter?" she said simply. "It doesn't do you any good."

She had never asked the Pentagon for any information on Ron. When I had pursued the matter, the Pentagon informed me that all the records of the 525 Military Intelligence Group in Hue had been lost. So, I asked her directly if she wished me to share with her what I found out from other, more direct sources.

"I guess I want to know everything you know," she said without enthusiasm.

—

The headquarters of the intelligence group in Hawaii from which Ron had fled and to which I arrived in the summer of 1967 was on Ford Island in the middle of the vast naval base at Pearl Harbor. Its shoreline encompassed the famous "battleship row" that was the target of the Japanese attack on December 7, 1941, and the subsequent graveyard for the USS *Arizona* and USS *Oklahoma*. Since 1962 the USS Arizona Memorial has been one of Hawaii's most visited sites. As it was with Maya Lin and Frederick Hart, the *curricula vitae* of the memorial's designer, Alfred Preis, was surprising. He was an Austrian Jew who had converted to Catholicism and had escaped his homeland in 1939, landing in Hawaii only to be interned there as a Nazi suspect once the war began. His memorial sits above the sunken wreck of the battleship and is meant to resemble a bridge. But with its white exterior and its sagging center roof it has been likened to a "squashed milk carton."

Preis's description of the structure resonates for the Vietnam Memorial: "Wherein the structure sags in the center but stands strong

USS Arizona Memorial (1962) by Alfred Preis, Pearl Harbor, Hawaii

and vigorous at the ends, [it] expresses initial defeat and ultimate victory . . . The overall effect is one of serenity. Overtones of sadness have been omitted to permit the individual to contemplate his own personal responses . . . his innermost feelings."

The commander of our Hawaiian unit was a blustering, unpleasant, uncouth colonel, stuck in this faraway army outpost at the end of his career, after having been passed over for promotion more than once. Bald and crude, a veteran of World War II, Korea, and Vietnam, he had no college education. His passion was sports, and he seemed to live and die for his small unit's performance on the dusty military ball fields of Hickam Air Force Base. Ron's misfortune lay in being a natural athlete, and the colonel insisted that he star on the unit's softball team. But Ron wanted to take courses at the University of Hawaii in his precious off-duty hours, and he refused to play. And so, the colonel harassed and tormented him, giving him kitchen and latrine duty and berating him in front of the troops. The tension grew worse and worse, until one day it became too much. After yet another violent quarrel over some trivial matter, Ron did the one thing that the colonel could not control: he volunteered for Vietnam.

With Ron long gone, I would have my own blowups with that gruff colonel. I too had been a pretty good athlete in high school and in college—All-Metropolitan in soccer and in baseball at my Washington, DC, high school, All-South in soccer at the University of North Carolina. So, I was the colonel's next hot prospect to star on his softball team and his next victim for harassment, but I, too, had no interest in spending my free time in intramural athletics. The colonel exerted considerable pressure, and several times I came very close to following Ron's lead in volunteering for the war. Perhaps they would send me to join Ron, and at last I would be doing the real work of intelligence. The lure of serving in the combat zone tantalized me as it had thousands of others. Duty stations in Baltimore, Monterey, and Hawaii did not sound so heroic. As the old saw goes, what was I to tell my grandchildren decades later about where I was during the Vietnam War? That simple juxtaposition, Ron's experience and my own, is at the heart of Maya Lin's artistic concept and power. When I look at Ron's name etched in the black granite of her wall, I see my own face.

Ron's first post was Da Nang, but soon enough he was reassigned to the Imperial City of Hue on the banks of the Perfume River. There he became "Mr. Reynolds," dressed in civilian clothes, outfitted in a small one-story house with a latticed portico, on a dirt street barely broad enough for a jeep.

His letters back home to us were upbeat. He liked Vietnam. His words reeked of Graham Greene and evoked the romance we had all signed up for. I was envious. His detachment was known officially as the Field Sociological Study Group, and the outfit was supposedly "studying" the culture and sociology of Hue.

But Ron's scholar-cover fooled no one—he was not the scholarly type—and eventually he was reassigned to a different job in Hue. He was now a "refugee employment liaison" to a US Navy employment office known as the Industrial Relations Division (IRD). His actual mission was worthy enough. The group was ordered to concentrate on the villages around Khe Sanh and in the A Shau Valley to the west of the city, through which a North Vietnamese invasion was sure to come, if there was to be one. They were to identify refugees whose hatred of the Viet Cong was great enough that they might be persuaded to return home to their villages as secret agents for the Americans. It was hoped that the agents would then provide "actionable" intelligence leading to productive combat missions for the twenty thousand US marines stationed nearby at Phu Bai.

Ron's team of four was housed in a classy, French-style villa on Ly Thuong Kiet Street, near the Truong Tien Bridge over the Perfume River and across from the citadel and the historic Imperial Palace of Peace. The name of their road honored a Vietnamese hero who had won great victories against a huge army of invading Chinese in the eleventh century. If one is to believe the information in the Museum of Vietnamese History in Hanoi, Ly Thuong Kiet, a eunuch in the service of the Ly Dynasty, skilled in literature and martial arts, faced an enemy force of one million Chinese soldiers, supported by two million laborers, and 100,000 horses across the Cau River forty kilometers north of Hanoi. In a brilliant nighttime raid across the river, General Kiet crushed the invasion and ushered in an era of independence for Vietnam. With great certainty, the display reports that only 23,400 invaders limped back to China along with only 3,174 horses. Vietnamese children are taught a sacred song about Kiet's glorious victory:

> The land of the Viet people must be for the Viet king
> That's admitted by Heaven's Empire
> Why was it invaded?
> The invaders would be sure to be defeated

Across the street from Ron's tiny detachment was the ruin of the former United States Information Agency (USIA) library. It had been torched along with the nearby American consulate, in Buddhist uprisings against the South Vietnamese government a year-and-a-half before.

On January 30, 1968, the first day of the Lunar New Year, General William Westmoreland in Saigon was receiving strong indications of enemy movement around. As he later wrote, regulations required that the information be passed routinely through channels, going first to the Third Marine Division in Phu Bai. Somehow, the channels north from Saigon were clogged, unless the intelligence was simply ignored or disbelieved. The capable commanding general of South Vietnam army's (ARVN) First Division, with its headquarters in the citadel, also had information of an imminent attack. On that day, to the dismay of his officers who were looking forward to a three-day holiday, he canceled all leaves and put soldiers under his command on full alert. American advisers including intelligence officers were integrated into ARVN command, but intelligence from that quarter did not make it across the Perfume River, much less to the boys on Ly Thuong Kiet Street at the end of the channel. So, the Americans knew the Tet offensive was coming. But this subsequent revelation of history did not help Mr. Reynolds. He went about a normal day, oblivious to the momentous event that was about to take shape all around him.

Had they been alerted and ordered to evacuate, the men of IRD could have thrown a few sensitive files into a shoulder bag and been on the road to Phu Bai in minutes. Or they could at least have sought refuge up the street in the small, walled American military compound of the Military Assistance Command Vietnam (MACV). It housed only about two hundred personnel, mainly administrative types and advisers, but no combat soldiers.

In the early evening, they strolled down to the river to carouse with the bar girls at a building known to the Americans as the Pink Pornography Palace, since it sported pre-World War I French pornographic images on the walls (although the women at another place called The Green Door were classier). Or if they were lucky enough to wangle an invitation to the Cercle Sportif on Le Loi Street, they might rub shoulders with old *patrons* from French colonial rule and ogle their graceful and beautiful women in white silk pants and tight high-collared tunics slit up to the hip. But at the down-low Pink Pornography Palace, they bought their favorite girl "Saigon tea" for less than a dollar, and a good deal of genuine flirting went on. (Had they wanted to take the flirting further, for an extra $15, they might have ended up with a girl on one of the sampans that floated languidly, awaiting them, in the middle of the Perfume River.) At the bar they might have burst into song, often an old standard composed by an American adviser in Hue that showed how a trooper with very little Vietnamese would communicate with a Vietnamese girl with very little English.

> *I walked into a bar, 'way down by the track.*
> *There stood a young co dep, long hair down her back.*
> *Her eyes, how they sparkled, in response to my touch*
> *And she told me she loved me, she loved me too much.*

> *Tai sao, tai sao, said she to me*
> *Tai vy, tai vy, said I.*
> *"In Saigon this morning, tonight I'm in Hue.*
> *If the VC don't get me tomorrow, makes one more day."**

Into the evening, as they knocked down bottles of *Ba Muoi Ba*, Vietnamese beer named "33"—"the one beer to have when you're having more than 33"—the conversation was relaxed and jovial. Perhaps there would be an attack on Hue someday, they mused. The enemy would sweep out of the A Shau Valley, take Hue, and then offer to negotiate. In the abstract, it was an interesting theory. But it did not translate into a premonition of imminent danger. Not now, not at Tet when there was always a three-day cease-fire between the sides to celebrate

---

*Translation: *co dep*: pretty girl/"too much" to a bar girl means "a lot"/ *tai sao*: why?/*tai vy*: because.

the holiday. And perhaps never. The North Vietnamese loved and respected the Imperial Capital too much, didn't they? It was hallowed ground, the soul of Vietnam, the capital of Vietnamese emperors for centuries, the historical, cultural, educational, and religious heart for all of Vietnam. Thus, it was virtually undefended as an "open city." Regulations forbade the use of heavy artillery or close air support within its confines. Hue was the moral equivalent of Kyoto, Japan, that had been spared American bombing during World War II because it was regarded as a global treasure.

At 3:40 a.m. Ron was startled awake by the sound of mortar passing over his house and landing near the MACV compound. The fluttering sound of larger shells followed shortly, 140 mm rockets. A few landed perilously close by. The bombardment lasted about an hour. To the west Ron could hear the crackle of machine gun fire, as flares lit up the sky. If the most effective NVA soldiers—called sappers—were actually going to attack, the team on Ly Thuong Kiet Street was sure they would have ample warning. At 4:30 a.m. there was a lull, and the men of IRD talked about walking over to MACV in the morning to inspect the damage. This was probably just another raid like those that had happened elsewhere in which the attackers returned to their jungle sanctuaries by daylight.

At 6:30 a.m. the scream of their guard—"VC! VC!"—shattered their serenity. Ron ran to the second-floor window. From there he could see only the ruined USIA library across the street. So, he scurried to the roof. From the west, already abreast of the CIA's pacification compound, two files of North Vietnamese regulars approached. In each file, there were about twenty men, dressed in jungle fatigues and slouch hats. As Ron peeked out his window in the glow of dawn, the NVA soldiers walked by the house with scarcely more than a glance. Shortly afterward, a fierce battle broke out in front of the police station up the street, barely out of sight. It lasted about fifteen minutes.

What Ron could not know was that these were the forward elements of the 804th Battalion of the People's Army of Vietnam that was

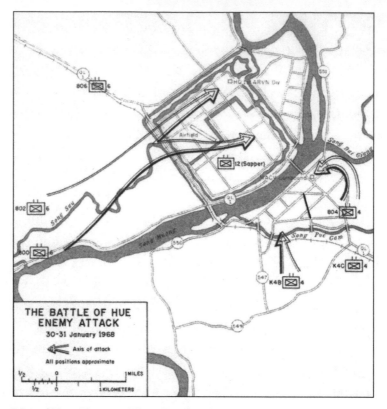

Map of Hue, Vietnam. The villa where Ron and his team were housed was on Ly Thuong Street, south of the Perfume (Huong) River, shown in bold.

sweeping in from the south, while the even more fearsome 12th Sapper battalion was attacking in force from west of the city. Eventually, the NVA force would number 8,000 soldiers.

At 10 a.m. the NVA attacked the South Vietnamese general's house that lay directly behind a rice paddy and the IRD house. Backed by mortars and a machine gun that had been set up in the Catholic Church four hundred yards to the west, the North Vietnamese formed a handsome line and moved smartly across the paddy toward the general's lair. At 1 p.m. hope sparked. In the distance from the southwest along Route 1, the road to Phu Bai, came the sound of tanks and trucks. Soon, the first American tank rattled into view, then two more tanks and twelve trucks. Ron could see US Marines walking behind the vehicles, but they were still the size of toy soldiers. The Americans inched forward, as Westmoreland put it in his memoirs, trying to relieve "the heroic little band that was still holding out in the MACV advisory compound." As he watched these initial skirmishes from his roof, Ron might have imagined that he was watching a Hollywood movie. But as the fighting became more intense and devolved into urban combat, street by street, house by house—for which the Marines were not trained—the action was more reminiscent of World War II.

From his grandstand, as the senior officer, Ron took charge, directing the other three men to positions at various windows and crevices, and rationing ammunition and food. Sheer instinct ruled him. To his mates, he seemed to operate without fear, almost cavalier in this unimaginable danger, as if it were merely a piece of bad luck, and this was a scrimmage on his high school football field. More than once, one of his soldiers warned him to keep down, as he darted about the room on frog's legs.

A half hour later, as he was parceling out ammunition to others, a sniper bullet smashed through the window and shattered his liver, passing through his side, and out his belly. He bled little. His pulse and breathing subsided rapidly. It was said later that he did not suffer. He had not fired a shot. For him there had been no heroic charge up a forgotten jungle hill, no fierce combat in a remote rice paddy. Just a random bullet. *Finito.*

—

Back at the Veterans Day ceremony at Arlington National Cemetery, the band played. Prayers were read before a broad-chested brigadier general in full regalia stepped forward to render words of comfort. Without much delay, he gravitated to the old well: Abraham Lincoln's letter to Mrs. Bixby, the mother of five dead soldiers.

"I feel how weak and fruitless must be any words of mine which should attempt to beguile you from the grief of a loss so overwhelming.

. . ." I can't remember what else the general said, except his banal closing line.

"Thank you for being players in Americanism."

When it was over, I bade Ron's mother farewell. I would not be going with her to the wreath-laying at the Tomb of the Unknown Soldier, nor to another ceremony with more minor dignitaries at the Vietnam Memorial. I preferred to visit Ron alone, later, without others making their dishonest uses of him. We lingered for a long handshake.

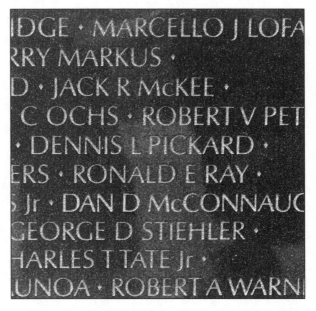

The name of Ronald E. Ray on Panel 35E of the wall

"Well, what did you think?" she asked. I muttered something.

"Don't shrug," she said maternally in gentle scold, and we shared a smile of understanding.

His Bronze Star citation read:

A large North Vietnamese Army force overran much of the city late on January 30, 1968, and Sgt. Ray's small unit was cut off from friendly military support. The enemy forces quickly discovered his team's position and attacked it. Time after time, Sergeant Ray exposed himself to ravaging enemy fire to repel the determined insurgent assaults with fierce rifle and grenade fire. The team's furious fighting diverted enemy troops from their primary targets and was far above the resistance to be expected from such limited manpower and weaponry. While fearlessly leading his men in a staunch defense of their position, he was hit by sniper fire and instantly killed.

Perhaps in memory that was the way it was, or should be.

—

I came to believe that there might have been a consolation in the suddenness of Ron Ray's demise. In all probability, a more gruesome fate was in store for him, had he survived the first night of Tet. It became known later that, from their extensive network of informants, the Communists knew exactly who was living in the French villa along Ly Thuong Kiet Street and what they were doing. In fact, blithe spirit that he was, totally innocent of the danger he was in, Ron stood out. What else could he be but an American intelligence agent? Of the twenty Americans who were living their apparently charmed life outside the MACV compound, only two survived. One of those did so by hiding in the muck of a pigsty for several days as scores of NVA soldiers passed by, holding their noses. The body of another American working outside the walls of a military compound, a USIA official, was soon discovered several days after January 30 with his hands tied behind his back and a bullet hole in the back of his head. He was only a harbinger.

Assassination squads, with lists of names, fanned out across the city and began their task of savagely eliminating their enemies, targeting political leaders, city officials, civil servants of the "puppet regime," as well as teachers, policemen, and intellectuals, and the few exposed American operatives like Ron, who were easy prey. For the most part, the assassins were local Viet Cong cadre, but they were assisted by North Vietnamese regulars. Perhaps upwards of 2,800 people were killed in the four weeks the NVA occupied the city. Their bodies were dumped in a mass grave. Only months later were the corpses exhumed and given a decent burial. In terms of face-to-face murder of civilians, the Hue massacre in February 1968 was the worst atrocity of the Vietnam War.

Meanwhile, the beleaguered MACV compound was able to hold out against a determined assault, until US Marines fought their way up Route 1 to rescue it. Ly Thuong Kiet Street became a strategic battle-ground with NVA soldiers occupying every house. Some of the fierc-est fighting took place along that thoroughfare. For days the sound of tank, recoilless rifle, and heavy machine gun fire resounded through the street, as Marines sought to clear each house and each room of its North Vietnamese defenders. But the Americans paid a high price. In the month-long battle, one of the bloodiest of the war, the three Marine battalions that fought sustained a 50 percent casualty rate; 216 American soldiers were killed and 1,609 were wounded. Five thousand attackers perished, and military historians regard their inability to cap-ture the MACV compound as a major factor in losing the battle.

The death of Ron Ray was merely a mundane footnote to a far larger struggle.

In the battle of Hue, and in the Tet Offensive that launched attacks against more than a hundred cities and towns, America lost its will to prosecute the war. Only a few months before, in November 1967, Gen-eral Westmoreland had come home to assure the American people that the tide had turned and the war at last was being won. But after Tet, CBS News anchor Walter Cronkite went to Hue and made a crucial observation.

"We have been too often disappointed by the optimism of the Amer-ican leaders, both in Vietnam and Washington, to have faith any longer in the silver linings they find in the darkest clouds. . . . We are mired in a stalemate," that can only be ended by negotiation, not victory.

Meanwhile, Hue itself, that exotic, once tranquil, romantic, untouch-able cultural jewel, lay in ruins. Of its 140,000 citizens, 116,000 became refugees.

In a matter of terrible bad luck, Ron Ray found himself, unwittingly and tragically, at the center of decisive historical events, but somehow that is cold comfort indeed. It is hard for me to believe that what he was doing in that little villa mattered very much. If he was a candidate for Maya Lin's wall, merely one of 58,000, he would not easily have seen his image reflected in Frederick Hart's soldiers, unless it was that awe-struck, thousand-yard stare down Ly Thuong Kiet Street in terror and hope, which he must surely have had in his final, harrowing hours.

—

I am sitting at a tea house beside the Hoan Kiem Lake in the Old Quarter of Hanoi. At last the week-long rain has stopped, and a full moon is rising through the mist. I'm waiting for Dr. Nguyen Ngoc Hung, a professor of English, a former government minister of education, and veteran of the battles around Hue. And for Bao Ninh. Ninh is Vietnam's most famous writer and the author of an astonishing, phantasmagoric novel called *The Sorrow of War*. When it was published in England in 1993, the *Independent* hailed the book as a masterpiece, saying it "vaults over all the American fiction that came out of the Vietnam War to take its place alongside the greatest war novel of the century, Erich Maria Remarque's classic, *All Quiet on the Western Front*."

These have been interesting days. They began with a trip to the old dividing line between North and South, the former DMZ, the most militarized "demilitarized zone" ever, and probably one of the most heavily bombed landscapes in the history of the world. My guide was Chuck Searcy, an ex-military intelligence officer like myself, who has lived in Vietnam since 1995 and has devoted himself to the overwhelming task of defusing unexploded ordnance, especially tennis ball-sized cluster bombs (now internationally banned) that are so attractive as playthings to children. His work is a kind of personal atonement for the sins of his country. American planes dropped more

Truong Son Cemetery, Vietnam

than eight million tons of bombs on Vietnam during the war, and the danger persists. Ten percent of those were unexploded. More than eight thousand deaths have resulted from delayed explosions.

Chuck had taken me to see the network of tunnels north of the Ben Hai River—the dividing line between North and South Vietnam—where villagers and North Vietnamese guerillas lived underground for years. From there we drove many miles through heavy rain, dodging children and cows, past flooded rice and cane fields to the Truong Son Cemetery, North Vietnam's equivalent of Arlington National Cemetery. Only a fraction of the one million NVA and VC dead are buried and memorialized there.

Sculptures in the mode of Soviet realism greet the visitor to the national cemetery. In the ornate pagodas that appoint the corners of the sacred burial ground, the names are engraved on black granite plaques. They remind me of a line in Bao Ninh's novel: "The fallen soldiers shared one destiny; no longer were they honorable or disgraced soldiers, heroic or cowardly, worthy or worthless. Now they were mere names and remains."

Statuary as "entrance experience," Truong Son Cemetery, Vietnam

Inevitably, I'd visited the Hòa Lo Prison Museum, the notorious "Hanoi Hilton," and read with interest the inscription on the wall outside the two rooms devoted to the American War, as the Vietnamese call it: "During the war the national economy was having difficulties, but the Vietnam government created the best living conditions they could for US pilots. They had a stable life during their temporary detention periods." A video portrayed the happy prisoners playing volleyball and ping pong. But in that prison museum the brutal French colonial occupation of the country is far more emphasized, including a grotesque guillotine that was regularly employed against resistance leaders. At first, I took the understatement as a sign of historical softening, driven by the newfound friendship between the United States and the Socialist Republic of Vietnam. I had heard that there was even a move afoot in the Politburo to change the name of Liberation Day—April 30, the date Saigon fell—to Unification Day.

If American transgressions are downplayed in Hanoi, nothing is glossed over at the gruesome War Remnants Museum in Saigon, formerly known as the American War Crimes Museum. The graphic, unrelieved portrayal of American massacres, tortures, poisonings, and bombings there is gut-wrenching, deeply upsetting, and profoundly sad. And yet even those pictures on the museum wall and the evocative plaques cannot put the viewer into the "jungle of screaming souls," the way Bao Ninh had done in his novel's description of what it was like to be on the ground when American helicopter gunships or napalm-bearing F-4 jet fighters or B-52 bombers were overhead. War, he wrote, was a world without romance. His protagonist, Kien, says of himself that it was "hard to imagine, hard to remember a time when his whole personality and character had been intact, a time before the cruelty and the destruction of war had warped his soul. A time when he had been deeply in love, passionate, aching with desire, hilariously frivolous and lighthearted, or quickly depressed by love and suffering. Or blushing in embarrassment. When he too was worthy of being a lover and in love."

Meanwhile, old Saigon is in the grip of Wild West Capitalism. Amid a forest of construction cranes, high-rises sprout across the city's landscape. There is even an impressive thirty-five-story skyscraper on the Saigon River, designed by César Pelli, Maya Lin's mentor at Yale. In the final stage of design, Pelli was encouraged to "Vietnamize" his building by adding a spire, evoking the hat of the Hung Kings, the founders of the nation in the year 2879 BC.

But mainly, I'd come all the way to Vietnam on a pilgrimage to Hue. There I'd holed up in an unpretentious hotel along Ly Thuong Kiet Street. The hotel promotions had promised a "nice clean hotel, nicely decorated, great food, friendly staff that speaks English well." That last part about speaking English well did not exactly turn out

Vietcombank Tower (2015) by César Pelli, Ho Chi Minh City, Vietnam

to be the case. My corner room on the seventh floor looked down on a vacant lot at the intersection of Ly Thuong Kiet Street and Dong Da Street where once an American consulate stood, before a thousand Buddhist students burned it down on June 1, 1966. That is how it was reported back then. Now we know that many of those "students" were Viet Cong. After all, Ho Chi Minh had lived under-cover as a Buddhist monk in Bangkok for four years from 1921 to 1925.

And in old Saigon, there is a shrine to Thich Quang Duc, the Bud-dhist monk who burned himself publically in 1963 and sparked the Buddhist Revolt against the Americans and their "puppet regime." It is widely supposed in Vietnam that Thich Quang Duc was a Viet Cong in monk's clothing. The English roadster that he drove from Hue to Saigon is preserved in the Hue pagoda as an artifact of his gruesome political suicide. Why would an atheist Communist state elevate a holy man to such heights of heroism, except for his service to the National Liberation Front?

It is remembered that the First Lady of South Vietnam, the noto-rious Madame Nhu (known as the Dragon Lady) had said before his immolation, "Let them burn, and we shall clap our hands."

Memorial to Thich Quang Duc, Ho Chi Minh City, Vietnam

Dr. Hung arrived alone, apologizing that he had been unable to reach his friend, Bao Ninh, who had apparently dropped out of sight and thrown away his cell phone. He had had enough of the taunting of other Vietnamese writers who were jealous of his international fame and of the Vietnamese government that had banned his book for ten years and now was denying him its highest literary prize. I was only mildly disappointed. I had heard that, despite his literary mastery, Bao Ninh in person was shy and incommunicative. Dr. Hung, white-haired with an oval brown face, a gentle affect and thoughtful manner, had earned a PhD in Australia, and his fluency was a great relief to me.

I told him I had seen the shrines: the tunnels in Viet Moc and Cu Chi, the museums in Hanoi and Ho Chi Minh City, the heroic statue of Thich Quang Duc, the tiger cages of the Con Son Prison. If collective fury existed, it seemed to be more directed against the Chinese and the French than the Americans. Among the people, as far as I could tell, there was no gloating about victory over the United States. Why was it, I asked him eventually, that there is so little triumphalism in Vietnam?

For an answer to that, he replied, you have to go deep into history. For a thousand years the Chinese invaded Vietnam, coming every thirty to fifty years to plunder this country and make it a vassal state. Then the French came for a hundred years with their arrogant quest to "civilize" the country through their brutal colonialism. After they left in 1954, there was only a brief respite before you came to impose your American brand of freedom and democracy. You stayed only fifteen years.

But why, I persisted, after all the bombing, several million deaths, and the poisoning of the land, was there not more anger and resentment?

Because, he replied, we fought the war differently than you. You measured success by how many soldiers you killed and how many weapons you seized. We lost every battle. Whenever thirty of us went out on an ambush, we were lucky if fifteen returned. But it was never our intention to defeat you. Indeed, 1968, the year when your friend was killed, was the worst year for us. There were no soldiers left, and the government had to scrape the barrel to find more men like me, students and women. But we fought only to make the Americans go away.

Why don't I see images of valiant heroic fighters everywhere? I asked. Because, he answered, we do not glorify soldiers. We remember the suffering of the women for their husbands and their sons. You will find no Rambos here. We only go to war when we can't avoid it. Our patriotism is like a lump of charcoal. When it is left alone, it is dormant and harmless. If you light it, it burns very hot. It can start a big fire and spread rapidly until it consumes a whole forest. But when it is over, it is over, and we focus on peace and development and rebuilding.

He looked out on the lake. This lake is called Ho Hoan Kiem, he said, and a legend is associated with it, the Legend of the Returned Sword. In 1428 a fisherman came here, and from the depths, a tortoise emerged and handed him a magical, golden sword from Heaven. On its simple wooden handle was written: "To Save the Nation." The fisherman became a great man, an emperor, to defend Vietnam against invasion from the Ming Dynasty of China. After many years, this king prevailed against the Chinese. After his victory, he returned here to this lake, magical sword in hand, and a giant golden tortoise surfaced from the depths and snatched it away, restoring it to its divine owners and leaving the king with only its wooden handle. The war was over. The sword was now useless.

We are proud of this legend, Dr. Hung said. Its message is deep in our culture and our character.

I thanked him for his time, and we parted with a warm handshake, and I watched him fearlessly navigate across the busy thoroughfare, through the swarm of motorbikes, without a backward glance.

ACKNOWLEDGMENTS

The *Rift in the Earth* was researched and written almost entirely within the grand precincts of the Library of Congress as a visiting fellow at John W. Kluge Center. For her unfailing assistance and good cheer, I want to thank Mary Lou Reker, the associate director of the Center, and for being such a good friend of this project. Others at the Center who provided help are Travis Hensley and Joanne Kitching. Concerning the art war over Vietnam memory, the Library has significant and unique holdings in the Manuscript Division, Prints and Photographs Division, and Motion Picture, Broadcasting and Recording Sound Division. The archives of the Vietnam Veterans Memorial Fund, all 132 boxes of material, are in the Manuscript Division. The Prints and Photographs Division has the slides of all 1,421 entries to the Memorial competition, as well as Maya Lin's original design boards. I have mined these treasures extensively.

In pointing me to the newspaper and television coverage of the controversy, I'm grateful to Professor Edward J. Gallagher at Lehigh University for his chronicle and his class notes. My main military advisers for the book were Dick Manuel, a retired captain in the US Marines, and Ray Wilkinson, both of whom fought in the battle of Hue during the Tet Offensive. When I saw Wilkinson in Hue, he was teaching English at a high school in Dong Ha, just south of the old DMZ. Lieutenant General Ron Christmas (Ret), who as a

Marine captain, commanded the salient force to retake Hue in early February and was badly wounded there, provided me with insights into the landscape of the city during the siege. And Ambassador James Bullington, who as a junior diplomat was stranded in Hue and rescued by Captain Christmas, also provided me with details about his ordeal, as well as information about the NVA massacre of civilians during the month-long occupation.

And I send special thanks to the incomparable Chuck Searcy, a former US Army Intelligence officer during the war. Searcy has lived in Vietnam for the past twenty years, and it is no wonder that he has often been called the unofficial US ambassador to Vietnam. He was my fascinating guide on our trip through the former "Demilitarized Zone" in December 2016 and was immensely helpful in arranging the logistics for that trip, as well as arranging important interviews. I thank Nguyen Luan Huu, Nguyen Quoc Tuan, and especially Dr. Nguyen Ngoc Hung for their insights.

From the beginning of this project I understood that the memory of the controversy was difficult and unpleasant for Maya Lin, even though her eventual triumph catapulted her into international fame. My questions to her were confined to specifics on design matters and to episodes where there were conflicts in the historical record. On December 2, 2016, she wrote to me: "I've never really wanted to talk about the controversy, [though] I've always been happy to talk about the design process. But I haven't really felt like talking about how tough that time was, as far as the machinations behind the scenes." So I thank her for her answers to my queries. Lin's mentor at Yale, César Pelli, and her professor at Yale in the fall of 1980, Andrus Burr, were also invaluable sources for me.

Lindy Hart, Frederick Hart's widow, was very generous with her time, and provided me with important letters and documents about her husband's involvement in making the memorial. He too was seared by the reaction to his statues. Were he still living, I suppose he would have been similarly circumspect and reluctant to revisit this difficult chapter of his life. His collaborators for his submission to the contest and its later execution, Joseph E. Brown and Michael Vergason, were also generous in giving me their time and thoughts. My friend, the prominent artist Craig McPherson, was my chief adviser on the culture of the art world. And Dr. Kathryn Fanning, a historian at the US Commission of Fine Arts, shepherded me through the voluminous proceedings of the Commission from 1981 to 1984.

Also at the Library of Congress, I'm immensely grateful to Becky Clark for her counsel, encouragement, and wisdom in marshaling the Library's specialists for the fact checking, image selection, and editing of the book in its final stages. These included the deft hand of a superior editor, Susan Reyburn; a true professional in image selection and rights acquisition, Athena Angelos; and a skillful researcher and fierce fact checker, Hannah Freece. To them I'm eternally grateful.

Finally, my heartfelt thanks goes to Cal Barksdale, my editor at Arcade, who saw the potential of the idea for this book from the beginning and embraced it enthusiastically, partly because he remembered the Art War over the Vietnam memorial vividly. He was trenchant in his advice about the large themes of the book. But he is also a stickler for using just right word. I will long remember his counsel to use the word *bogus* instead of *false* and *patinated* instead of *patinaed*. How much better that corrected sentence of the foundry man for the Hart statues now sounds:

"We could have patinated the piece with tears."

PERMISSIONS ACKNOWLEDGMENTS

The author and publisher would like to thank the following for permission to reprint copyrighted materials:

For the poetry:

Excerpt from "The Young Dead Soldiers" from *Collected Poems, 1917–1982* by Archibald MacLeish. Copyright © 1985 by The Estate of Archibald MacLeish. Reprinted by permission of Houghton Mifflin Harcourt Publishing Company. All rights reserved.

"Facing It" from *Dien Cai Dau* © 1988 by Yousef Komunyakaa. Published by Wesleyan University Press. Used by permission.

For the illustrations:

7	Prints & Photographs Division, Library of Congress.
10, left	Courtesy of the Stetson University Library Archives.
10, right	US National Archives and Records Administration, Courtesy: Jimmy Carter Library.
19	Courtesy of the US Senate Historical Office .
26	Prints & Photographs Division, Library of Congress.
39	Courtesy of Andrus Burr.

42	Prints & Photographs Division, Library of Congress.
43	Prints & Photographs Division, Library of Congress.
48	Prints & Photographs Division, Library of Congress.
57	© *The Washington Post*/Getty Images.
64	Prints & Photographs Division, Library of Congress.
74	Prints & Photographs Division, Library of Congress.
78	Diana Walker/ The LIFE Images Collection/ Getty Images.
79	Reprinted with permission of the DC Public Library, Star Collection, © *Washington Post*.
84	Photograph by Ed Malcik.
85	Prints & Photographs Division, Library of Congress.
98	Photograph by Ed Carlos/Courtesy of Lindy Lain Hart.
100	Sisse Brimberg/National Geographic Creative.
103	MacNelly Ed: © 1982 MacNelly, Inc, Distributed by King Features Syndicate.
108	Courtesy of the Digital Archive of Fort Benning and the Maneuver Center of Excellence.
122	Photograph by C. Bruce Forster.
141	*Washington Post*, © *The Washington Post*/ Getty Images.
140	From *The Courier Journal*, 11/14 © 1982 Gannett-Community Publishing. All rights reserved. Used by permission and protected by the Copyright Laws of the United States. The printing, copying, redistribution, or retransmission of this Content without express written permission is prohibited.
151	Motion Picture, Broadcasting & Recorded Sound Division, Library of Congress.
155	Courtesy of Lindy Lain Hart.
164	Courtesy of Lindy Lain Hart.
165	©1994. Courtesy of Darrell Acree.
167	©1994. Courtesy of Darrell Acree.
169	Detail of photograph by Carol Highsmith. Courtesy of Chesley, LLC.

171	Photo by Mark Gulezian/QuickSilver Photographers, Takoma Park, MD.
176	© Thomas S. England/ The LIFE Images Collection/ Getty Images.
178	© Leigh Vogel/ WireImage Collection/ Getty Images.
180	Prints & Photographs Division, Library of Congress.
182	Prints & Photographs Division, Library of Congress.
186	By permission of the United States Postal Service. My thanks to Champion Stamp Co. for providing the image file.
188	Courtesy of Gail Stiltner.
192	US Navy photo by Photographer's Mate 3rd Class Jayme Pastoric.
198	Courtesy of the U.S. Army Center of Military History.
200	Prints & Photographs Division, Library of Congress.
204	Photograph by James Reston, Jr.
205	Photograph by James Reston, Jr.
207	Courtesy of Pelli Clarke Pelli Architects.
208	Photograph by James Reston, Jr.

All photographs in the color insert are courtesy of the Prints & Photographs Division, Library of Congress, with the exception of the design entry panels by Joseph E. Brown with sculpture designs by Frederick Hart on pages 14 and 15, for which the credit is as follows: A Memorial to the Veterans of Vietnam: Competition Entry 579, Courtesy of EDAW, Inc.

Every effort has been made to locate copyright holders and to obtain their permission for the use of copyrighted material. The publisher apologizes for any errors or omissions in the above list and would be grateful to be notified of any corrections that should be incorporated in future reprints or editions of this book.

NOTES

Chapter One

3 **Vietnam War casualty figures**: America's Wars (War Statistics). Fact sheet published by the Office of Public Affairs, Department of Veterans Affairs, accessed November 30, 2016, https://www.va.gov/opa/publications/factsheets/fs_americas_wars.pdf; Philip Shenon, "20 Years After Victory, Vietnamese Communists Ponder How to Celebrate," *New York Times*, April 23, 1995: 12.

3 **Agent Orange victim claims**: Joseph P. Fried, "Judge Rules on Allocation of the Agent Orange Fund," *New York Times*, May 29, 1985: B3.

4 **Statistics on those who served and didn't**: Eligible men: 26.8 million; did not serve: 15.4 million were deferred, exempted, or disqualified; total deployed: 2.1 million. Francis X. Clines, "To Ex-Deserter, Urban War Should Be the Real Debate: Off the Trail Visits with Americans," *New York Times*, September 29, 1992: A20.

4 **Gallup polling on American attitudes toward the war, 1965–71**: "American Public Opinion and the War in Vietnam," William L. Lunch and Peter W. Sperlich, *Western Political Quarterly*, March 1979.

4 **President Carter's pardon**: Proclamation 4483: Granting Pardon for Violations of the Selective Service Act, U.S. Department of Justice, January 21, 1977, accessed 3 February 2017, https://www.justice.gov/pardon/proclamation-4483-granting-pardon-violations-selective-service-act and Executive Order 11967: Relating to Violations of the Selective Service Act, August 4, 1964 to March 28, 1973, US Department of Justice, January 21, 1977, accessed 3 February 2017, https://www.justice.gov/pardon/federal-register-executive-order-11967.

4 **Carter's pardon of draft evaders**: "According to Justice Department figures, the pardon would cover about 2,600 draft dodgers still under indictment, about 9,000 who were convicted or pleaded guilty and who could have their records erased, and about 1,200 who were under investigation." This totals 12,800 eligible under Carter's pardon. Lee Lescaze, "President Pardons Viet Draft Evaders," *Washington Post*, January 22, 1977: A1.

4–5 **The debate over pardon versus amnesty**: James Reston, Jr. articles and books: "Is Nuremberg Coming Back to Haunt Us?," *Saturday Review*, July 18, 1970; "Vietnamize at Home," *New York Times*, April 10, 1971; "Amnesty for Arrested Goes of War," *Chicago Tribune*, October 8, 1971; "A Proposal to the President: Vietnam Amnesty," *New Republic*, October 9, 1971; "Universal Amnesty," *New Republic*, February 5, 1972; *The Amnesty of John David Herndon* (New York: McGraw-Hill, 1972); "The Case for Amnesty," *World*, July 17, 1973; "Resisting Was Moral," *Newsday*, 1974; "Needed: A General Reconciliation," *Newsday*, September 3, 1974; "Limited Amnesty: Not Easy, President Carter Has a Difficult Job," *New York Times*, September 8, 1974; "Real Amnesty Would Be Good for America," *Newsday*, March 1, 1975; "On Carter's Amnesty and Pardon Views," *New York Times*, October 2, 1976; "A Wall Honoring Not Only Vietnam Veterans," *New York Times*, November 6, 1984; *Sherman's March and Vietnam* (New York: Macmillan, 1984); "Iraq, anyone?", *USA Today*, January 5, 2008

5 **Total Americans deployed to Vietnam (2.1 million)**: Francis X. Clines, "To Ex-Deserter, Urban War Should Be the Real Debate: Off the Trail Visits with Americans," *New York Times*, September 29, 1992: A20.

7 **Anti-war protests**: Tom Wicker, "Dissent: Deepening Threat of a Sharply Divided Nation," *New York Times*, November 16, 1969: E1.

8 *Hearts and Minds:* Peter Davis, director, 1974.

9 **"Now that it was all over, truce signed, and the dead buried, he had, especially in the evening, these sudden thunderclaps of fear. He could not feel"**: Virginia Woolf, *Mrs. Dalloway*, G. Patton Smith, ed. (London: The Hogarth Press, 1990), 76.

9 **Max Cleland's "readjustment therapy"**: Max Cleland Collection (AFC/2001/001/03512), Veterans History Project, American Folklife Center, Library of Congress, updated July 9, 2016, http://memory.loc.gov/diglib/vhp/bib/loc.natlib.afc2001001.03512.

10 **Cleland's request to Congress for aid for veterans**: Cleland's proposal would cost $10 million in the first year and a total of $43 million over the first five years. Jack Anderson, "Vietnam Veterans' Needs Unfulfilled," *Washington Post*, April 28, 1979: E37; Associated Press, "VA Chief Asks More Counseling for Vietnam Vets," *Baltimore Sun*, January 26, 1979: A5; Colman McCarthy, "Vietnam Veterans Stumble On, Their Hidden Wounds Ignored," *Los Angeles Times*, February 8, 1979: D7.

10 **World War II veterans in Congress**: William H. Stringer, "Sixty-Nine World War II Vets Go to Congress," *Christian Science Monitor*, November 9, 1946: 17.

10 **Exposing GIs to Agent Orange**: Michael Uhl and Todd Ensign, *GI Guinea Pigs: How the Pentagon Exposed Our Troops to Dangers More Deadly Than War: Agent Orange and Atomic Radiation* (New York: Playboy Press, 1980).

11 **Fonda and the definition of treason**: Aid and comfort, Article 3, Section 3, Clause 1, US Constitution.

11 **Fonda at the Academy Awards, 1972**: Bronwyn Cosgrave, "Jane Fonda: The Reluctant Fashionista," *New York Times*, September 22, 2016: D5.

11 **McCain refusing to see Fonda in Vietnam**: George F. Will, "Asian Communism—Without Romance," *Washington Post*, April 15, 1979: B7.

13 **"Depoliticization" quotation in review of *The Deer Hunter***: "Locating the War," *Washington Post*, April 11, 1979: A26.

13 **Stephen Rosenfeld column**: Stephen S. Rosenfeld, "Still Coming Home from the War," *Washington Post*, April 20, 1979: A15.

13 *Going After Cacciato:* Tim O'Brien, *Going After Cacciato* (New York: Delacorte Press/Seymour Lawrence, 1978), 25.

13 *A Rumor of War:* Philip Caputo, *A Rumor of War* (New York: Holt, Rinehart and Winston, 1977), 5, 192, 305, 332.

14 *Dispatches:* Michael Herr, *Dispatches* (New York: Alfred A. Knopf, Inc., 1977), 152, 153, 154–155

14 **"The creative fact or the fertile fact"**: Virginia Woolf, "The Art of Biography," *The Death of the Moth and Other Essays* (New York: Harcourt, Brace and Company, 1942), 197.

15–17 **"Cold, Stone Man"**: Lewis W. Bruchey, "Cold, Stone Man," *Washington Post*, August 10, 1980: C4. Only a portion of the poem is quoted here.

Chapter Two

18 **President Carter remarks, May 30, 1979**: Memo, Anne Wexler and Stu Eizenstat to President Jimmy Carter, May 29, 1979, "5/30/79" folder, Container 119, Records of the Office of the Staff Secretary, Presidential Files, Jimmy Carter Library; Memo, Bernie Aronson to President Jimmy Carter, May 29, 1979, "5/30/79" folder, Container 119, Records of the Office of the Staff Secretary, Presidential Files, Jimmy Carter Library.

19 **Scruggs's biography**: Jan Scruggs, "'We Were Young. We Have Died. Remember Us,'" *Washington Post*, November 11, 1979: B4; Jan C. Scruggs and Joel L. Swerdlow, *To Heal a Nation: The Vietnam Veterans Memorial* (New York: Harper & Row Publishers, 1985), 7; Robert W. Doubek, *Creating the Vietnam Veterans Memorial: The Inside Story* (Jefferson, North Carolina: McFarland & Company, Inc., 2015), 8.

19 **"Perhaps a national monument is in order"**: Jan Craig Scruggs, "Forgotten Veterans of 'That Peculiar War'," *Washington Post*, May 25, 1977: A17.

20 **Scruggs on "continued indifference"**: Jan C. Scruggs, "Continuing Indifference to Vietnam Veterans," *Washington Post*, August 5, 1978: A15.

20 **Scruggs on *The Deer Hunter***: Scruggs and Swerdlow, *To Heal a Nation*, pp. 7–8; Phil McCombs, "War in Memories: Gathering to Honor Vietnam's Soldiers," *Washington Post*, October 13, 1980: B9.

20 ***Friendly Fire ratings***: Les Brown, "ABC's 'Friendly Fire' Drew 64 Million," *New York Times*, April 25, 1979: C22.

20 **$2,800 of Scruggs's own money**: Jan Scruggs, Vietnam Veterans Memorial Fund, accessed January 3, 2017, http://www.vvmf.org/jan-scruggs.

21 **Scruggs's early days planning the memorial**: Scruggs and Swerdlow, *To Heal a Nation*, pp. 8–9, 12, 15–16; Doubek, *Creating the VVM*, 11.

21 **Press conference on Memorial Day, 1979**: "Around the Nation—Vietnam Veterans to Seek $1 Million for a Monument," *New York Times*, May 28, 1979: A8.

21 **$144.50**: Robert W. Doubek, "The Story of the Vietnam Veterans Memorial," *The Retired Officer* 39, no. 11 (November 1983): 18; Doubek, *Creating the VVM*, 15.

21 **Comedian making fun of Scruggs**: Scruggs and Swerdlow, *To Heal a Nation*, 9.

21 **Joseph Brown/Frederick Hart collaboration**: Joseph E. Brown and Michael Vergason, interview with the author, 2016; Lindy Hart, interview with the author, 2016.

21 **Dinner with von Eckardt**: Judith Martin, interview with the author, January 19, 2016.

21 **Von Eckardt on Hart's sculpture at the Washington Cathedral**: Wolf von Eckardt, "The Creation of Adam: Frederick Hart's Sculpture for the Washington Cathedral Blends Science and Theology," *Washington Post*, September 23, 1978: B1.

22 **Building the Washington Monument**: Robert Belmont Freeman, Jr., "Design Proposals for the Washington National Monument," *Records of the Columbia Historical Society, Washington, D.C.* 49 (1973/1974): 151–186; Mary Kay Ricks, "Washington Monuments that Never Quite Made It," *Washington Post*, January 13, 1999: HO3; Kirk Savage, "The Self-Made Monument: George Washington and the Fight to Erect a National Memorial," *Winterthur Portfolio* 22, no. 4 (Winter 1987): 225–242.

22 **Twain quotation ("a factory chimney with the top broken off")**: Mark Twain and Charles Dudley Warner, *The Gilded Age: A Tale of Today* (New York and Toronto: Signet Classic, 1969), 177.

23 **Building the FDR Memorial**: Grace Glueck, "Roosevelt Memorial: Finally, a Plan is Set," *New York Times* (July 18, 1978): C1, C17.

23 **Von Eckardt column on need for national competition**: Wolf Von Eckardt, "The Making of a Monument: Planning for the Vietnam Vet's Memorial," *Washington Post*, April 26, 1980: C7.

23–24 **Buy-in from Senators Mack Mathias and John Warner, early fundraising**: Scruggs and Swerdlow, *To Heal a Nation*, 13, 21, 23–24; Doubek, *Creating the VVM*, 72.

24 **Scruggs column ("violence-prone, psychological basket cases")**: Jan Scruggs, "'We Were Young. We Have Died. Remember Us,'" *Washington Post*, November 11, 1979: B4.

24 **Archibald MacLeish poem**: Archibald MacLeish, "The Young Dead Soldiers Do Not Speak," Washington, 1940, Library of Congress, accessed December 8, 2016, https://www.loc.gov/item/rbpe.24204400.

25 **Chorlton, "If the memorial is to serve any purpose at all"**: Tom Chorlton, "Victims of War," *Washington Post*, November 30, 1979: A14.

25 **Suggestion memorial be at Arlington Cemetery**: Scruggs and Swerdlow, *To Heal a Nation*, 15.

26   **History of Constitution Gardens**: History & Culture, Constitution Gardens, National Park Service, accessed January 10, 2017, https://www.nps.gov/coga/learn/historyculture/index.htm; Kay Fanning, US Commission of Fine Arts, interview with the author, 2015.

26–27   **Joint resolution approving the building of a memorial**: A joint resolution to authorize the Vietnam Veterans Memorial Fund, Inc. to erect a memorial. S. J. Res 119, 96th Cong. (1979–1980); Joint Resolution to authorize the Vietnam Veterans Memorial Fund, Inc., to establish a memorial, Pub. L. 96–297, 94 Stat. 827 (1980).

27   **J. Carter Brown's letter on Constitution Gardens**: Letter from J. Carter Brown to Ronald Peterson, Assistant Director, Legislative Reference, regarding S. Res 119, February 22, 1980. US Commission of Fine Arts.

27   **Carter signs bill authorizing memorial**: Memo, Al McDonald, Gordon Stewart, and Achsah Nesmith to President Jimmy Carter, July 1, 1980, "7/1/80" folder, Container 168, Records of the Office of the Staff Secretary, Presidential Files, Jimmy Carter Library.

27   **Clergyman's invocation at consecration of Constitution Gardens**: Transcript from *60 Minutes*, volume XV, number 4, broadcast October 10, 1982, page 8, VVMF Records, LCMD.

27   **Scruggs call to Perot**: Chronology of H. Ross Perot's involvement with the Vietnam Veterans Memorial Fund, box 32, Vietnam Veterans Memorial Fund records, 1965–1994, Library of Congress Manuscript Division, Washington, DC. See also Doubek, *Creating the VVM*, 56.

28   **H. Ross Perot's attempts to rescue POWs in Vietnam and EDS employees in Iran**: Gerald Posner, *Citizen Perot: His Life and Times* (New York: Random House, 1996): pp. 100–122.

28   **Senator Warner's breakfast**: Scruggs and Swerdlow, *To Heal a Nation*, p. 21; Warner in film, "The Story of the Vietnam Veterans Memorial—The last landing zone," directed and produced by Bob Muller, 1994. Library of Congress Motion Picture Division, Washington, DC.

28   **Warner dinner at Pension Building**: Phil McCombs, "War in Memories: Gathering to Honor Vietnam's Soldiers," *Washington Post*, October 13, 1980: B1, B9.

29   **Perot, "You take these young guys out"**: McCombs, "War in Memories," B9.

29   **Elizabeth Taylor and the blonde**: McCombs, "War in Memories," B1, B9; Doubek, *Creating the VVM*, 107–108.

29   **"If they'd given him what he wanted over there"**: McCombs, "War in Memories," B9.

30   **Scruggs, "I basically think that the war was a serious mistake"**: McCombs, "War in Memories," B9.

30   **Jim Webb, "The key thing that's been missing is simply according to the people who served, the dignity of their experience"**: McCombs, "War in Memories," B9.

30   **Webb's book given as prizes at fundraiser**: Statement by Jim Webb, page 3, enclosed in letter from Webb to Jan Scruggs, January 17, 1984, VVMF Records, LCMD.

30   **Funds raised at Pension Building event**: Doubek, *Creating the VVM*, 108.

Chapter Three

31   **Mood of the Yale campus, 1967–1980**: Andrus Burr, interview with the author and subsequent email exchanges, August 8, 2015.

32   **Barry Commoner**: Paul J. Bass, "A clever cover-up of the Iranian crackdown," *Yale Daily News*, September 22, 1980: 3; John B. Harris, "Commoner Asks Iran Ties Be Resumed," *Hartford Courant*, September 17, 1980: A14.

32   **Casualties between 1967 and 1969**: Statistical information about casualties of the Vietnam War, Vietnam Conflict Extract Data File of the Defense Casualty Analysis System (DCAS) Extract Files, National Archives and Records Administration, accessed January 10, 2017, https://www.archives.gov/research/military/vietnam-war/casualty-statistics.html.

32   **National protests**: James Doyle, "100,000 March in War Protest," *Boston Globe*, October 22, 1967: 1; Richard Harwood, "Largest Rally in Washington History Demands Rapid End to Vietnam War," *Washington Post*, November 16, 1969, 1.

32   **William Sloan Coffin, Jr.**: author recollections and Paul Moore, "Coffin Gives Yale CO's Sanctuary," *Yale Daily News*, October 3, 1967: 1.

32   **May 1970 protests at Yale**: Stuart Rosow, "SDS Protestors Fail to Stop US Marine Recruiting Squad," *Yale Daily News*, February 18, 1970: 1; "Weekend of Demonstrations Ends with Second Night of Disorder" and "May Day Mixes Many Moods," *Yale Daily News*, May 4, 1970: 1; "Study Options: More Attend Class," *Yale Daily News*, May 7, 1970: 1; Warren Goldstein, *William Sloan Coffin, Jr.: A Holy Impatience*

(New Haven: Yale University Press, 2004), 256. For other campus protests, see: Robb Baker, "Columbia U Students Cut Their Classes, Call Off Activity for Rest of Year," *Chicago Tribune*, May 10, 1970: 26; Parker Donham, "300 Occupy Harvard . . . For Five Hours," *Boston Globe*, April 22, 1969: 1; "Nation Picks Up Pieces at Kent State Seeking to Find Causes of Death," *Hartford Courant*, May 10, 1970: 28A, 35.

33   **More on William Sloan Coffin, Jr.**: Fred P. Graham, "Spock, Coffin Indicted for Activity Against Draft," *New York Times*, January 6, 1968: 1; "U.S. Court Overturns Conviction of Spock," *Chicago Tribune*, July 12, 1969: W1; "The New Man at Riverside," *Hartford Courant*, August 16, 1977: 14.

33   **Bobby Seale**: Robert Enstad and Robert Davis, "Seale is Bound, Gagged as He Disrupts Trial," *Chicago Tribune*, October 30, 1969: 1; William Chapman, "Seale Is Held in Contempt, Gets 4 Years," *Washington Post*, November 6, 1969: A1; John Darnton, "New Haven Is Looking with Foreboding to the Murder Trial of Bobby Seale," *New York Times*, March 22, 1970: 57; Trudy Rubin, "Yale Moves to Damp Seale Trial Tensions," *Christian Science Monitor*, April 30, 1970: 1, 14; "Chicago 7 Principals Plan Seale Vigil in New Haven," *Hartford Courant*, May 19, 1971: 42A; "The Seale Case—A Chronology," *Boston Globe*, November 14, 1971: B1.

33   **Coffin, "All of us conspired to bring on this tragedy"**: Warren Goldstein, *William Sloane Coffin, Jr.: A Holy Impatience* (New Haven: Yale University Press, 2004), 254.

33   **Crosby, Stills, Nash, and Young song, "Chicago"**: "Mr. Fish in Conversation with Graham Nash," Truthdig.com, April 3, 2010, accessed December 12, 2016, http://www.truthdig.com/report/item/an_interview_with_graham_nash_20100403.

34   **1977 strike at Yale**: Ruth Marcus, David Berreby, and David Lauter, "Workers vote to end strike," *Yale Daily News*, December 19, 1977: 1.

34   **Professor Burr's summer, 1980 and funerary architecture course**: Andrus Burr, interview with the author, 2015.

34   **Inscription on Oscar Wilde's tomb**: Richard Ellman, *Oscar Wilde* (New York: Alfred A. Knopf, 1988), 588–589.

37   **Spreiregen and the competition**: Paul Spreiregen, interview with the author, July 20, 2015. On Spreiregen, see also: Doubek, *Creating the VVM*, 86; Scruggs and Swerdlow, *To Heal a Nation*, 50; Sarah Rowley, "Investing in the Future: A Gift to Ennoble Everyday Life," *PLAN* 65 (August 2006).

37 **Selecting jurors**: Doubek, *Creating the VVM*, 93–94; Paul Goldberger, "Pietro Belluschi, 94, an Architect of Major Urban Buildings, Dies," *New York Times*, February 16, 1994: A19; Julie V. Iovine, "Garrett Eckbo is Dead at 89; Pioneer of Modern Landscape," *New York Times*, June 18, 2000: 32; Anne Raver, "Hideo Sasaki, 80, Influential Landscape Architect, Dies," *New York Times*, September 25, 2000: B9.

37–38 **Design competition rules**: The Vietnam Veterans Memorial Design Competition, VVMF Records, LCMD; Doubek, *Creating the VVM*, 95–96, 114, 121; Scruggs and Swerdlow, *To Heal a Nation*, 53; Paul Spreiregen, interview with the author, July 2015.

38 **Burr's class assignments and jury process**: Andrus Burr, interview with the author; email from Andrus Burr to the author, September 28, 2016.

38 **Maya Lin's development of her idea**: Maya Lin, *Boundaries* (New York: Simon and Schuster, 2000): 4:10 –4:11.

38 **Lin, "Some people were playing Frisbee that day"**: Phil McCombs, "Maya Lin and the Great Call of China," *Washington Post*, January 3, 1982: F11.

40 **Burr's bitterness**: Letter from Andrus Burr to Robert Doubek, July 29, 2002, US Commission of Fine Arts.

41 **Questions from entrants**: Typed document by design competition staff listing entrants' questions and subsequent answers, VVMF Records, LCMD.

42–43 **Competition submissions**: Library of Congress Prints and Photographs Division, Washington, DC.

45 **Von Eckardt's comment about the design submissions ("architectural stunts to sculptural theatrics")**: Wolf Von Eckardt, "Storm over a Viet Nam Memorial," *Time*, November 9, 1981.

45 **Jury deliberations**: Letter from Grady Clay to James Watt, December 1, 1981, U.S. Commission of Fine Arts; Paul Spreiregen, interview with the author, July 2015; Grady Clay, "The art of choice," *Harvard Magazine* (1985): 56A–H; Doubek, *Creating the VVM*, 119, 121–122; Scruggs and Swerdlow, *To Heal a Nation*, 58, 62.

45 **"an expression of human tragedy" and "forward to life"**: Grady Clay, "Jury comments," VVMF Records, LCMD.

46 **"I think there are several that might just work!"**: Paul Spreiregen, interview with the author, July 2015.

46 **Anecdote about Rosati finding a signature**: Clay, "The art of choice," 56F; Interview with Grady Clay, January 25, 2003, Oldham

County Veterans Oral History Project, Louie B. Nunn Center for Oral History, University of Kentucky Libraries.

46 **Hart/Brown third place finish:** Joseph E. Brown, interview with the author, February 23, 2016; Frederick Hart and Joseph E. Brown, Design drawing for the Vietnam Veterans Memorial, 1980, in the collection of Michael Vergason; Doubek, *Creating the VVM*, 127.

47 **Krosinsky second place finish**: full boards, Library of Congress Prints and Photographs Division, Washington, DC; Doubek, *Creating the VVM*, 127.

48 **Lin's design as "naïve"**: Lin, *Boundaries*, 4:12.

49 **Quotation's from Lin's statement**: Maya Lin, Design drawing for the Vietnam Veterans Memorial, 1980, Library of Congress Prints and Photographs Division, Washington, DC. Reprinted in Lin, *Boundaries*, 4:05.

49 **Clay calls Lin's design "sketchy"**: Interview with Grady Clay, January 25, 2003, Oldham County Veterans Oral History Project.

49 **"Deceptive simplicity" of Lin's design**: Clay, "The art of choice," 56F.

49–50 **Jurors' comments on Lin's design**: Grady Clay, "Jury comments," VVMF Records, LCMD; Grady Clay to James C. Watt, secretary of the Interior, December 1, 1981; Doubek, *Creating the VVM*, 127–128.

50 **Belluschi comments on Lin's design (a family's background "has a way to penetrate and show in her work")**: McCombs, "Maya Lin and the Great Call of China," F9–F10.

51 **Antoine de Saint-Exupéry**: Antoine de Saint-Exupéry, *Terre des Hommes* (Paris: Gallimard, 1939), 60.

Chapter Four

52 **"We believe it should be built as designed"**: Grady Clay to James C. Watt, secretary of the Interior, December 1, 1981.

52 **Planning announcement of the winning design**: Paul Spreiregen, interview with the author, July 2015; Paul Goldberger, "Vietnam War Memorial to Capture Anguish," *New York Times*, June 6, 1981: 7.

53 **Scruggs, "I like it"**: Doubek, *Creating the VVM*, 129; Scruggs and Swerdlow, *To Heal a Nation*, 66.

53 **Wheeler, "I think it is a work of genius"**: Scruggs and Swerdlow, *To Heal a Nation*, 65.

53 **Scruggs's worries**: Mock, *Lin: A Strong Clear Vision*; Scruggs and Swerdlow, *To Heal a Nation*, 64–66.

54   **Colonel Schaet tells Lin she won**: Lin, *Boundaries*, 4:12; Mock, *Lin: A Strong Clear Vision*; Doubek, *Creating the VVM*, 116.

54   **Joseph Brown wants to know if he should prepare acceptance speech**: Paul Spreiregen, interview with the author, July 2015; Doubek, *Creating the VVM*, 132.

54   **Harry Weese offers to build models of Lin's design**: Paul Spreiregen, interview with the author, July 2015.

55   **"It has to be love at first sight" and reaction from Lin ("You have changed my design!")**: Paul Spreiregen, interview with the author, July 2015.

55–56   **Von Eckhart and Martin meeting with Lin**: Judith Martin, interview with the author, 2015.

56   **Scene at announcement**: Film footage of the announcement, Library of Congress Motion Picture Division; Mock, *Lin: A Strong Clear Vision*; Doubek, *Creating the VVM*, 131–133.

57   **Weaknesses of Hart/Brown design**: Joseph Brown, interview with the author, 2016.

58   **"Student Wins Vietnam Memorial Contest" headline**: Don Shannon, "Student Wins Vietnam Memorial Contest," *Los Angeles Times*, May 7, 1981: E11.

58   **"For the dead whom few wanted to remember"**: Henry Allen, "Epitaph for Vietnam: Memorial Design Is Selected," *Washington Post*, May 7, 1981: F1, F3.

58–59   **Maya Lin family background**: Donald Langmead, *Maya Lin: A Biography* (Santa Barbara: Greenwood, 2011), 1–9, 11, 28–29, 31–34, 60; Maya Lin, interview by Bill Moyers, *Becoming American: The Chinese Experience*, Public Affairs Television, March 2003, accessed February 6, 2017, http://www.pbs.org/becomingamerican/ap_pjourneys_transcript5 _print.html; McCombs, "Maya Lin and the Great Call of China," F9; Maya Lin, interview with the Academy of Achievement, June 16, 2000, last modified January 17, 2017, accessed February 6, 2017, http://www .achievement.org/achiever/maya-lin/#interview; Lin, *Boundaries*, p. 4: 10–4:12.

59   **Lin, "I've been an artist from probably the first time I stepped into my dad's ceramics studio"**: Lin, interview by Bill Moyers, 2003.

61   **Thiepval Memorial's "yawning archway"**: Lin, *Boundaries*, 4:11.

61   **Popularity of Vincent Scully's class at Yale**: Paul Spreiregen, interview with the author, July 2015.

61   **Experience in Denmark**: Lin, interview by Bill Moyers, 2003.

61   **"No matter how long you've been here"**: Lin, interview by Bill Moyers, 2003.

62   **"All my artworks deal with nature and the environment"**: Lin, interview by Bill Moyers, 2003.

62   **"I imagined taking a knife and cutting into the earth"**: Lin, interview by Bill Moyers, 2003 and Lin, *Boundaries*, 4:10.

62   **"Literally as you read a name, and touch a name"**: Mock, *Lin: A Strong Clear Vision*.

62   **"The cost of war is these individuals"**: Mock, *Lin: A Strong Clear Vision*.

63   **The interface "between our world and the quieter, darker, more peaceful world beyond"**: Lin, *Boundaries*, 4:10.

63   **"I did not want to civilize war"**: Lin, *Boundaries*, 4:09.

63   **"That abstraction can be human and relate to you"**: Lin, interview by Bill Moyers, 2003.

63   **"It wasn't a politically glorified statement about war"**: Mock, *Lin: A Strong Clear Vision*.

63   **"Writing is one of the purest arts"**: Lin, interview by Bill Moyers, 2003.

64   **"I have just dealt with the facts"**: Lin, interview by Bill Moyers, 2003.

Chapter Five

67   **Reagan's speech**: Speech for the Veterans of Foreign Wars Convention, August 18, 1980. Ronald Reagan Presidential Library, accessed February 6, 2017, https://reaganlibrary.archives.gov/archives/reference/8.18.80.html.

68   **Harris Poll**: Louis Harris and Associates, *Myths and Realities: A Study of Attitudes Toward Vietnam Era Veterans* (Washington, DC: Veterans Administration, 1980), 91, table IV-5.

68   **James Watt and the Mall**: "Chronology of Events: Involvement of Secretary of Interior in Approval of Design," memo, VVMF Records, LCMD.

68   **Watt and the Beach Boys**: Phil McCombs and Richard Harrington, "Watt Sets Off Uproar with Ban on Music," *Washington Post*, April 7, 1983: A1, A17; Bob Cannon, "Beach Boys banned," *Entertainment Weekly*, April 9, 1993, accessed February 1, 2017, http://ew.com/article/1993/04/09/beach-boys-banned.

69 **Public reception**: Doubek, *Creating the VVM*, 136–137.

69 **Critical reception**: Paul Goldberger, "Vietnam War Memorial to Capture Anguish of a Decade of Doubt," *New York Times*, June 6, 1981: 7; Wolf Von Eckardt, "Of Heart & Mind: The Serene Grace of the Vietnam Memorial," *Washington Post*, May 16, 1981: B1, B4; Paul Gapp, "Clouds of Doubt Engulf Viet Nam Memorial," *Chicago Tribune*, June 28, 1981: D12; Paul Gapp, "Sculpture to Be Scuttled? Viet Memorial Fight Flares Up," *Chicago Tribune*, September 29, 1982: D1-D2; Raymond Coffey, "America's Neglected War Vets," *Chicago Tribune*, May 21, 1981: 19; Charles Krauthammer, "Washington Diarist: Memorials," *New Republic* 184, no. 21 (May 23, 1981): 43.

70 **Perot reaction**: Chronology of H. Ross Perot's involvement with VVMF, VVMF Records, LCMD; Doubek, *Creating the VVM*, 132; Scruggs and Swerdlow, *To Heal a Nation*, 67–68.

71 **Egg roll**: Patrick Hagopian, interview with the author, 2015.

71 **Lin's relationship to Spreiregen**: author interviews with Paul Spreiregen, July 2015; and Kent Cooper, March 2, 2016.

72 **"crawling back on my hands and knees"**: Lin, *Boundaries*, 4:13.

72 **Scully, "There's really nothing like it at all"**: Mock, *Lin: A Strong Clear Vision*.

72–73 **Lin and César Pelli**: César Pelli, interview with the author, 2015.

73 **Kent Cooper and Lin**: Kent Cooper, interview with the author, July 25, 2015.

73 **Cooper, "There hasn't been a commemorative piece before or after"**: Steve Davolt, "Edifice Rex: Architect Kent Cooper keeps coming up with new ideas to change D.C.'s attitude toward newfangled building design," *Washington Business Journal*, November 4, 2004, accessed February 1, 2017, http://www.bizjournals.com/washington/stories/2004/11/08/story8.html.

75 **Spreiregen, "working with Lin had no great appeal for me"**: Paul Spreiregen, notes from interviews with Kim Murphy, January 29 and February 2, 2007, for *The Wall: Twenty-Five Years of Healing and Education*, MT Publishing, 2007, page 17.

75 **Lin, "You have no responsibility for the memorial"**: Kent Cooper, interview with the author, July 25, 2015.

75 **"Maya did not walk away from Washington with a single friend"**: Paul Spreiregen, interview with the author, July 2015.

75 **Challenges of execution**: Cooper interview with the author, July 25, 2015; Lin, *Boundaries*, 4:13–4:14; Scruggs and Swerdlow, *To Heal a Nation*, 78–79; Lin, interview by Bill Moyers, 2003.

76 **Lin, "I knew that the timeline was key to the experience"**: Lin, *Boundaries*, 4:14.

76 **Problem of listing names in alphabetical order**: Scruggs and Swerdlow, *To Heal a Nation*, 78–79.

76 **Thickness of stone walls**: Kent Cooper, interview with the author, July 25, 2015; Lin, *Boundaries*, 4:14.

76 **Lin, "I always saw the wall as a pure surface"**: Lin, *Boundaries*, 4:14

76 **Lin on the color black**: Lin, *Boundaries*, 4:14; McCombs, "Maya Lin and the Great Call of China," *Washington Post*, F10.

77 **Lin's later statement that the memorial was not just for veterans**: Maya Lin, interview on the *Today Show*, July 12, 1982. Transcript, page 2, VVMF Records, LCMD.

77 **Lin on her political beliefs**: Lin, *Boundaries*, 4:14.

77 **J. Carter Brown**: Neil Harris, *Capital Culture: J. Carter Brown, the National Gallery, and the Reinvention of the Museum Experience* (Chicago: University of Chicago Press, 2013), 8, 18, 20, 27, 160, 191–218, 257; Michael Kimmelman, "J. Carter Brown, 67, Is Dead; Transformed Museum World," *New York Times*, June 19, 2002: A1, C14.

77–78 **Brown as "arbiter of excellence"**: Scruggs and Swerdlow, *To Heal a Nation*, 73.

78 **US Commission of Fine Arts Meeting, July 7, 1981**: Transcript and Minutes of the U.S. Commission of Fine Arts (CFA), July 7, 1981; Doubek, *Creating the VVM*, 144.

78 **Lin, "Walking through this park-like area, the memorial appears as a rift in the earth"**: Lin, *Boundaries*, 4:05.

78 **Excerpt from Lin's journal ("Fine Arts went superbly")**: McCombs, "Maya Lin and the Great Call of China," F12.

79 **Scott Brewer's statement ("abstract, anonymous, inconspicuous")**: Scott Brewer, "Statement Delivered before the Commission of Fine Arts on July 7, 1981, in Washington, DC," Minutes, CFA, July 7, 1981.

79 **Brown on Lin's design (Nobility "is the great hallmark of this design")**: Transcript, CFA, July 7, 1981, 31–32.

Chapter Six

81 **Lin/Cooper collaboration**: Kent Cooper, interview with the author, July 25, 2015.

81 **Flap over inscriptions**: Lin, *Boundaries*, 4:14; Doubek, *Creating the Vietnam Memorial*, 155; Kent Cooper, interview with the author, July 25, 2015; Scruggs and Swerdlow, *To Heal a Nation*, 79–80.

83 **Egg field in Austin**: Susan Duffy, "The Egg War," *Texas Monthly* (March 1980), 136–148; Statement by Jim Webb, page 3, VVMF Records, LCMD.

84–85 **Wheeler vs. Webb**: Doubek, *Creating the VVM*, 171–174; Patrick Hagopian, *The Vietnam War in American Memory: Veterans, Memorials, and the Politics of Healing* (Amherst: University of Massachusetts Press, 2009), 106; Statement by Jim Webb, page 6, VVMF Records, LCMD.

86 **Tom Carhart's background**: Doubek, *Creating the VVM*, 57, 159.

86 **Carhart did not expect to win the competition**: Tom Carhart, "Statement to the U.S. Fine Arts Commission, 13 October, 1981," Minutes, CFA, October 13, 1981.

86 **Carhart calls Lin a "gook"**: Doubek, *Creating the VVM*, 159.

86 **"Fucking gook"**: Carlton Sherwood called Lin a "fucking gook." Statement by David Christian, September 23, 1983, enclosed in a letter from Terrence O'Donnell, Williams & Connolly, to George R. Clark, Pierson, Ball & Dowd, Sherwood's lawyer, November 7, 1983. VVMF Records, LCMD.

86 **The South Boston memorial**: Myra McPherson, "Taps in Southie: South Boston's Homage to its Vietnam Dead," *Washington Post*, September 15, 1981: D1, D8; Joan Vennochi, "A monument in Southie: Viet Dead Remembered," *Boston Globe*, September 14, 1981: 1, 20; "Southie and Vietnam," *Boston Globe*, September 27, 1981: A6.

87 **Statistics about Harvard student casualties**: Mary Preston, Harvard Alumni Office, interview with the author.

87 ***National Review* article ("If the current model has to be built, stick it off in some tidal flat")**: "Stop That Monument," *National Review* 33, no. 18 (September 18, 1981): 1064.

88 **Webb letter to Commission of Fine Arts**: Letter from James Webb to Members of the U.S. Fine Arts Commission, October 12, 1981. Minutes, CFA, October 13, 1981.

89 **Selection of granite**: Doubek, *Creating the VVM*, 161, 182, 286; Lin, *Boundaries*, 4:15; Transcript, CFA, October 13, 1981.

89   **"black hole of Calcutta"**: 129 Cong. Rec. 2254 (February 15, 1983).

89   **Carhart's testimony ("black gash of shame and sorrow")**: Tom Carhart, "Statement to the U.S. Fine Arts Commission, October 13, 1981," Minutes, CFA, October 13, 1981.

89   **Scruggs's testimony**: Transcript, CFA, October 13, 1981, 49–54.

90   **Brown's testimony**: Transcript, CFA, October 13, 1981, 45–48.

91   **Fallout from the October 13 meeting**: "If you didn't support the memorial you were crazy," Statement by Jim Webb, page 9, VVMF Records, LCMD; "the Army's lowest award for valor," Letter from James Webb to Jan Scruggs, December 11, 1984; "a cocky platoon leader," Letter from Jan Scruggs to Jim Webb, December 18, 1984; "My men nominated me for every award I received," Letter from James Webb to Jan Scruggs, undated. VVMF Records, LCMD.

91   **Carhart's editorial**: Tom Carhart, "A Better Way to Honor Viet Vets," *Washington Post*, November 16, 1981: C5.

91   **Webb's editorial ("a wailing wall for future anti-draft and anti-nuclear demonstrations")**: James H. Webb, Jr., "Reassessing the Vietnam Veterans Memorial," *Wall Street Journal*, December 18, 1981.

92   **Questioning Eckbo's past**: Doubek, *Creating the VVM*, 171, 198; "pro-Viet Cong movement," Hagopian, 174.

93   **Pat Buchanan article**: Patrick Buchanan, "An insulting memorial," *Chicago Tribune*, December 26, 1981: A11.

93   **Perot "folding [his] tent"**: Chronology of H. Ross Perot's involvement with the VVMF, VVMF Records, LCMD; Hagopian, 114; Doubek, *Creating the VVM*, 178.

93   **"We could argue aesthetics forever"**: Editorial, *Cleveland Plain Dealer*, November 1981.

93   **William Greider article ("neutral and soft-spoken monument")**: William Greider, "Memories That Shape Our Futures," *Washington Post*, November 8, 1981, C1–2.

94   **James J. Kilpatrick, "Far from being an outrage"**: James J. Kilpatrick, "Letters: Vietnam War Memorial," *National Review* 33, no. 20 (October 6, 1981): 1170.

94   **Kilpatrick, "This will be the most moving war memorial ever erected"**: James J. Kilpatrick, "Finally We Honor the Vietnam Dead," *Washington Post*, November 11, 1981: A2.

94   **Excerpts from Lin's journal ("Beginning to vanquish the devils")**: McCombs, "Maya Lin and the Great Call of China," F1.

95   **Henry Hyde**: Doubek, *Creating the VVM*, 183, 186; Letter from
      Henry Hyde to Republican Congressmen, December 30, 1981, VVMF
      Records, LCMD; Scruggs and Swerdlow, *To Heal a Nation*, 87.

95   **Hyde, "War memorials may be too important"**: Doubek, *Creating
      the VVM*, 204.

95   **Letter from Henry Hyde to President Ronald Reagan**: January 12,
      1982. VVMF Records, LCMD.

Chapter Seven

96–97 **Hart's early years**: Frederick Turner et al., *Frederick Hart: The Com-
       plete Works* (Louisville, Butler Books: 2007), 283–284; Michael Novak
       et al., *Frederick Hart: Changing Tides* (New York: Hudson Hills Press,
       2005), 170–171; Homan Potterton et al., *Frederick Hart: Sculptor* (New
       York: Hudson Hills Press, 1994), 19–20; Lindy Hart, interview with
       the author, March 31, 2016.

97   **Hart, "the best experience of my learning life"**: Homan Potterton,
       "Metamorphosis: Stone Carver to Artist," in Potterton, *Hart: Sculptor*, 19.

97–98 **His anti-war activities**: Lindy Hart, interview with the author, 2017.

99   **Cathedral design competition and *Ex Nihilo***: Mary Yakush and Erik
       Vochinsky, "Washington National Cathedral: The Creation of Fred-
       erick Hart's Personal Style" in Novak, *Hart: Changing Tides*, 20; Pot-
       terton, "Metamorphosis: Stone Carver to Artist" in Potterton, *Hart:
       Sculptor*, 20, 26; Frederick Turner, "On *Ex Nihilo*" in Turner, *Hart: The
       Complete Works*, 17–28; Sarah Booth Conroy, "A Genesis in Stone,"
       Horizon 22, no. 9 (September 1979): 28–37.

99   **"I don't think of myself as an architectural sculptor"**: Potterton,
       "Metamorphosis: Stone Carver to Artist," in *Hart: Sculptor*, 32.

99   **Comparing *Ex Nihilo* to Jean Delville**: Craig McPherson, interview
       with the author.

99   **Creation myth of Pierre Teilhard de Chardin**: Michael Novak,
       "Beauty is Truth: The Changing of the Tides" in Novak, *Hart: Chang-
       ing Tides*, 7.

99   **Conversion to Catholicism**: Chronology in Turner, *Hart: The Com-
       plete Works*, 286–287.

99   **Rev. Dr. Stephen Happel's eulogy**: "A Memorial Tribute," in Novak,
       Hart: Changing Tides, 215.

100   **Duration of work on *Ex Nihilo***: Michael Kernan, "Re-Creating the
       Creation in Just 4 Years," *Washington Post*, February 12, 1982: C7.

100   **Hart looking for his next project, reading Scruggs's column**: Jan Scruggs, interview with the author, January 19, 2017.

101   *National Geographic* **article on National Cathedral featuring Hart**: Robert Paul Jordan, "Washington Cathedral: 'House of Prayer for All People,'" *National Geographic* 157, no. 4 (April 1980): 552–555, 561–573.

101   **July 1979 dinner with Wolf von Eckhart**: Judith Martin, interview with the author, January 19, 2016.

101   **Hart never imagined he would have to compete**: Lindy Hart, interview with the author, 2016.

101   **Hart/Brown submission**: Joseph Brown and Michael Vergason, interview with the author, 2016.

101   **Hart felt there was a way to get back in the game**: Lindy Hart, interview with the author, 2016.

102   **"It's like everything is up in my head," "Everyone thinks I'm morbid," and journal excerpts**: McCombs, "Maya Lin and the Great Call of China," F1, F9–F12.

102   **Lin appeared in gossip columns**: Doubek, *Creating the VVM*, 184.

102   **Lin, "I knew what he meant"**: McCombs, "Maya Lin and the Great Call of China," F11.

102   **"An Asian artist for an Asian war"**: McCombs, "Maya Lin and the Great Call of China," F9.

103   **Veterans wished they could control Lin's press access**: Doubek, *Creating the VVM*, 184.

103   **Jim Webb remark about scorpions in a jar**: Statement by Jim Webb, page 10, VVMF Records, LCMD.

104   **Phyllis Schlafly column**: Phyllis Schlafly, "Viet Memorial Insults Vets," *San Gabriel Valley Tribune*, January 11, 1982.

104   **James J. Kilpatrick accuses Buchanan of taking cheap shots**: James J. Kilpatrick, "In the Eye of the Beholder," *The Sun*, January 14, 1982: A15.

104   **Westmoreland's support of the design**: on book royalties, see Hagopian, 117; letter from Westmoreland to James Webb quoted by Scruggs in Jan C. Scruggs, "In Defense of the Vietnam Veterans Memorial," *Wall Street Journal*, January 14, 1982.

104   **Perot's poll**: Hagopian, 125; Statement by Jim Webb, page 12, VVMF Records, LCMD.

104   **Perot demands an audit of the VVMF**: Doubek, *Creating the VVM*, 178, 187, 190, 217.

105 **White House discussions, including National Security Council memo ("A role other than that of a 'fair arbiter'")**: Hagopian, 113, 114, 116–117, 121–122; "Present Status of Vietnam Veterans Memorial," December 11, 1981, and note from Craig L. Fuller to Mike Deaver, December 19, 1981, VVMF Records, LCMD.

105 **Scruggs, "Some liked it. Some did not."**: Scruggs and Swerdlow, *To Heal a Nation*, 97.

105 **Ashbrook letter to Reagan**: Rep. John M. Ashbrook to Ronald W. Reagan, January 27, 1982, casefile 057761, Ronald Reagan Presidential Library. Quoted in Hagopian, 116.

106 **Watt, "an act of treason"**: Philip Geyelin, "The Vietnam Memorial (Cont'd.?)," *Washington Post*, January 11, 1983: A15.

106 **Meeting on January 27, 1982, and the proposed compromise**: Milt Copulos, "Background to Betrayal: Viet Vets Want Their Memorial Back," Soldier of Fortune (May 1983): 18–21, 85–88; Doubek, *Creating the VVM*, 191–194; Hagopian, 119–120; Scruggs and Swerdlow, *To Heal a Nation*, 99–101; Jan Scruggs, interview with the author, January 19, 2016.

107 **Price on the color black**: Doubek, *Creating the VVM*, 193; Scruggs and Swerdlow, *To Heal a Nation*, 100. General Price was the brother of the opera singer Leontyne Price.

108 **Perot, "A statue for the living and a wall for the dead"**: Doubek, *Creating the VVM*, 194.

108 **Scruggs and his colleagues had been outmaneuvered**: Scruggs and Swerdlow, *To Heal a Nation*, 101.

109 **Press release from Senator John Warner**: "Vietnam Veterans' War Memorial Compromise Reached, Warner Says," Press release from Senator John Warner's office, March 24, 1982.

109 **Lin and Cooper respond to compromise**: Kent Cooper, interview with the author, July 25, 2015; Doubek, *Creating the VVM*, 195.

109 **"Patriotic claptrap"**: Scruggs and Swerdlow, *To Heal a Nation*, 106.

109 **"Aesthetically, the design does not need a statue"**: Scruggs and Swerdlow, *To Heal a Nation*, 101.

Chapter Eight

110 **"Maudlin" changes to the memorial; Weese, "Putting these elements in that design is a spoiled brat approach"**: "Critics of Viet Memorial Demand Serviceman Statue and Flagpole," *AIA Journal* 71, no. 4 (April 1982): 46, 52.

110 **"Monumental absurdity"**: Benjamin Forgey, "Monumental 'Absurdity,'" *Washington Post*, March 6, 1982: C5.

110 **"Commemorating the war in Vietnam is likely no simpler than fighting it"**: Rick Horowitz, "A Vietnam Epitaph," *Boston Globe*, April 4, 1982: SM13.

111 **Cooper, a statue "tends to weaken the powerful formality—the necessary inhumanity—of the memorial"**: Doubek, *Creating the VVM*, 213.

111 **Cooper's long summer**: Kent Cooper, interview with author, July 25, 2015.

111 **Outcome of the Warner compromise**: Doubek, *Creating the VVM*, 198, 202; Scruggs and Swerdlow, *To Heal a Nation*, 105–106.

111 **Watt responds**: Doubek, *Creating the VVM*, 201; Hagopian, 126–127; Scruggs and Swerdlow, *To Heal a Nation*, 106–107.

111 **A sculpture that would be "prideful, but not glorify the war"**: Scruggs and Swerdlow, *To Heal a Nation*, 115.

111 **There should be "artistic tension"**: Statement by Jim Webb, page 16, VVMF Records, LCMD.

111 **Sculpture panel**: Doubek, *Creating the VVM*, 211–213; Hagopian, 127; Scruggs and Swerdlow, *To Heal a Nation*, 115; Lindy Hart, interview with the author, 2016; Joseph Brown, interview with the author, 2016; Statement by Jim Webb, page 14, VVMF Records, LCMD.

112 **Hart's selection as sculptor**: "Sculptor Is Selected for Vietnam Statue," *New York Times*, July 2, 1982: A12; Milt Copulos, "Background to Betrayal: Viet Vets Want Their Memorial Back," Soldier of Fortune (May 1983): 86; Doubek, *Creating the VVM*, 212–213.

112 **Hart approach to his commission**: Lindy Hart, interview with the author, 2016.

113 **Hart and Cooper**: Kent Cooper, interview with the author

113 **"They emerge from a thicket"**: Doubek, *Creating the VVM*, 213.

113 **Webb's understanding of the January 27 compromise agreement**: Remarks of Jim Webb, press conference of 4 November, 1982. VVMF Records, LCMD.

113 **Lin, "This farce has gone on too long"**: Rick Horowitz, "Maya Lin's Angry Objections: Vietnam Memorial Artist on Changes: 'This Farce Has Gone on Too Long,'" *Washington Post*, July 7, 1982: B1, B6.

114 **Lin, "It's a question of who 'they' are"**: Lin, interview on the *Today Show*, 1982, 1. VVMF Records, LCMD.

114 **Lin, "I designed something—it's not mine":** Lin, interview on the *Today Show*, 1982, 2. VVMF Records, LCMD.

114 **Lin's legal representation:** Doubek, *Creating the VVM*, 229.

115 **"one hundred percent better" and Weese's Michelangelo quip:** Isabel Wilkerson, "'Art War' Erupts Over Vietnam Veterans Memorial," *Washington Post*, July 8, 1982: D3.

115 **"Instead of a daringly simple memorial":** Greer B. Gilka, letter to the editor, "Decisions and Revisions: The Vietnam Memorial," *Washington Post*, July 12, 1982: A14.

115 **"A memorial to the indecision, political meddling, and lack of principle":** Chips Johnson, letter to the editor, "Vietnam Memorial: Drawing the Line," *Washington Post*, July 17, 1982: A22.

115 **A grove of weeping willows: Rose Wilson, letter to the editor, "Vietnam Memorial: Drawing the Line,"** *Washington Post*, July 17, 1982: A22.

115 **"A great privy, an outside urinal":** David De Vaull, letter to the editor, "Vietnam Memorial: Drawing the Line," *Washington Post*, July 17, 1982: A22.

115 **Robert Lawrence response ("ill conceived," "breach of faith"):** "Viet Memorial Designer, AIA Strongly Denounce Alterations," *AIA Journal* 71, no. 9 (August 1982): 9–10.

115 **Lin, "It really fits in":** "Personalities," *Washington Post*, July 13, 1982: C2.

116 **Cooper and Brown contention over placement of statue:** Kent Cooper, interview with the author, July 25, 2015.

116 **Kilpatrick moved ("nothing I had heard or written prepared me"):** James J. Kilpatrick, "The Names," *Washington Post*, September 21, 1982: A19.

116 **Hart's selection announced:** "Sculptor Is Selected for Vietnam Statue," *New York Times*, July 2, 1982: A12.

116 **Hart's fee:** Doubek, *Creating the VVM*, 215.

116 **"I realize that there is an existing design":** Kathryn Buxton, "Personalities," *Washington Post*, July 2, 1982: D2.

116 **Lin views Hart's maquette:** Doubek, *Creating the VVM*, 232.

116 **Unveiling of Hart's sculpture, September 20, 1982:** Benjamin Forgey, "Hart's Vietnam Statue Unveiled," *Washington Post*, September 21, 1982: B1, B4. video: "Compromise Statue Unveiled," VVMF, producer, Library of Congress Motion Picture, Broadcast, and Recorded Sound Division, Washington, DC.

117 Hart, "The gesture and expression of the figures are directed to the wall": Statement from Frederick Hart read to the US Commission of Fine Arts, October 20, 1982. Note this document is dated October 20, but was read from at the statue unveiling on September 20 and at the CFA meeting on October 13.

117 Sasaki, "Often works of other artists, if sensitively done, enhance the totality of the design": Letter from Hideo Sasaki to Jan Scruggs, October 6, 1982, VVMF Records, LCMD.

117 Weese, "I view the adulteration of Maya Lin's design by any dissident group as arbitrary": Telegram from Harry Weese to the VVMF, copy of message sent to J. Carter Brown, October 13, 1982, VVMF Records, LCMD.

117 Paul Goldberger article ("It tries to shift this memorial away from its focus on the dead"): Paul Goldberger, "Vietnam Memorial: Questions of Architecture," New York Times, October 7, 1982: C25.

118 Response from Lin: Doubek, Creating the VVM, 234.

118 Dedication of Ex Nihilo: Joe Brown, "Behold, 'The Creation,'" Washington Post, October 4, 1982: C2.

118 Prince Philip attends the dedication of Ex Nihilo: Potterton, et al., Hart, Sculptor, 40.

118 60 Minutes broadcast: 60 Minutes, volume XV, number 4, broadcast October 10, 1982. Transcript, page 8, VVMF Records, LCMD.

119 Perot's Poll: "Most Ex-POWs Polled Dislike Vietnam War Memorial Design," Washington Post, Oct. 12, 1982

Chapter Nine

120 Tom Wolfe's Washington Post article: Tom Wolfe, "Art Disputes War: The Battle of the Vietnam Memorial," Washington Post, October 13, 1982:B1, B3–B4.

121 Lin's design as "skill-proof" and quotation of Tom Stoppard: Tom Wolfe, "The Artist the Art World Couldn't See," New York Times, January 2, 2000.

122–123 Comparing Hart to Giotto di Bondone and his work to that of Raymond Kaskey, Eric Parks, and Audrey Flack: Tom Wolfe, "The Idealist: A Commentary," in Potteron, Hart: Sculptor, 12–16.

123 A. E. Housman, "Here Dead Lie We": A. E. Housman, More Poems (London: Jonathan Cape, 1936), 54.

123 **US Commission of Fine Arts Meeting, October 13, 1982**: Transcript and Minutes, CFA, October 13, 1982.

124 **Hart's testimony**: Statement from Frederick Hart read to the US Commission of Fine Arts, October 20, 1982. See also, transcript, CFA, October 13, 1982, 66.

124 **Hodel's testimony**: Transcript, CFA, October 13, 1982, 87–90.

125 **Plan to site sculpture by tree line**: Transcript, CFA, October 13, 1982, 70–73.

125 **Cooper, "Aesthetics in itself is an important component message"**: Transcript, CFA, October 13, 1982, 68.

125 **Cooper, "powerful symbolic element"**: Transcript, CFA, October 13, 1982, 76.

125 **Cooper's argument against putting the flagpole near the wall**: Transcript, CFA, October 13, 1982, 77.

125 **Carhart's testimony**: Transcript, CFA, October 13, 1982, 138.

125 **General Price's testimony**: Transcript, CFA, October 13, 1982, 127.

125 **General Davison's testimony**: Transcript, CFA, October 13, 1982, 141.

126 **Bailey's testimony**: Transcript, CFA, October 13, 1982, 95–96.

126 **Lin's testimony**: Transcript, CFA, October 13, 1982, 152–154.

127 **Spreiregen's testimony**: Transcript, CFA, October 13, 1982, 166–172.

127 **Carter Brown's commentary**: Transcript, CFA, October 13, 1982, pages 7–10 after meeting reconvenes.

128 **Carter Brown says Hart saved the memorial**: J. Carter Brown, "Introduction," in Potterton, *Hart: Sculptor*, 11.

128 *US News and World Report*: "Vietnam Memorial: Peace at Last," *US News & World Report*, October 25, 1982: 12.

128–129 **ABC News *Nightline* broadcast**: ABC News *Nightline*, broadcast October 14, 1982. Transcript in VVMF Records, LCMD.

130 **Brown's summary of the CFA's decision**: J. Carter Brown, "The Vietnam Memorial Decision: 'Part of the Healing,'" *Washington Post*, October 16, 1982: A15.

130 **Letter from senators**: Senators Steven Symms, James A. McClure, John P. East, Chuck Grassley, Representatives Don Bailey, Larry E. Craig, Phil Crane, and Henry Hyde to James G. Watt, October 15, 1982, box 29, VVMF Records, LCMD.

131 **Letter from Lawrence**: Robert M. Lawrence to J. Carter Brown, October 20, 1982, VVMF Records, LCMD.

131   **Lin's design can survive additions**: Ralph Bennett, "Viet Nam Veterans Memorial: Abstract or Representational?" *Design Action* 1, no. 2 (November/December 1982): 5.

131   **J. Carter Brown and Secretary Watt meeting**: J. Carter Brown to Secretary James G. Watt, October 27, 1982 and Secretary James G. Watt to J. Carter Brown, November 24, 1982, VVMF Records, LCMD; Doubek, *Creating the VVM*, 251.

132   **Bailey urges Reagan to intervene**: Remarks by Congressman Don Bailey at press conference, November 4, 1982. VVMF Records, LCMD.

132   **Carhart "We fear that the black wall will be left on the field"**: November 4 Press Conference on Viet Vets' Memorial. VVMF Records, LCMD.

132   **Webb, "Like Moby Dick, this is more than a story about a whale"**: Remarks of James Webb, press conference of 4 November, 1982, 1–3. VVMF Records, LCMD.

133   **Webb on wearing his son's combat boots**: Robin Toner, "As Senator Falters, a Democrat Rises in Virginia," *New York Times*, September 18, 2006.

134   **Maya Lin's acknowledgment of naiveté**: Lin, *Boundaries*, 4:17.

Chapter Ten

135   **Lin and Grady Clay at memorial**: Clay, "The art of choice," 56H.

136   **"Is this the best they can do?"**: Dick Manuel, interview with the author, 2016.

136   **Lin on seeing the memorial**: Lin, *Boundaries*, 4:16.

136   **"Why did you do such a thing? This memorial is to you, not to us!"**: Clay, "The art of choice," 56H.

136   **"Why didn't you put in a flag? Why did you try to bury us?"**: Bob Brewin, "Laying the War to Rest," *Village Voice*, November 23, 1982: 30–31.

136   **Celebrating at the Cosmos Club**: Doubek, *Creating the VVM*, 262.

136   **Copulos's editorial**: Milt Copulos, "An Effort to Victimize Vietnam Vets One Last Time," *Washington Times*, November 12, 1982.

137   **Copulos talks about blowing up the memorial**: Doubek, *Creating the VVM*, 254–255, 262.

137   **Threatening call to the VVMF offices**: Scruggs and Swerdlow, *To Heal a Nation*, 135.

137 **Carhart talks about blowing up the memorial**: Doubek, *Creating the VVM*, 254.

137 **National Salute**: Francis X. Clines, "Tribute to Vietnam Dead: Words, a Wall," *New York Times*, November 11, 1982: A1, B15; Doubek, *Creating the VVM*, 259–261, 264; Scruggs and Swerdlow, *To Heal a Nation*, 141–151.

138 **McGrory piece**: Mary McGrory, "Remembering the fallen," *Boston Globe*, November 10, 1982: 23.

138 **Lin, "a parade would not, in the long term, help them overcome the enormous trauma"**: Lin, *Boundaries*, 4:16.

138 **The parade and the dedication ceremony**: film footage, "Maya Lin: A Strong, Clear Vision"; Kenneth Bredemeier, "Preparations for Salute to Vietnam Vets Nearly Done," *Washington Post*, November 9, 1982: B1, B3; Judy Mann, "Remembering," *Washington Post*, November 12, 1982: C1; Doubek, *Creating the VVM*, 264–266; Scruggs and Swerdlow, *To Heal a Nation*, 150–152; Phil McCombs, "Veterans Honor the Fallen, Mark Reconciliation," *Washington Post*, November 14, 1982: A1.

138 **Westmoreland libel suit**: Laura A. Kiernan, "Westmoreland Accuses CBS of Libel in $120 Million Suit," *Washington Post*, September 14, 1982: A1, A12.

139 **Bu Dop**: Bu Dop is a village and encampment, 90 km. north of Saigon close to the Cambodian border. A fierce battle took place there on November 29–30, 1967. Neil Henry, "Reunion: Joined in Soul by Vietnam," *Washington Post*, November 14, 1982: A1.

139 **Casualties at Hue**: Erik Villard, *The 1968 Tet Offensive Battles of Quang Tri City and Hue* (Fort MacNair, Washington, D.C.: U.S. Army Center of Military History, 2008), 78.

140 **"So many guys on the same day, it's incredible"**: Mock, *Lin: A Strong Clear Vision*.

140 **"A real good lieutenant"**: Francis X. Clines, "Tribute to Vietnam Dead: Words, a Wall," *Washington Post*, November 11, 1982: A1.

141 **Artifact collection at the wall**: Vietnam Veterans Memorial Collection, Museum Resource Center, National Capitol Region, accessed January 24, 2017, https://www.nps.gov/orgs/1802/vive.htm.

142 **"Buttering up Vietnam veterans"**: Elizabeth Hess, "A Tale of Two Memorials," *Art in America* 71, no. 4 (April 1983): 126.

142 **Vietnam War creating addicts**: Doubek, *Creating the VVM*, 270.

142   **Richard Cohen**: Richard Cohen, "Roll Call," *Washington Post*, November 14, 1982: B1.

142   **Service at Washington Cathedral**: Doubek, *Creating the VVM*, 270–271.

142–143   **General Nguyen Ngoc Loan**: Patricia Camp, "Saigon Police Chief Now Runs Burke Café," *Washington Post*, April 28, 1976: C1; Caryle Murphy, "Onlookers: Area Vietnamese View Memorial With Interest," *Washington Post*, November 13, 1982: B1; Source: Robert McG. Thomas, Jr., "Nguyen Ngoc Loan, 67, Dies; Executed Viet Cong Prisoner," *New York Times*, July 16, 1998: A27; Andrew Friedman, *Covert Capital: Landscapes of Denial and the Making of a U.S. Empire in the Suburbs of Northern Virginia* (Berkeley: University of California Press, 2013) 196.

143   **Christopher Hitchens column**: Christopher Hitchens, "Minority Report," *Nation* 235, no. 16 (November 13, 1982): 486.

143–144   **William Broyles, Jr. essay**: William Broyles, Jr., "Remembering a War We Want to Forget," *Newsweek*, November 22, 1982: 82.

144   **Robert Kaiser piece**: Robert G. Kaiser, "We Can't Bury 'Nam Under the Memorial," *Washington Post*, November 28, 1982: C1, C3.

145–146   **Yusef Komunyakaa poem**: Yusef Komunyakaa, "Facing It," *Pleasure Dome: New and Collected Poems* (Middletown, CT: Wesleyan University Press, 2001): 234–235.

Chapter Eleven

147   **Hart's identification with the Renaissance**: Lindy Hart, interview with the author, 2016; Frederick Hart, "Contemporary Art is Perverted Art," *Washington Post*, August 22, 1989: A19; Esther and Franklin Schmidt, "Passion for Tradition: Renowned Sculptor Frederick Hart Led a Charge to Revive Classical Art," *Art & Antiques* XXII, no. 9 (October 1999): 84–93;] Stephen Happel, "The Arts as a Matrix of Spiritual experience: Frederick Hart's *Three Soldiers* and the Vietnam Veterans Memorial", manuscript, summer 1995; Barbara Matusow, "The Passion of Frederick Hart," *The Washingtonian* 34, no. 2 (November 1998): 54–61, 164.

148   **Veterans Committee visit to Hart's studio**: Hugh Drescher, "At Rick's Studio," audio recording #RXB 0469, Library of Congress Recorded Sound Reference Center.

149   **Hart's model for the black soldier**: Lindy Hart, interview with the author, 2016.

150–151   **Rep. Bailey's legislative proposal**: H.J. Res. 636, Directing Completion of Vietnam Veterans Memorial in West Potomac Park in the District of Columbia, 128 Cong. Rec. 32938 (December 20, 1982); 128 Cong. Rec. 33251 (December 21, 1982) (statement of Representative Don Bailey); Bailey press conference, December 20, 1982: "Flag, inscription and statue must be placed as originally intended, as integral part of the memorial rather than off to the side of the memorial as the Commission dictated."

151   **Duncan Hunter's proposal**: Cosponsors, H.J.Res.636 - A joint resolution directing the completion of the Vietnam Veterans Memorial in West Potomac Park in the District of Columbia, accessed January 25, 2017, https://www.congress.gov/bill/97th-congress/house-joint-resolution/636/cosponsors; Press release from Representative Duncan Hunter, February 7, 1983.

151   **Geyelin, "rekindle the war"**: Philip Geyelin, "The Vietnam Memorial (Cont'd.?)," *Washington Post*, January 11, 1983: A15.

151–152   **Watt intercedes**: Letter from James Watt to Mrs. Helen Scharf, Chairman, National Capital Planning Commission, February 1, 1983; Phil McCombs, "Watt Stalls Addition to Vietnam Memorial," *Washington Post*, January 29, 1983: C1; Phil McCombs, "Watt's Memorial Turnabout," Washington Post, February 2, 1983: D1.

152   **Representative Hunter**: Press release from Representative Duncan Hunter, February 7, 1983.

152   **US Commission of Fine Arts Meeting, February 8, 1983**: video, Library of Congress Motion Picture, Broadcast and Recorded Sound Division, Washington DC. Transcript and Minutes, CFA, February 8, 1983.

152   **Hunter's testimony**: Transcript, CFA, February 8, 1983, 30.

153   **Brown's response to Hunter ("governed by laws, not by press releases")**: Transcript, CFA, February 8, 1983, 32–35.

153   **Scruggs's testimony**: Transcript, CFA, February 8, 1983, 95.

153   **Scruggs calls Webb, Carhart, and Copulos "evil"**: Mock, *Lin: A Strong Clear Vision*.

153   **Cooper and Joseph Brown, "the utmost reverence"**: Transcript, CFA, February 8, 1983, 20.

153   **Brown delivers the commission's verdict**: Transcript, CFA, February 8, 1983, 101.

154   **Dr. Steven Silver's testimony**: Testimony of Steven M. Silver, Ph.D., before the US Commission of Fine Arts, enclosed in letter to Robert

Doubek, January 7, 1983, 1–2. VVMF Records, LCMD. See also, Transcript, CFA, February 8, 1983, 84–88.

154 **"Before any President may commit American forces to combat"**: Letter from Steven Silver to Robert Doubek, January 7, 1983. VVMF Records, LCMD.

155–156 **Hart's equanimity amid furor and his development of his work**: Lindy Hart, interview with the author, 2016.

Chapter Twelve

157 **Alliance of Figurative Artists**: Craig MacPherson, interview with the author.

158 **Hess article**: Elizabeth Hess, "A Tale of Two Memorials," *Art in America* 71, no. 4 (April 1983): 120–127.

158 *Spotlight* **article**: J. P. Passinault, "Proposed Vietnam Memorial Attacked by Veterans, Patriots," *Spotlight* (January 18, 1982): 16.

158 **Hart, "exercise in ideological squatters' rights"**: Frederick Hart, letter to the editor, *Art in America* 71, no. 10 (November 1983): 5.

158–159 **Lin quotations in Hess article**: Hess, "A Tale of Two Memorials," 123.

159 **Sorkin article**: Michael Sorkin, "What happens when a woman designs a war monument?" *Vogue* 173, no. 5 (May 1983): 120, 122.

160 **"Greatest aesthetic achievement"**: Christopher Knight, "Modern Art as National Healing," *Los Angeles Times*, April 16, 2000.

160 **Paul Gapp apology**: Lin, interview by Bill Moyers, 2003.

160 **Hart, "Once under the banner of beauty and order, art was a rich and meaningful embellishment of life"**: Frederick Hart, "Contemporary Art is Perverted Art," *Washington Post*, August 22, 1989: A19.

160 **Hart's response to Hess article**: Frederick Hart, letter to the editor, *Art in America* 71, no. 10 (November 1983): 5.

160 **Hart quotations in Hess article**: Hess, "A Tale of Two Memorials," 124.

161 **Additional Lin quotations in Hess article**: Hess, "A Tale of Two Memorials," 123.

161 **Hart, "There's nothing more powerful than an ingénue"**: Hess, "A Tale of Two Memorials," 124.

162 **Purported meeting between Lin and Hart at the foundry**: Tom Wolfe, "The Artist the Art World Couldn't See," *New York Times*, January 2, 2000.

162 **Questioning the meeting at the foundry**: Lindy Hart, interview with the author, 2016.

162 **Lin, "Hart looked me straight in the face"**: Robert F. Howe, "Monumental Achievement," *Smithsonian Magazine*, November 1, 2002;

163 **Lin, "Obviously, it was very traumatic and upsetting"**: Lin, interview by Bill Moyers, 2003.

163 **Hart's process**: Lindy Hart, interview with the author, 2016.

163–164 **Experience of Jim Connell, Hart's Marine model**: email from Connell to Lindy Hart, November 20, 2014.

166 **"I have the eerie feeling they are searching for their own names"**: Letter from Charles S. W. Berl to Frederick Hart, September 13, 1982. Collection of Lindy Hart.

166 **Casting the sculpture**: Lawrence Van Gelder, "Casting History in Bronze," *New York Times*, June 9, 1985: LI2.

166 **Artist's technique**: Lindy Hart, interview with the author, July 21, 2014.

166 **The press's first look at Hart's statue**: Barbara Gamarekian, "The Vietnam War Comes Home Again, in Bronze," *New York Times*, October 30, 1984: A20.

167 **Hart on the quality of the sculpture**: Benjamin Forgey, "The Statue and the Wall," *Washington Post*, November 10, 1984: A1, D1, D8.

167 **Webb's gift of sword to Hart**: Christopher Buckley, "The Wall," *Esquire* (September 1985): 73.

167–168 **Carhart interview in** Washington Post: Elisabeth Bumiller, "The Memorial, Mirror of Vietnam," *Washington Post*, November 9, 1984: F10.

168 **Carhart's response**: Tom Carhart, letter to the editor, "'The Memorial, the Mirror': A Reply," *Washington Post*, November 12, 1984: A18.

168 **Dedication of the memorial in 1984**: Arthur S. Brisbane, "Reconciliation Theme Voiced in Mall Ceremony," *Washington Post*, November 12, 1984: A1, A14; Ben A. Franklin, "President Accepts Vietnam Memorial," *New York Times*, November 12, 1984: A1, A16; Remarks at Dedication Ceremonies for the Vietnam Veterans Memorial Statue, November 11, 1984. Ronald Reagan Presidential Library, accessed January 25, 2017, https://www.reaganlibrary.archives.gov/archives/speeches/1984/111184a.htm.

168 **Secretary Watt's firing**: Steven R. Weisman, "Watt Quits Post; President Accepts with 'Reluctance,'" *New York Times*, October 10, 1983:

A1. His offense had been to give a tawdry speech to the US Chamber of Commerce containing a racial and handicap slur. In boasting about the complexion of his coal leasing panel, he said, "I have a black, a woman, two Jews and a cripple. And we have talent." It was the final straw. He was gone within a few weeks. Later, *Time* magazine would rank Watt as one of the ten worst cabinet members in all of American history.

170 **Forgey's assessment of the statue**: Benjamin Forgey, "The Statue and the Wall," *Washington Post*, November 10, 1984: A1, D1, D8.

170 **"Perhaps Hart should visit"**: Max Roesler, letter to the editor, "A 'Perverted' Perspective on Art," *Washington Post*, August 26, 1989: A19.

170 **Helprin letter**: Letter from Mark Helprin to Frederick Hart, September 11, 1995. Collection of Lindy Hart.

171 **Kuspit essay**: Donald Kuspit, "Tragic Beauty and Human Wholeness: Frederick Hart's Reparation of the Figure," in Turner, *Hart: The Complete Works*, 9–10.

Epilogue

173 **Epigraph**: G. K. Chesterton, *A Defense of Nonsense and Other Essays* (New York: Dodd, Mead, and Company, 1911), 8.

174 **The maturing of Maya Lin**: Andrus Burr, interview with the author, 2015.

174–176 **Building the Civil Rights and Yale memorials:** Lin, *Boundaries*, 4:26–4:29, 4:38–4:39; Lin, interview with Bill Moyers, 2003; Civil Rights Memorial History, Southern Poverty Law Center, accessed January 26, 2017, https://www.splcenter.org/what-we-do/civil-rights-memorial/history; Civil Rights Martyrs, Southern Poverty Law Center, accessed January 26, 2017, https://www.splcenter.org/what-we-do/civil-rights-memorial/civil-rights-martyrs; 40 Lives of Freedom, Southern Poverty Law Center, accessed January 26, 2017, https://www.splcenter.org/sites/default/files/d6_legacy_files/downloads/publication/40lives.pdf; Alexi Sargeant, "The story of a surface," *Yale Herald*, November 11, 2011; Mock, *Lin: A Strong Clear Vision*.

177 **Lin on her work ("to make people aware of their surroundings")**: Lin, *Boundaries*, 2:03.

177 **Lin's other works**: Lin, *Boundaries*, 5:03–12:13; Maya Lin Studio, accessed January 26, 2017, http://www.mayalin.com/; Joshua Barone, "Maya Lin Unveils Redesign of Smith College Library," *New York Times*, October 16, 2016.

177–178   **Lin on her work ("I feel I exist on the boundaries")**: Lin, *Boundaries*, 0:01–0:05.

178   **Presidential Medal of Freedom ceremony**: Remarks by the President at the Presentation of the Presidential Medal of Freedom, November 22, 2016, accessed January 26, 2017, https://obamawhitehouse.archives.gov/the-press-office/2016/11/22/remarks-president-presentation-presidential-medal-freedom.

179   **Lin and the 9/11 Memorial**: Edward Wyatt, "In 9/11 Design, Rules Are Set To Be Broken," *New York Times*, April 29, 2003: B1.

179   **Xin Wu interview with Lin**: Xin Wu, "Maya LIN (USA)—between art creation and form," from *The New Art of Landscape—Conversations between Xin WU and Contemporary Designers* (2012), 174–175; Xin Wu, interview with the author, 2016.

179–180   **Influence of Lin on the 9/11 Memorial**: Martin Filler, *Makers of Modern Architecture*, vol. 2 (New York: New York Review of Books, 2013), 266, 274, 276.; David W. Dunlap and Glenn Collins, "How Greening of Design Swayed Memorial Jury," *New York Times*, January 8, 2004: B1–B2; Ted Loos, "Architect and 9/11 Memorial Both Evolved Over the Years," *New York Times*, September 4, 2011: AR1.

181   **Hart's political sculptures**: Novak, *Hart: Changing Tides*, 72–75, 83, 90–91.

181   **Hart's success**: Barbara Matusow, "The Passion of Frederick Hart," *The Washingtonian* 34, no. 2 (November 1998): 54.

181   **Heroic Spirit**: Turner, *Hart: The Complete Works*, 296.

181   **Cross of the Millennium**: Novak, *Hart: Changing Tides*, 84, 114–115.

181–182   **Daughters of Odessa**: Novak, *Hart: Changing Tides*, 53–54.

182   **Hart and the Prince of Wales**: Novak, *Hart: Changing Tides*, 82, 85.

182   **Hart called an "art fascist"**: Esther and Franklin Schmidt, "Passion for Tradition: Renowned Sculptor Frederick Hart Led a Charge to Revive Classical Art," *Art & Antiques* (October 1999): 84.

182   **On building Hart's mansion, Chesley**: Schmidt, "Passion for Tradition," 84–93; Matusow, "The Passion of Frederick Hart," 61.

184   **Lawsuit over *Ex Nihilo* in *Devil's Advocate***: Gustav Niebuhr, "Sculpture in a Movie Leads to Suit," *New York Times*, December 5, 1997: A26; James Reston, Jr., "Inspired Art or Stolen Art?," *New York Times*, February 11, 1998: A29; "Washington National Cathedral Files Lawsuit Against Warner Brothers," *The Living Church* 215, no. 26 (December 28, 1997): 7. On an artist's moral rights, see Judith Bresler, letter to

the editor, "Depictions of Art Earn No Protection," *New York Times*, February 17, 1998.

184 **Settlement of lawsuit**: Sylvia Moreno, "Studio Settles Suit Brought by Sculptor," *Washington Post*, February 14, 1998: C3.

184 **Hart's stroke**: Matusow, "The Passion of Frederick Hart," 164.

184 **Hart's last public address on Vietnam memorial**: Novak, *Hart: Changing Tides*, 194.

184 **Hart's death**: Louie Estrada, "Sculptor Frederick Hart Dies," *Washington Post*, August 15, 1999: C8.

185 **National Medal of Arts**: Novak, *Hart: Changing Tides*, 92.

185 **Spreiregen, "To put art in the service of memory"**: Paul Spreiregen, Additions to testimony for the National Capital Memorial Advisory Commission, May 2001. Provided by Spreiregen to the author.

186 **Spreiregen, "If the flagpole and the statue were to disappear this afternoon" and comments about Lin**: Paul Spreiregen, notes from interviews with Kim Murphy, January 29 and February 2, 2007, for *The Wall: Twenty-Five Years of Healing and Education*, MT Publishing, 2007, pages 6, 8, 13; Paul Spreiregen, review of *Creating the Vietnam Veterans Memorial* by Robert W. Doubek, 2015.

Author's Reflection

187 **Secretary Udall's quiet opposition to the Vietnam War**: Maeve Reston, "The Dining Table Wars: The Decision Makers in the Vietnam Conflict and Their Dissenters at Home," (master's thesis, Dartmouth College, 2014; UMI 1568547). Udall's opposition to the Vietnam War was a major source of contention for him within President Lyndon Johnson's cabinet, especially in the latter years of the Johnson Administration. Several of Udall's children, especially his daughter Lori, were active in the anti-war movement.

After Udall left the government, his son, Scott, was drafted into the US Army in 1969. As news of huge American losses and the devastating destruction of Vietnam's landscape from bombing and toxic chemicals filled the newspapers, he became profoundly distraught and disaffected. After the My Lai massacre was revealed, and without consulting his parents, Scott Udall deserted the army and fled to Canada. He slipped back into the country for a family vacation and, given all the distress and anxiety over his deserter status, he attempted to commit suicide by driving his car off Key Bridge in Washington.

Miraculously, he landed on a sand bar and survived. Promptly arrested and charged, he was cashiered out of the Army with a dishonorable discharge. Throughout the entire ordeal, his family gave him unqualified love and support. "Udall Son Deserted, Is Living in Canada," *Washington Post*, November 13, 1971; Interview with Stewart Udall, M. Reston, "The Dining Table Wars"; author's recollection.

187–188 **Johnson's press conference**: Press Conference, President Lyndon B. Johnson, July 28, 1965, accessed January 26, 2017, http://millercenter. org/president/lbjohnson/speeches/speech-5910.

191 **Alfred Preis and the USS *Arizona* Memorial**: Donald Langmead, *Icons of American Architecture*, vol. 2 (Westport, Conn.: 2009), 465–466; Treena Shapiro, "Arizona Memorial Seen as a Dedication to Peace," *Honolulu Star-Bulletin*, May 27, 2002, accessed January 36, 2017, http:// archives.starbulletin.com/2002/05/27/news/story4.html; Paul Joseph Travers, *Eyewitness of Infamy: An Oral History of Pearl Harbor* (Lanham: Madison Books, 1991), 269–270.

194 **Ly Thuong Kiet**: Museum of Vietnamese History, Hanoi, December 2016.

195 **Intelligence about an impending NVA attack at Tet**: James R. Bullington, *Global Adventures on Less-Traveled Roads: A Foreign Service Memoir* (CreateSpace Independent Publishing Platform, 2017); James R. Bullington, interview with the author, 2016.

197 **Ronald E. Ray and the NVA attack during Tet**: author interview with survivor of the attack who remains anonymous.

198 **The attack on Hue, January 30–31, 1968**: Bullington, interview with the author; Lieutenant General Ron Christmas (Ret) interview with author, April 2017; US Marine Captain Dick Manuel, interview with the author; Bullington, *Global Adventures*; Eric Hammel, *Fire in the Streets, The Battle for Hue, Tet 1968*

199 **Westmoreland quotation, "the heroic little band"**: William C. Westmoreland, *A Soldier Reports* (Garden City, New York: Doubleday & Company, 1976), 330.

199 **The Marines and urban combat**: Bullington, *Global Adventures*: "This was deadly, destructive urban combat of the sort the U.S. military had not engaged in since the Battle of Seoul during the Korean War, and for which the Marines were not trained. But they improvised, learned quickly, and broke the back of the North Vietnamese resistance by February 10." From that point forward training for urban warfare

became standard, and would be needed four decades later in the battle for Faluja, Iraq. The best dramatization of the urban combat that took place in Hue City during the Tet Offensive is the Stanley Kubrick film *Full Metal Jacket* (1987). The film is based on the 1979 novel *The Short Timers* by Gustav Hasford, who co-wrote the screenplay with Michael Herr, author of *Dispatches* (1977).

201 **Number of civilians killed at Hue**: Olga Dror, "Translator's introduction," Nha Ca, *Mourning Headband for Hue*, trans. Olga Dror (Bloomington, Ind.: Indiana University Press, 2014), xxx–xxxi.

202 **American and South Vietnamese military casualties at Hue**: Villard, *The 1968 Tet Offensive Battles of Quang Tri City and Hu*, 78.

202 **Cronkite's February 27, 1968, remarks**: "Final Words: Cronkite's Vietnam Commentary," All Things Considered, July 18, 2009, accessed February 7, 2017, http://www.npr.org/templates/story/story.php?storyId=106775685.

202 **Refugees**: Jack Shulimson, *US Marines in Vietnam: The Defining Year, 1968*, (Washington, DC: History and Museums Division, Headquarters, U.S. Marine Corps: 1997), 164, 219.

203 ***The Independent* review of *The Sorrow of War***: Geoff Dyer, "Book Review: Deadly bees among the peanut plants: Geoff Dyer on a magnificent Vietnamese story of love and death, *The Sorrow of War*," *The Independent*, January 28, 1994, accessed 30 January 2017, http://www.independent.co.uk/arts-entertainment/books/book-review-deadly-bees-among-the-peanut-plants-geoff-dyer-on-a-magnificent-vietnamese-story-of-love-1403327.html.

203–204 **American bombs dropped on Vietnam**: The War Remnants Museum, Saigon, December 2016. Chuck Searcy, interview with the author, December 2016.

204 **"The fallen soldiers shared one destiny"**: Bao Ninh, *The Sorrow of War: A Novel of North Vietnam*, trans. Phan Thanh Hao (New York: Riverhead Books, 1993), 25.

206 **"Hard to remember a time when his whole personality and character had been intact"**: Source: Ninh, *The Sorrow of War*, 30.

207 **1966 burning of American consulate by Viet Cong posing as Buddhist students, Ho Chi Minh's life undercover as a Buddhist monk, and Thich Quang Duc's affiliation with the Viet Cong**: Tony Nong, agent and guide from tour company, Ann Tours, December 18, 2016.

SELECTED BIBLIOGRAPHY

Bullington, James R. *Global Adventures on Less-Traveled Roads: A Foreign Service Memoir*. CreateSpace, 2017.

Caputo, Philip. *A Rumor of War*, New York: Holt, Rinehart, and Winston, 1977.

Clay, Grady. "The Art of Choice," *Harvard Magazine* (1985): 56A–H.

Doubek, Robert W. *Creating the Vietnam Veterans Memorial: The Inside Story*. Jefferson, NC: McFarland & Company, 2015.

Filler, Martin. *Makers of Modern Architecture*, vol. II. New York: New York Review Books, 2013.

Goldstein, Warren. *William Sloane Coffin, Jr.: A Holy Impatience*. New Haven, CT: Yale University Press, 2004.

Hagopian, Patrick. *The Vietnam War in American Memory: Veterans, Memorials, and the Politics of Healing*. Amherst: University of Massachusetts Press, 2009.

Hammel, Eric M. *Fire in the Streets: The Battle for Hue, Tet 1968*, Pacifica, CA: Pacifica Military History, 1991.

Harris, Neil. *Capital Culture: J. Carter Brown, the National Gallery, and the Reinvention of the Museum Experience*. Chicago: Chicago University Press, 2013.

Herr, Michael: *Dispatches*. New York: Alfred A. Knopf, 1977.

Langmead, Donald. *Maya Lin: A Biography*. Santa Barbara: Greenwood, 2011.

Lin, Maya. *Boundaries*. New York: Simon and Schuster, 2000.

Lin, Maya, interview by Bill Moyers, *Becoming American: The Chinese Experience*. Public Affairs Television, March 2003, accessed February 6, 2017, http://www.pbs.org/becomingamerican/ap_pjourneys_transcript5_print.html.

McCombs, Phil. "Maya Lin and the Great Call of China." *Washington Post*, January 3, 1982: F1, F9–F12.

Mock, Frieda Lee. *Maya Lin: A Strong Clear Vision*. 1994. Los Angeles: New Video Group, 2003. DVD, 83 min.

Nha, Ca. Trans. by Olga Dror. *Mourning Headband for Hue: An Account of the Battle for Hue, Vietnam, 1968*. Bloomington: Indiana University Press, 2014.

Ninh, Boa: *The Sorrow of War: A Novel of North Vietnam*. New York: Pantheon, 1995.

Novak, Michael et al. *Frederick Hart: Changing Tides*. New York: Hudson Hills Press, 2005.

O'Brien, Tim: *Going After Cacciato*, New York: Delacorte Press, 1978.

Posner, Gerald: *Citizen Perot: His Life and Times*. New York: Random House, 1996.

Reston, James, Jr. *The Amnesty of John David Herndon*. New York: McGraw Hill, 1972.

Reston, James, Jr. *Sherman's March and Vietnam*. New York: Macmillan, 1987.

Reston, James, Jr. *To Defend, To Destroy*. New York: W. W. Norton, 1971.

Potterton, Homan et al. *Frederick Hart: Sculptor*. New York: Hudson Hills Press, 1994.

Scruggs, Jan C., and Joel L. Swerdlow. *To Heal a Nation: The Vietnam Veterans Memorial*. New York: Harper & Row, 1985.

Transcripts and minutes of meetings of the US Commission of Fine Arts (CFA), various dates.

Turner, Frederick, et al. *Frederick Hart: The Complete Works*. Louisville: Butler Books, 2007.

Uhl, Michael and Ensign, Todd: *GI Guinea Pigs: How the Pentagon Exposed Our Troops to Dangers More Deadly Than War: Agent Orange and Atomic Radiation*. Playboy Press, 1980.

Vietnam Veterans Memorial Fund. *The Wall: Twenty-Five Years of Healing and Education*, Evansville, IN: MT Publishing, 2007.

Vietnam Veterans Memorial Fund Records, 1965–1994, Library of Congress Manuscript Division, Washington, DC.

Webb, James H: *Fields of Fire*. New York: Prentice Hall, 1978.

Westmoreland, William C. *A Soldier Reports*. New York: Doubleday, 1976.

Wolfe, Tom. *Painted Word*. New York, Farrar, Straus and Giroux, 1975.

Wu, Xin: *The New Art of Landscape—Conversations between Xin Wu and Contemporary Designers*, Beijing: China Architecture and Building Press, 2012.

INDEX

Bold page numbers indicate photo or illustration.